Making Do:
Women, Family, and Home
in Montreal during the
Great Depression

Making Do:
Women, Family, and Home in Montreal during the Great Depression

Denyse Baillargeon

translated by
Yvonne Klein

Wilfrid Laurier University Press

We acknowledge the support of the Canada Council for the Arts for our publishing program. We acknowledge the financial support of the Government of Canada through the Book Publishing Industry Development Program for our publishing activities.

Canadä

Canadian Cataloguing in Publication Data

Baillargeon, Denyse
  Making do: women, family, and home in Montreal during the Great Depression

(Studies in childhood and family in Canada)
Translation of: Ménagères au temps de la crise.
Includes bibliographical references and index.
ISBN 0-88920-326-1

1. Housewives – Quebec (Province) – History. 2. Housewives – Quebec (Province) – Montreal – History. 3. Depressions – 1929 – Quebec (Province). 4. Women – Quebec (Province) – Social conditions. 5. Women – Quebec (Province) – Economic conditions. I. Klein, Yvonne M. II. Title. III. Series.

HQ1459.Q8B3412 1999   305.43′649′09714   C99-930689-8

© 1999
Wilfrid Laurier University Press
Waterloo, Ontario N2L 3C5

Cover design by Leslie Macredie
Cover illustration: view-23308 *New triplex development, Montreal, QC, 1925*. Notman Photographic Archives, McCord Museum of Canadian History, Montreal

Printed in Canada

In memory of Alma and Marie-Rose

Table of Contents

List of Tables

Table

Acknowledgments

I would like first of all to thank the thirty respondents whose precious accounts permitted me to enter into the very heart of the domestic sphere; without their contribution, this study would quite simply never have taken shape. I would also like to express my gratitude to the representatives of the various organizations and institutions that I approached. Their support and cooperation proved indispensable not only in tracking down these women but also in establishing with them the atmosphere of confidence necessary to eliciting a good interview. Lauréanne Collin, information technician at the Council of Health and Social Services of the Metropolitan Region of Montreal (CSSSRMM), provided me with a list of nursing homes, Centres locaux de services communautaires (CLSCs), and people to contact, which facilitated my research a great deal and for which I should like to thank her.

Many persons read the manuscript and their comments allowed me to improve its contents. I should particularly like to thank Jacques Rouillard, professor in the Department of History at the University of Montreal, who directed my doctoral thesis which was the origin of this work; his unfailing availability and his repeated encouragement were largely responsible for my bringing this study to its conclusion. My thanks also go to Bettina Bradbury, Lorraine Gadoury, and Dominique Jean, whose constructive criticisms provided food for thought. Daniel Bédard provided a first review of the manuscript which permitted me to improve its form, and for which I am very grateful. Finally, I should like sincerely to thank my partner, Guy Marleau, for his technical advice (as a newcomer to computers, my appeals for his help were frequent!) and especially for his moral and emotional support throughout the five years that I devoted to the research and editing of my thesis and the book.

I am also indebted to the Fonds pour la Formation de Chercheurs et l'Aide à la Recherche (FCAR) of the government of Quebec for its financial support.

Introduction

The Great Depression of the 1930s has entered our collective imagination as a period synonymous with unemployment, as a kind of
yardstick to which we inevitably refer when trying to assess the strength
of a new recession. Yet again, even at the beginning of the 1980s, newspapers were making the point that the number of unemployed in Canada
was as great as at the beginning of the Depression, as if that event provided an absolute reference to convey the gravity of the problems which
were besetting the country.[1]

Our comprehension of the Depression, however, remains fragmentary.
The political history of the period primarily recounts the constitutional
debates which led to the establishment of the Canadian welfare state and
the emergence of third parties on the left and the right, whereas other
studies pay close attention to organizations and to demonstrations of the
unemployed and to the measures put in place by various governments to
counter unemployment—in short to the consequences of the Depression
that are the most evident and most easy to document.[2] The soup kitchens,
the lines waiting at the doors of the Meurling Refuge, public works sites
where men worked with picks and shovels rather than machines in order
to increase the number of jobs, the drought and the plague of grasshop-
pers which descended on Saskatchewan, the single men who rode the
Canadian rails in search of work, all are shocking images popularized in
the press of the day and more recently in the film *La Turlutte des années
dures*.[3] The anecdotal thread of various oral histories, like those collected
by journalist Barry Broadfoot, in *Ten Lost Years*,[4] reminds us of what the
Depression might have meant to those who lived through it. But outside

---

Notes to the Introduction are on p. 193.

of a few distinctive strategies that catch the imagination, like jumping the electric meter, doing a midnight move, or swiping coal from the railroad tracks for the stove—we know next to nothing about daily life in the days when La Bolduc was a star.

The constitutional conflicts, the deeds and posturings of political men and the brilliant feats recorded in the press certainly did not constitute the ordinary texture of life during the Depression. For the thousands of working-class families that were stricken with unemployment, it was more a matter of hanging on at all costs until the next job or until the economic recovery that would finally occur at the beginning of the Second World War. Most studies of this period, while recognizing that the aid extended to the unemployed was insufficient to their needs, have nothing to say about the means these families used to assure their survival. Some deplore the absence of information in this regard, but despite a constantly growing number of studies and a broadening of the range of themes that they address, studies of the Depression continue to pay little attention to everyday life.

For some years, however, women's history and the history of the family have underscored the importance of the domestic sphere and of the work which women do in it in order to understand the totality of historical reality. The work undertaken in these fields has provided evidence of the connections which exist between the family and the world of work and of the central role played in this dynamic by women. Whereas students of women's history place at the centre of their analysis the interdependence between the subordinate position of women in the labour market and their assignment to the function of reproduction and to the responsibility for life within the domestic sphere, those studying the history of the family pay close attention to all the possible strategies undertaken by families to adapt to the industrial context.[5] Women, who organize and manage daily life and who are responsible for the well-being of the family, emerge as the principal architects of these strategies. At present, their domestic labour is seen as an important contribution to the family economy, that is, to the range of resources contributed collectively by all the members of the family—women, men, and children—to ensure their survival.

These two fields of research have opened up new and particularly rich pathways of investigation into the 1930s. If we are to understand how working-class families managed to survive this era of profound economic and social upheaval, we must obviously scrutinize the private sphere and ask about the functioning of the family economy and the role played by women's work within the home. What indeed was the domestic labour of working-class housewives at the beginning of the Depression? How and to what degree did these women increase or modify their labour in order to ensure the economic survival of their families through the period of unemployment and underemployment? What consequences did the Depression have on the various elements of their work at home? These are the principal questions this study hopes to answer.

An investigation of the private sphere can turn out to be a disappointing exercise if one tackles it solely by means of conventional sources. In fact, these contain very little information about daily life and domestic labour. Admittedly, students of women's history have developed a certain expertise in the rereading and reinterpretation of archival documents, newspapers, reports of commissions of inquiry, and other governmental publications familiar to historians. Especially in regard to the history of domestic labour, they have learned to use profitably new and less conventional sources like illustrations, studies of material culture, and even cookbooks and department store catalogues. Although these documents have not been ignored, it became quickly apparent that, to gain access to daily life during the Depression years, it would be necessary to turn to the first-person accounts of those who had lived through it.

The main source on which this study rests is a set of thirty interviews undertaken in 1986 and 1987 with women who were already married at the beginning of the 1930s and who agreed to relate their experiences of the Depression. By the time this study took shape, this period represented the earliest decade for which it was still possible to find women who had lived through it as wives and mothers. Their recollections made it possible to shed light not only on the impact of the economic crisis on their domestic labour, but also on their entire development from childhood to the Second World War, and on the living conditions of the working class from which most of them came. This material is all the more valuable because it proceeds from a generation of women that will soon disappear and that has left very little in the way of written evidence behind.

The first chapter of this study, which includes a brief description of working-class living conditions in Montreal at the beginning of the Depression and an account of the evolution of domestic labour from the dawn of industrialization until the 1930s, also devotes space to a consideration of the methodology of oral history on which this work is based. The chapters following contain analyses of the interviews. Chapter 2, devoted to the childhood and youth of the women interviewed, allows us to develop a profile of the sample while at the same time gives information about their school attendance and the work experience, both waged and in the home, that they acquired before they married. Chapter 3 talks about dating and marriage and describes the couples' possessions at the beginning of their life together (property, furniture, wedding presents, bride's trousseau) while the fourth chapter examines motherhood, sexuality, and contraception.

Chapter 5 analyzes the contribution made by salaried and paid work, of men as well as of women, and the management of the family budget and patterns of consumption. In chapter 6, the subject is housework and a review of its various aspects: where it was performed, how it was organized, what tasks were involved, and what implements were available to women to do it. Finally, chapter 7 considers the contribution of government, strategies of mutual aid, such as the help of relatives and neighbours, and the use of credit. The final chapters then examine more specifically the impact of the Depression on various aspects of women's domestic labour and on the family economy. Considering the Depression from the point of view of those who had to deal with it, this study will make evident the indispensable role played by women as they did their best to overcome the poverty in which they found themselves.

Chapter 1

Domestic Labour and Economic Crisis

*T*he New York stock market crash of 1929 is generally considered the beginning of an unprecedented economic crisis that would spread to every capitalistic country before it finally ground to a halt shortly before the start of the Second World War. A decade of destitution, unemployment and poverty separates these two events. The language which historians have chosen to describe that period—*The Great Depression, Ten Lost Years, La Décennie des naufragés* (Decade of Castaways), *The Winter Years, The Dirty Thirties*, to mention the titles of only the best known works—is meant to reflect the scale of the socio-economic upheavals the crisis produced and the trauma borne by those who lived through it.

An examination of the principal economic indicators confirms this rather catastrophic perception of the period. With an economy largely dependent on exports and with the United States as its primary market, Canada indeed ranks second among the countries most affected by the Depression. Thus, between 1929 and 1933, Canadian manufacturing production was reduced by more than a third, the consumer price index is estimated to have dropped 25 to 30 percent, while salaries in non-export industries fell 37 percent. Meanwhile, the numbers of unemployed rocketed in the other direction. According to even conservative estimates, between 27 and 33 percent of the workforce was looking for work in the winter of 1933, which meant that 1.5 million Canadians, 15 percent of the entire population of the country, had to live on public assistance.[1]

Quebec, despite its industrial structure centred on light industry and the production of primary consumer goods, was one of the provinces most affected by unemployment. The city of Montreal, which was at that time at the centre of industrial activity, recorded the worst performances. With a population of 800,000, the city represented 28 percent of the population of Quebec, but 60 percent of those on relief in the province. In February 1934, at the height of the Depression, more than 240,000 persons, that is 28 percent of the population of Montreal, were living on public assistance; among Francophones, the proportion increased to 38 percent.[2] These statistics, though impressive enough, probably do not convey the entire reality of unemployment as they do not take into account those without work who did not ask the municipality for assistance nor do they include those who saw their workweek lopped to one or two days or who were subjected to wage cuts. Despite their deficiencies, however, the figures clearly show that, out of all occupational categories, it was the workers who were the most affected by unemployment. In Montreal, for example, although they represented about two-thirds of all paid labour, they made up 87 percent of the family wage earners on relief, with unskilled labourers alone representing 54.9 percent of the total.[3]

The data we have on wages and relief payments demonstrate that this period was especially difficult for the working class. In 1931, for example, although the Canadian Welfare Council fixed the figure of $1040 as the absolute annual minimum required to support an average family of five and $1500 as the amount required to attain a certain level of comfort, that body remarked that almost half of the heads of Montreal families earned less than $1000 a year. Four years later, although the subsistence level was pegged at $1200 a year, an inquiry undertaken by the Montreal Board of Trade revealed that 68 percent of the 180,000 employed heads of families in the city were earning less than $1000 a year—and more than 50 percent of them were making less than $850—leaving aside the 40,000 families who were dependent on public assistance.[4] The latter group did not receive even half the amount required to assure their subsistence. The scale of grants established by the city of Montreal fixed the sums of $36.88 a month in summer and $39.48 in winter as the amounts allowed to cover costs of food, heating, rent, and clothing for a family of five.[5]

Very clearly, it was impossible to live decently on such meagre resources. Morover, the low wages condemned a significant proportion of these families to rent unhealthy lodgings. The report of a municipal inquiry carried out in 1936-37 in seven working-class districts of the city in fact deemed that the general condition of 54 percent of some 5000 lodgings visited ranged from only fair to outright bad. Some were infested with vermin, a number were situated in basements, attics, back alleys, or even old stables and the majority were badly lit, badly ventilated and lacked a bath and hot running water. In 73 percent of these cases, the housing rented for less than $16 a month, but for the majority of families living there, this sum represented more than 30 percent of their monthly budget. Crowding constituted another problem, since 25 percent of Montreal households had to be satisfied with fewer than one room for each person.[6]

Low wages and bad housing conditions evidently went hand in hand with poor health. Even though infant mortality was decreasing throughout the Depression, going from 132.3 per thousand in 1929 to 59.3 per thousand in 1940, the rate remained higher in the working-class districts than elsewhere. It was much the same story for infectious diseases like tuberculosis which continued to wreak havoc.[7] An investigation undertaken in 1933 into people living on home relief in Montreal likewise concluded that these were more likely to exhibit respiratory troubles as well as problems with their teeth, eyesight, hearing, and even mental illness. The problem of malnutrition appeared particularly acute: in 1933, for example, it was observed that only 55 percent of adults and 47 percent of youths living on public assistance were adequately nourished. After five years on relief, the percentage of individuals exhibiting dietary deficiencies rose to 49 percent. To be precise, the amount allocated by the Unemployment Relief Commission in Montreal for the feeding of a family of five totalled $21.88 a month while a balanced diet would have required $35.17 and even the "restricted diet for emergency use" would have cost $25.90.[8]

These data, though extremely useful in giving a sense of urban misery during the Depression, have still to be seen in perspective. It must be admitted indeed that the inadequate income and problems of housing and health linked to the poverty and unemployment that affected the working-class population during the 1930s already represented the daily lot of many during even the "prosperous" 1920s. The number of families assisted by the Saint Vincent de Paul Society between 1920 and 1929, which amounted to three or four thousand each year, represents a good indication of the economic difficulties experienced in the course of the decade preceding the Depression.[9]

In fact, from the beginning of the process of industrialization and urbanization in the nineteenth century, workers' families had to learn how to cope with low wages, seasonal unemployment, and periodic slowdowns of industrial activity. If there is no doubt that the Great Depression distinguished itself from its predecessors in terms of its sheer duration and by the fact that it occurred in a society that was more industrialized than it had ever been before, it is no less true that for large sections of the working class, particularly for the families of unskilled workers, precarious living conditions were part and parcel of their daily life and they had already developed various strategies to deal with them. Child labour, which was widespread as witnessed by the statistics for school attendance during the period preceding the Second World War, represented one of the means most commonly employed by these families to increase their income and counteract the effects of underemployment. But these families counted just as much on other kinds of work and other strategies which depended to a large degree on mothers at home. The entire range of responsibilities assumed by women at home, the income they brought in, the savings they effected, though long overlooked by historians, now appear very much one of the elements to which attention must be paid if we wish to achieve a better appraisal of the standard of living of working-class families and appreciate their capacity to survive.

The nature and importance of these responsibilities have varied according to era and economic circumstances. Thus in the course of the period marked by the beginning of industrialization in Montreal, the different kinds of contribution women made to the family income, as identified by Bettina Bradbury, cover a broad range of activities which permitted their families to escape an absolute dependence on paid work and thus improve their standard of living. Raising livestock, cultivating a patch of land, making cloth, clothing, and foodstuffs for family use or to exchange for the money necessary for household upkeep, taking in boarders or sharing the house with another family represented the kind of strategies to which they had always turned.[10]

By the time the Great Depression broke out, industrialization and urbanization had already eliminated a number of these practices. In particular, keeping livestock within the city limits had been prohibited for some time, while the population density of the working-class districts had seriously reduced the possibilities of tending a garden. At the same time, domestic production of many basic items, like bread, cloth, and soap, to name only a few, had clearly diminished. But despite a greater dependence on the part of workers' families on wages and on the consumer goods market, the labour of women in the home still comprised a whole host of tasks altogether necessary to support the family. It fell to women to manage the available money so as to get the most out of every cent; they were likewise responsible for the feeding, clothing, and upkeep of the family, and for doing it as cheaply as possible. Finally, they had both to find sources of supplementary income to balance the budget and to maintain the informal networks of mutual aid and exchange with relatives that would allow them to achieve precious economies. All of these responsibilities—as well as pregnancy, the care and raising of children, not to speak of the management of family conflicts, and the emotional support of its members, especially the partner,[11] are now included in the term "domestic labour." The study of this particular kind of work turns out to be indispensable if we are to go beyond the statistical, and frequently reductive, portrait of working-class living conditions during the Great Depression.

Housework Is Also Work

Not so long ago, the aggregation of tasks carried out by women in the home was seen as nothing more than a collection of trivial occupations, passed on to them by reason of their biological capacity to bear children and completely disconnected from the great events that form the historical framework of a nation. In our industrial societies where "work" has become synonymous with employment and with wages, it was that much easier to deny the economic and social importance of women's work in the home since it was unpaid and because the domestic sphere, where this sort of work was done, appeared a place isolated from the rest of the social organization.

Feminist analysis over the last twenty years has overturned all of these notions. In particular, the debates surrounding the conceptualization of domestic work have made it possible to demonstrate that it is indeed labour in the sense that it is as essential to the maintenance and reproduction of the economic and social organization as is the production of goods and services.[12] Indeed, in addition to assuring, without pay, the physical maintenance and the biological and social reproduction of the labour force, domestic labour ensures the transformation and circulation of market-produced commodities and takes over the multiple services that neither industry nor the state can provide but which are nonetheless essential to the survival of both, as well as to that of the familial group and the welfare of the individuals which it comprises.[13]

Most feminist theorists also take the view that, from the dawn of industrial capitalism, this form of labour allowed men to reinforce their position of domination. Work at home had been assigned to women by virtue of a sexual division of labour that well predated industrialization and in which women had already been subordinated. Work carried out inside the home in fact relieved men of responsibilities related to their own care and the care of their children and allowed them to enter the labour market and, more generally, to devote themselves to activities in the public sphere that in turn became new bases for their power over women.[14] This is not to maintain that women were altogether excluded from paid employment, but the wage discrimination to which they were (and still are) subjected meant that they had no other choice than to make themselves economically dependent on a man, even though this dependence—and the familial and domestic constraints which ensued from it—became the pretext for the low wages which they were (and still are) paid. Thus, the domestic labour of women both serves the needs of capitalism and patriarchy, which derive genuine material benefit from it, and permits us to understand the subordinate position of women in the labour market. Domestic labour is indeed at the heart of the very functioning of society itself and of gender relations and thus can in no way be considered an epiphenomenon. Quite the contrary, it constitutes "the basis and complement of this society that can neither do without it nor reduce it to a simple commercial transaction."[15]

The assignment of women to household tasks and the care of children does not begin with industrial capitalism, but this new mode of production produced profound upheavals in the organization of the family and considerably modified the role of women within it. In pre-industrial societies, where the workplace and the home characteristically coincided, the family constituted a unit of production in which women's work included numerous tasks related to the production of goods consumed by the family or sold on the market. In addition to preparing the daily meals, doing the laundry, cleaning house, and caring for the children, women in rural areas also were responsible for the farmyard animals, as well as the dairy and pigpens, the garden, the weaving of cloth, the making of clothes and household linens, and so on. In town, artisans' wives helped their husbands conduct business, if they were not directly involved in the production itself. The presence in the household of various relatives, apprentices, and domestic servants also meant that the responsibility for the socialization of children did not fall exclusively on their mothers; the children were, moreover, quickly integrated into adult life following a period of apprenticeship that was often served outside the family.

An effect of the shift of production to the workshop and then to the factory was to institute a new spatio-sexual division of labour: relying on their old form of domination, men were integrated en masse into market production, a new source of power in industrialized societies, while women, especially married women, were relegated to the home, bringing into being the housewife, in the modern sense of the term.[16] Technological developments and the industrial production of many common consumer goods little by little led housewives to abandon their domestic production and to use new and improved tools and appliances, which accordingly lightened their toil. At the same time, the role of wife and mother took on a whole new dimension and became narrowly associated with "feminine nature," to such a degree that tasks performed by women within the home disappeared under the cover of maternal and conjugal love. This is the reason why the fact that domestic labour plays a key role in the functioning of our societies has long been obscured.

The Evolution of Domestic Labour before the Depression

Between the appearance of factory work in the nineteenth century and the Great Depression, every element comprising women's domestic labour underwent numerous transformations. Present research does not always permit us to focus squarely on the consequences of these changes for housewives of the poorest classes, but it is evident that these women, despite their meagre incomes, did not remain completely untouched by the numerous developments that we observe over the course of this period. Household chores, for example, were certainly facilitated by the introduction of electricity and cold running water in the working-class districts of Montreal during the first two decades of the twentieth century. Likewise, we may suppose that the majority of these housewives developed the habit of buying various products available on the market, like bread, cloth, and soap, and acquired certain household appliances that appeared in the course of this period, like manual washing machines. It must be pointed out, however, that electric appliances like irons, washers, stoves, and refrigerators were not offered in the department store catalogues before the 1920s and that, despite often flashy advertising campaigns touting their time and labour-saving advantages, they were slow to make their appearance in the home on account of their rather high cost.[17] Thus, according to the study undertaken by the Metropolitan Commission in certain working-class districts of the city in 1937, the majority of housewives in these areas possessed only a wood or coal stove that was also used for heating and only 67 percent of them had an icebox. As well, the investigators noted that 91 percent of these homes had softwood floors which were difficult to take care of, and that less than half the families used one of their rooms as a parlour.[18] Indeed, the data available regarding wages, housing conditions, and the spread of domestic technology lead us to the conclusion that, for poorer urban housewives, the family remained a site of production well after industrialization, while household chores were always performed by hand and represented a heavy burden at least until the Second World War.

At the turn of the century, the performance of housework also became the object of numerous recommendations which went hand in hand with the new industrialized context and the domestic technology it had given rise to. In order to care for their families better, urban housewives were urged to plan their work and to familiarize themselves with the new sciences, like food chemistry and nutrition. The movement for the scientific management of housework reached its peak at the beginning of the twentieth century, when, under the influence of Taylorism, there was an attempt to convince women to reduce their motions and time their jobs.[19] According to historian Ruth Schwartz Cowan, the First World War marked a turning point in regard to this attitude. Housework, until recently considered a science, became an art, the expression of the housewife's love for her family.[20] One must always wonder to what degree housewives of the poorest classes were able to conform to these new standards, considering their limited access to domestic technology and to decent housing.

Motherhood as well underwent numerous transformations in the course of this period. On the one hand, women were having fewer children. Whereas French-speaking Quebec women born in 1867 gave birth on average to 6.4 children, their granddaughters, born at the beginning of the century, on average had two fewer children.[21] This reduction in the birth rate was accompanied by a trend toward the nuclearization of the home, which meant that women found themselves more isolated than they previously had been and henceforth would be on their own in shouldering the responsibility for childcare. Furthermore, toward the end of the nineteenth century, we witness a virtual exaltation of the maternal role which comes to epitomize female destiny. In this new context, infant mortality became unacceptable and of greater and greater concern to social reformers. Fostered by new medical developments, the discourse on hygienics which was taking shape in this period served to justify the increasing intervention of doctors in women's lives, especially during pregnancy and childbirth. Various organizations (*Goutte de Lait, L'Assistance maternelle*, and the visiting nurse service of the Metropolitan Life Insurance Company) were thus created to give free aid and advice to women about the best methods of caring for their children.[22] Of course, the first priority of these services was to educate women of the poorest classes, who were seen to be most at risk and at the same time the least likely to consult a doctor, due to lack of money. To the volunteers, doctors and nurses associated with these organizations, the medical supervision of mothers and their newborn babies, as well as breast-feeding, became virtually their theme song. The repetition of the same recommendations throughout the course of the opening decades of the twentieth century is a clear indication that working-class women either could not conform to them or were reluctant to.[23] Indeed, the reduction in the rates of infant mortality registered in these years must be largely attributed to the improvement in sanitary facilities and to the pasteurization of milk that was made obligatory in 1926.[24] These statistics ought not obscure the fact that women of the poorest classes well up until the Second World War very commonly experienced the loss of one or more young children and frequently miscarried as a result of malnutrition.

At the same time, this period saw the development of the bourgeois model of the woman economically dependent on her husband/-breadwinner;[25] from now on the family was expected to offer a peaceful haven to the husband/breadwinner, a refuge against the harshness of the outside world, while the woman was to become more and more focussed on supporting her husband emotionally, caring for her children, and keeping the house. For working-class women, however, the line between the public and private spheres was not so clearly drawn.[26] Although very few of them were actually working for wages during this time, more and more indications suggest that women were contributing financially to the household economy by performing one or several paid occupations at home. The links between the market and the family were all the more evident for these women in that they were the ones who administered the family budget and it fell to them to make up, one way or another, the shortages produced by insufficient wages. It is extremely difficult, however, to define the evolution of those activities which took place in the secrecy of the private sphere. We know, for example, that the clothing trade in Montreal, at least up until the Depression, depended on a significant workforce in the home, but it is almost impossible to quantify a phenomenon like this.[27] Keeping boarders, making various products for sale, or making money from their services (like doing laundry) represent many of the means to which women resorted in order to balance the budget, though we cannot determine to what extent. Likewise, it is difficult to assess women's participation in networks of family support, though we do know that industrialization did not eliminate these.[28] It is quite evident, however, that the wife-mother-housewife model offered to women did not yet correspond to the experience of life among housewives of the poorest classes at the time of the Great Depression. The analysis of the interviews will reveal particulars about each element of their domestic labour and highlight the impact of the Depression on each of them.

Oral Sources

In the last fifteen years, studies grounded in whole or in part on oral sources have become increasingly numerous. This new approach, fostered by the concerns of social history and *histoires des mentalités* intends to take into account the experience of groups which are absent from the public sphere and from the written record; thus it is a highly desirable, if not indispensable, tool to bring women back into history. Oral narratives are also central to the creation of women's history in that they give voice to those who have been suppressed, constituting them as historical subjects, and making it possible to go beyond the usual discourse of the elites who have been especially prolific in regard to women.[29] Finally, these oral testimonies also help us better to apprehend certain particularly complex realities, such as the family, and to disclose the often unsuspected interaction between the public and the private spheres by revealing the ubiquity of ordinary daily experience at the heart of what official history calls "the great events," like wars and economic crises.[30] Therefore, to interview women in itself makes them actors and restores them to history; it also provides the sole means of access to a vast range of information about the family that often only women keep and chronicle.

Whatever the object of the research, the complex nature of oral sources must be kept in mind. They are in fact constructed within the framework of an interpersonal relationship, thanks to the workings of memory. The information collected thus depends on the quality of the questions, the contact established between the interviewer and the interviewee, and on the functioning of the subject's memory. These various constituent elements of oral history require that we bring as critical an eye to bear on the preliminary steps of formulating the problem and the questionnaire as to the conditions under which these narratives were elicited.

As for memory, it is certainly important to point out that the memories of old people, as long as they are in good health, are no less reliable than those of young adults and that the loss of memory associated with old age primarily affects recent memory, leaving intact those recollections of childhood and youth which are of particular interest to the historian.[31] On the other hand, it is clear that memory works selectively and is conditioned by the present. That is, memories are rekindled only to the degree that they represent a particular significance to respondents while being questioned and that their perceptions are modified as much by their subsequent experience as by the changes at work in society.[32] Thus, the effects of the Great Depression on family life and domestic labour remain vivid for the women interviewed not only because of the inconveniences and deprivations which they suffered but also because those years frequently offered a striking contrast to their present living conditions, which acted as a marker to which they could compare the situation of the past. Likewise, the resurgence of the feminist movement at the end of the 1960s and the development of new styles of life centred on consumption impacted more particularly on their conception of their lives. The number of pregnancies, male-female relations, the sharing of domestic tasks, the grip exercised by the Catholic Church on society in those days, or the lack of material comfort they experienced when young, all are themes which aroused many comments and criticisms. The accounts collected, however, record a clear distinction between present and past judgements. This ability to distinguish between what was thought then and what now is absolutely necessary to a good interview and constitutes an excellent indicator by which to evaluate the credibility of the subjects questioned and the information obtained.[33]

If memory is not, strictly speaking, sexually determined, the way it is structured depends on individual experience, which is itself determined by gender. Thus, the place occupied in social relationships and the sexual division of labour gives rise to a time-specific relation and fosters the recollection of certain kinds of experiences.[34] An existence passed almost entirely within the confines of the domestic sphere, as was the case for the majority of the women interviewed, favours the recollection of events and deeds associated with that area of activity. So it is not surprising that they supplied often very precise details about daily life, more than their husbands would have been able to do, right down to the price of groceries and their husbands' wages during the early years of their marriage.[35] This "family memory" does not, however, operate according to the same dates or points of reference as does official history. On many occasions during the course of the interviews, the framework of events was reconstructed around the years when children were born, a close relative died or a move took place.

At the beginning, the interview guide included certain questions relevant to the social and political context, what the respondents thought at the time about the measures taken by the government to deal with the crisis, or the position of the Church regarding unemployment, etc. It became evident very quickly, however, that women of this generation had not been especially interested in what was happening outside the domestic sphere; only those who had been closely involved in certain "public" events had retained memories of them. Thus, one of the women recalled a women's demonstration outside the Montreal city hall, organized by the *Ligue de solidarité féminine*,[36] because one of her neighbours had taken part in it and had told her all about it. Nevertheless, she did not know who had organized the event. Another woman remembered demonstrations by the unemployed because her husband had been involved, but no more than that, while a third recalled very clearly that the Taschereau government had promised a cash payment to those who would move back to the country to so-called "regions of colonization" because, in her case, the promised sum was never paid! For the majority, however, the events which unfolded in the public sphere passed almost unnoticed, leaving hardly a trace; questions relating to them raised only faint echoes, confirming the relationship between involvement in an area of activity and the subject of memory.

Because of the peculiar way that memory works and the limitations which follow from it, oral sources cannot be substituted for written ones for certain kinds of information. Written sources thus turned out to be indispensable in developing a relevant questionnaire and played an essential role in the chronological reconstruction of the period used as a framework for the interviews. As well, for each theme taken up, the accounts collected were analyzed in the light of sources, studies, and monographs of various origins. Documents drawn from the archives of the Metropolitan Insurance Company, certain newspapers and periodicals, Eaton's catalogues, a number of governmental publications (census figures, statistical yearbooks, publications of various government departments, memoranda and reports of commissions of inquiry, and the like), as well as studies of the Great Depression, women, and the family carried out in Quebec, in English Canada, the United States and England made it possible to quantify certain phenomena and to situate the experience lived by the informants within a broader perspective. Comparing one interview with others and the different parts of the response of a single witness allowed us to validate certain information when the written sources could not do so.

The women were questioned more about how they had lived rather than what they had witnessed of the events which took place around them, an approach which, in theory, minimizes the risk of mistakes or oversights. We ought not, however, overlook the fact that respondents generally attempt to preserve the image they have of themselves or of the group to which they belong. This image refers to a socially and sexually oriented construction, but one whose elements may change according to the historical period. Even if these variations alter what was taboo into what is now acceptable, behaviours that were deemed deviant in previous years—premarital pregnancy, for example—can be more difficult to ascertain. Despite present-day tolerance of behaviour of this kind, the person being questioned knows that she transgressed the norm that was in force at the time and may still feel so embarrassed that she seeks to disguise the fact, even if it means lying about the date of her marriage or the year her first child was born. Rather than a deliberate and conscious lie, experience reveals that omissions and evasive responses are the means used to avoid an embarrassing question that has revived painful memories. Whether conscious or not, these "oversights" and "mistakes" are as significant as the memory of an event and ought to be submitted to analysis when they can be identified.

The relationship between the interviewer and the subject remains the great unknown in this process. It is difficult to determine precisely what are the exact consequences but even if the interviewer intervenes as little as possible, her very presence influences the content of the material, which will more or less conform to the "norm," depending on how she is seen. The sex, age, race, and social class of two persons facing one another are further factors that enter into the equation. Thus, it has been fairly easy for me, as a woman, to ask participants about their sexuality, their childbirths, and to approach subjects like contraception, but the mere fact of being a woman offers no absolute guarantees as differences in generation and social class may erect formidable obstacles. The fact that the interviewer was a stranger probably encouraged a subject to confide what she might feel too ashamed to share with those closer to her, like her children. The same is true for certain astonishingly virulent comments about relations between men and women or parents and children, which can be attributed to a propensity on the part of some older people to a wounding mode of speech that they display as though it were a privilege of old age.[37] Nevertheless, my being a young woman and a stranger may have hindered me from obtaining other kinds of information, although it is clearly difficult to determine what sorts.

A minimum level of trust must be established and the two participants must discover a pleasure in talking to one another and listening to one another in order to assure the success of each interview: "a good interview is one where both take mutual pleasure in the conversation."[38] This relationship of trust ought not, however, permit us to forget that the principal danger of this approach is to lead the subject into saying what the interviewer wants to hear. Particular attention must therefore be given to the composition of the interview guide and the formulation of the questions.

The interview guide comprised a hundred points divided into three sections which corresponded to the different stages of the respondents' lives from their birth to the end of the 1930s.[39] Beyond the questions about family origin, the first section of the interview asked about schooling and paid and domestic work experience prior to marriage. Collecting this kind of information was intended both to determine the profile of the sample and to put the later experience of the respondent into perspective. The second part asked questions about courtship, marriage, and motherhood. These stages do not simply represent important transitions in the women's lives, which in themselves demand our attention, but the questions relating to them allow us to understand the familial framework (husband's occupation, number of children, place of residence, etc.) within which they experienced the Depression. Finally, the last section of the questionnaire involved questions about the contributions to the family economy made by different forms of work (paid and domestic), institutions like the government and the family, and other strategies of survival during the 1930s. A combination of specific questions in order to elicit factual information and broader, more open questions in order to sketch in motivations, values, attitudes, and behaviours seemed to me most likely to stimulate the subjects' memories without inducing answers while procuring the desired information.

The choice and number of subjects likewise determines the value of the information collected and the analysis that can be made of it. In this regard, we must emphasize that historians, unlike sociologists, have to take into account that death has already struck down a group of potential contributors.[40] Additionally, the very nature and the scope of the data that the qualitative interview produces makes it difficult to analyze too large a number of interviews. It was a question, therefore, of being sure of a qualitative representation, of knowing that the testimonies collected present a sufficient number of points in common to permit a certain degree of generalization. To put it another way, it was necessary to reach and then go beyond the "saturation point." This concept, borrowed from Daniel Bartaux, starts from the point of view that "beyond a certain number of interviews (biographical or not), the researcher or the team gets the impression that nothing new is being learned, at least insofar as the sociological object of the research is concerned."[41] The interviews have been pursued to the point where it became evident that further interviews would yield little in the way of new information regarding practices already identified, the recurrence of which was no longer in doubt. Thirty interviews were completed. According to a number of writers, this figure marks a significant stage: "it is unusual to learn new information after the twentieth or thirtieth interview."[42]

A homogenous sample constitutes a prior condition to any meaningful analysis of the data collected in this way. The informants thus had to fit certain criteria. The area of investigation, centred on domestic labour in the context of the depression of the 1930s, involved a sample of women who were already married at the beginning of that decade. The most catastrophic year according to the economic indicators, 1933, was used as a reference point. The probability that women who married much after this date would have felt the effects of the Depression on their domestic labour was indeed less great. Nevertheless, in order to be able to establish comparisons, it was necessary to find women who had spent the early years of their marriages before the Depression (this is clearly the case for eighteen of the respondents married in 1929 or before) or whose husbands had been working during the first months of the marriage (which is the case for all but one of the respondents).

The influence of the Depression and of unemployment was felt largely in urban areas and it was the men of the working class, especially unskilled labourers, and tradesmen who were primarily affected. These factors thus determined the selection of respondents who had to have lived in a working-class district of Montreal in the years between 1929 and 1939. The residence qualification, while it may seem rather vague, permitted us to enlist women who, because of their partners' occupations, had shared the living conditions of the working class without necessarily presuming their own class affiliations.[43] In order to maximize the chance of finding informants from this era, no particular district was selected.[44] Finally the respondents had to be French Canadian in origin (and therefore Catholic), their ethnic

and religious uniformity determining the community of culture essential
to a comparison and analysis of the material elicited. In the end, the sample consisted of the thirty women born between 1897 and 1916 and married between 1919 and 1934.

The interviews, which lasted on average for three hours, were all conducted in the respondents' homes, for the most part in the absence of wit-
nesses. Twenty-six of the women were widowed and lived by themselves,
while one lived with her daughter, who was present for a good part of the
interview. Four women lived with their husbands; of these men, two were
present off and on during the interview and intervened at greater or lesser
length, particularly when unemployment or their occupations were under
discussion. Their presence did not turn out to be so intrusive, however,
that the interviews completed under these circumstances had to be
rejected. On the contrary, it permitted us to deal with certain subjects
from their point of view (for example, women working for wages after
marriage, childbirth, the sharing of household chores and the like) and to
obtain information unknown to their wives (about their occupations,
their youth before they married, their feelings regarding unemployment
and the Depression, and so on). Moreover, it was not always possible to
avoid the unexpected visit of a daughter, a son, or a sister, but these people were present for part of the interview in only three cases.

Before the meeting, the subjects had been informed about the general
aim of the study and the principal points which would be touched upon.
The open-ended questions extended considerable latitude to the interviewee, who often recalled various stages of her life according to the reminiscences and stories which came to mind. In general, a good proportion of
the interviews unfolded in this manner, without the intervention of questions. This mode of procedure requires considerable skill in guiding an
interview so as to follow the rhythm and structure of the informant's narrative without losing track of the point which she has or has not dealt
with. But it yields the greatest amount of information, even if digressions
can be rather frequent. Ultimately, it might be said that an essential condition to a good interview is that the subject takes charge of it. "A life-nar-
rative does not exist until questions are no longer being answered and the
pleasure of telling one's story, of transmitting one's experience to another,
takes over."[45]

Appendix B presents thumbnail biographies of the informants which,
while respecting their anonymity, permit the extracts drawn from the
interviews to be repositioned in the larger life course of each individual. In

the chapters which follow, each of these extracts will be identified by a capital letter E followed by the number of the interview to which it corresponds. Finally, it should be noted that the order of the chapters in this study follow the order of the questions in the interview guide, which is reproduced in Appendix A. The analysis of the responses begins with two chapters on the childhood and youth of the informants up until their marriage, followed by close attention to the details of the life of the couple until the end of the thirties, especially in regard to the responsibilities that these women assumed within the family and to the impact of the Depression on different aspects of their domestic labour.

—————— *Chapter 2* ——————

From Birth to Marriage

> *"I certainly know that you get used to the role you take on." (E3)*

W hen the stock market crashed in 1929, the majority of the women interviewed for this study were at least twenty years old. Eighteen of them were already married or would get married that year; the rest married their husbands in the next few years. The decade of economic crisis that affected the Western world thus coincided with that stage in their lives when they began to assume their role as wife and mother. Before analyzing the impact of an economic crisis of this size on the assortment of tasks that they were called upon to shoulder within the family, a study of their previous history will permit us better to draw their profiles and take a look at the formative years that prepared them to take on their adult female roles.

Birth Families

It is during childhood and youth that we learn what we need to know, internalize behavioural norms, and adopt the role models and social values specific to our gender. For women born at the beginning of this century, this period of training and preparation for adult life was marked by the intensification of various winds of change that had been blowing through Quebec society for some decades. While imposing a new sexual division of labour based on the couple as provider/homemaker, the developing industrialization and urbanization that was becoming more pronounced

———————

Notes to Chapter 2 are on pp. 197-98.

during this period significantly modify traditional female life-courses and apprenticeships. Of course, the socialization of girls remains a function of their attributes as mother and wife, but the apprenticeship into these social roles does not cover the same realities as previously. In urban working-class families, at the very least, the market economy fosters the abandonment of the production of certain goods in the home and imposes new practices, while strategies of survival encourage more and more frequent integration of young women into the labour market. The typical life path of women of this generation follows the course of early socialization at home, then at school, followed by several years of waged work preceding marriage. Place of birth and early residence and the composition and stability of the birth-family are as important as how social roles are learned. This is why these elements deserve to be the object of detailed scrutiny.

Place of Birth and Residence

Twenty-six of the women interviewed were born in Quebec, two in the United States, and two in Ontario. Sixteen were born in urban areas, eleven of them in Montreal, and fourteen in rural areas. Of these, six were born on farms. A description which limited itself to these facts would, however, be misleading. Actually, the pulse of urbanization, which was accelerating at the beginning of the century, meant that a number of these women, though born in the countryside or outside of Quebec, came to Montreal during their childhood or adolescence and thus grew up, to a greater or lesser extent, in an urban context; a few of them, born in the city, travelled in the opposite direction.

These moves must be taken into account in order to understand the progress of the informants, since school attendance, training in household work, and the possibility of waged work vary according to social circumstances. The following table compares the birthplace of the informants with their place of residence upon marriage.

Table 1
Birthplace and Place of Residence at Marriage

	Urban			Rural		
	Montreal	Other	Total	Farm	Non-farm	Total
Place of birth	11	5	16	6	8	14
Res. at marriage	18	2	20	4	6	10

When taking the geographical mobility of the informants into account, we notice that two-thirds of them were already living in an urban setting (in Montreal or Verdun) by the time they were married. Leaving aside those whose families had left Ontario and the United States to move to the city when they were still children, four of them who were born in a rural area came to Montreal between the ages of thirteen and fifteen years.

More often than not, the motive for these moves was economic and actually aided the integration both of themselves and of other members of their families into the labour market. But these migrations also represented an uprooting and a radical change in lifestyle to which it was often difficult to adapt. "I was bored stiff. I didn't like the city at all. Everything was different—when you're fifteen, you have lots of friends in the villages, you know everybody" (E11). Some went back and forth between city and country several times. This is particularly true of one informant who was born in the United States and who lived in Montreal until the age of three, after which she migrated to a region of colonization before returning to Montreal ten years later. Another, born in Montreal, lived for several years in Ontario, then in a small town in the Montérégie, on the south shore off the island of Montreal, before marrying a man from the city. A Montreal family went to live at Pont Viau, north of the city, for several years in order to hide their sons and protect them from the Conscription Act of 1917. These frequent moves, important in regard to the socialization of the informants, seem also to indicate that urbanization, far from being a linear phenomenon, was instead accompanied by very various patterns of movement that were a function of the families' needs or particular circumstances.[1]

Father's Occupation and Standard of Living

The following table indicates the principal occupation of the informants' fathers (the occupation that they followed for the longest period while they were head of the household), listing whether they owned their own businesses, the nature of the work (manual or not) and the qualifications attained.

It is important to point out that this table provides a rather simplified view of the facts, since half of these men had more than one job, sometimes at the same time. Moreover, the job category of the father does not necessarily reveal the family's standard of living. Earnings provided by a particular job (which the informants did not always know), number of dependent or working children, and the seasonal nature of certain jobs are all factors which must be considered in evaluating the family's financial situation. In general, the families of unskilled workmen, casual labourers, and farmhands, despite the contribution of working children and even at times of working wives, achieved a very low standard of living:

> In those days, you know, as long as you had a kitchen, a table and chairs, and beds and chests of drawers.... We only had what was absolutely necessary, no luxuries. No living-room suites. Living-room suites and pianos were for the rich.... What I had was my little room. I had my little bed and my stepfather made me a little dresser out of orange crates. (E16)

Table 2
Father's Occupation

Occupation	Number
Farmer	6
Small business/self-employed tradesman	4
Office work/white collar	2
Skilled workman	12
Semi-skilled, unskilled, labourer	6
Total	30

Skilled workers were not, however, necessarily much better off in terms of an income sufficient to support a large family. In one weaver's case, for example, his family of seven children was crammed into a four-room flat. His daughter's recollections shed light not only on the poverty in which she grew up, but also on her mother's contribution to the family's survival:

> We didn't have electricity until I was twelve years old. We used lamps. We had a toilet in the house but no bathtub. We took baths in the laundry-tub. We had four rooms but there were seven of us children and that made nine with my father and mother. There was a large room in the back. There were two double beds in it—three of the girls slept in one and two in the other ... the washing machine was behind the door to the room and then there was a bureau between the two beds.... I don't know how my mother could get through. We really had to make miracles when there wasn't any money coming in. My father didn't care. It was my mother who had to see about getting coal, wood, food for the table. She sewed hand-me-downs so that we had dresses to wear. It was amazing what my third sister could get out of old clothes.... But we weren't unhappy—we didn't know anything better.... We always had clothing, we were never cold, we were never hungry, and we were always decently dressed. (E6)

The father of another woman, who, as a furrier, enjoyed quite a good salary as well as a certain prestige, nevertheless was unemployed for almost half the year. The relative comfort in which this family lived was the result of the financial contribution made by the older children and by two maternal aunts who lived with them:

> That meant that my father had to stop working in November and did not go back until after the fur market in New York was held in April. Then I had my sister and brother who were working regularly and who brought home what we needed.... We were fortunate to have my mother's two unmarried sisters living with us. One of them was a forewoman ... in a garment factory, the other was a lead milliner.... We had the advantage of having these two aunts dressing the two of us girls. We were always turned out looking much better off than we really were. (E15)

Having a skilled trade was thus far from being synonymous with having a sufficient or comfortable income, even when the father was working regularly, as the daughter of a painter employed by a railway company explained:

> We weren't rich, not even comfortable. It took everything we had to get by. In those days, my father ... the wages weren't very high. We came through all right. We never lacked anything, but you couldn't say we were comfortable.... In those days, nobody was rich. We went to work early. I think my oldest sister was twelve when she went to work. (E29)

According to certain of the respondents, rural families generally had larger living quarters and conditions which were less precarious because the farm produce assured they had something to eat. But the standard of life, on subsistence farms, was no higher for all that. In summer, the family often had to be content with a monotonous diet based on salt pork while the lack of cash reduced the purchase of manufactured goods to a bare minimum and eliminated any possibility of material comfort.

Whether they were born in the country or in town, the majority of the informants grew up in decidedly modest circumstances, that is, in families where the contribution made by children working either on the farm or in the factory was deemed essential to family survival. Lacking any other easily applicable standard, this indication indeed appears as one of the most relevant in determining the living standard of their families. If we add to it the information collected from these women regarding years of schooling, the age at which they first went to work, and their descriptions of their living quarters, we are able to conclude that only four had the benefit of a youth spent in comfortable circumstances. To the contrary, some experienced extreme poverty, often because of the death, illness, or alcoholism of their father. "Mama didn't bother to unpack because we knew that we'd have to move from one month to the next because if Papa didn't pay the rent, they would put us in the street" (E18). Not all of them experienced such extreme situations, but five of the families had to depend on charitable organizations like the Saint Vincent de Paul Society and on the mothers working for wages for a greater or lesser period of time. With the exception of one mother, who took in boarders to improve the family's lot, the paid work of the women always coincided with the father's absence or his inability to fulfil his role as provider. Only when pressed by direst necessity did mothers take jobs in factories or as domestics.[2] In general, however, when it came to supplementing the paternal income, the preference was to count on the waged work of the children, a subject that we will return to later.

Number of Children and Place in Family

The women interviewed came from families in which the number of children varied from one to fifteen, with an average of 7.2 children per family. We must note, however, that this average is based on the number of brothers and sisters with whom the informant grew up. Some could not in fact recall precisely how many children were born alive, how many were stillborn, and how many miscarriages their mother had had, which seems to have been a fairly common event.[3] As can be seen from the following table, whether they came from the city or the country, most came from families where there were between six and nine children, six being the most frequent number.[4]

Table 3
Number of Children Per Family Per Place of Residence

Number of children	Urban	Rural	Total
1-2	2	1	3
3-5	3	1	4
6-9	9	7	16
6	4	2	6
7	2	1	3
8	2	1	3
9	1	3	4
10 and more	2	5	7

Families of more than ten children, though frequently presented as the norm among Quebec francophones of this period, represent only a minority of the sample.[5] Furthermore, a majority, five out of seven of these families, lived in rural areas and it is interesting to note that the two urban families of more than ten children went to live outside of Montreal after the birth of the informants, both of whom were born fifth in their families.

In contrast, the small size of certain families is explained, in four cases out of the seven, by the death of one of the parents and by the infertility of a fifth couple who decided to adopt a single child. In the other cases, whether the parents sought to limit the size of the family or whether it was a question of chance is something which the informants did not know, but in a majority of cases, we cannot observe the results of birth control practices.

Seventeen of the informants knew that the number of pregnancies their mothers had conceived was greater than the number of infants carried to term and surviving to adulthood. In the thirteen other cases, either the number of children corresponds to the number of pregnancies or the informant did not know if her mother had miscarried or had lost children in early infancy. If we suppose that in these thirteen cases, there were no miscarriages or infant mortality, the number of pregnancies of the mothers of the respondents then rises to an average of 9.4; one of them had twenty-four pregnancies and ten others between ten and sixteen. Taking into account their place of residence, whether urban or rural, the following portrait emerges:

Table 4
Average Number of Children and
Pregnancies by Area of Residence

Origin	Number of women	Children	Pregnancies
Urban	16	6.3	8.2
Rural	14	8.2	10.7
Total	30	7.2	9.4

As we might expect, we can see that mothers of urban families raised fewer children and had fewer pregnancies than those from the countryside. Yet five of the women who raised between six and nine children in an urban setting had more than ten pregnancies. That is to say that if the majority of the informants grew up in families smaller than ten children, that was largely due to the deaths of parents or infants or to miscarriage.

In chapter four, which deals with the informants' experience of mother-hood, we will be able to evaluate the changes that these two generations experienced.

The birth position of children can influence their life course, in particular determining the length of schooling they acquire and the age at which they enter the workforce, and, if the child is a girl, the role she must play in regard to her mother and brothers and sisters. Where lack of money dictated, the eldest children were taken out of school at a very early age so that they could make their contribution to the family at the time when it consisted mostly of dependents. This was generally the case for women who were among the eldest, that is, the first three born into the less fortunate families. But when the eldest went to work, the younger members of the family were more likely to follow in their footsteps, even if they had a somewhat greater latitude to continue their education.[6] Thus several informants born fourth, fifth, or sixth in their families went to work at the age of fourteen, like their elder siblings before them.

Eldest daughters were frequently recruited to help their mothers when there were younger children to care for, but in the absence of a son, they might find themselves on the labour market sooner so that the task of helping the mother would devolve on a younger sister. The role of mother's helper could be assumed in turn—as the older girls grew up, they would go to work to be replaced by the next sister in line, who would then quit school. Finally, if the mother fell ill or died and the oldest girls were already married, a younger sister who was old enough would have to take charge of the house for her widowed father and her unmarried brothers. This was the case for four of the five younger sisters among the informants. There is indeed no direct or automatic relationship between birth order and remaining at home to help the mother. If the eldest daughters of large families were more frequently recruited for this position, various factors might come to bear so that any of the daughters would be called upon to play her part as right hand or substitute for the mother.

The presence of other people in the home was another factor that modified family life. Eleven informants lived with various relatives, uncles, aunts, but most often, grandparents, for a greater or lesser period of time.

> My two maiden aunts, my grandfather and his brother all lived with us. So, you see, at our house if we had a booboo or something, there was always a grown-up around to spoil us or sing us a lullaby. I was always well surrounded when I was a child. (E15)

The presence of these people could thus translate into additional attention and affection for the children in the family, as well as contributing additional income,[7] but they could also represent an additional restriction, especially in terms of living space. "The children were pushed around" (E2), explained one informant whose grandmother occupied a bedroom to herself, which meant that three of the children had to sleep in the diningroom while three others had to share one bed. A woman spoke this way about her sister who had returned home to live:

> It was during the 1914 war when my sister came to stay with us with her two children. Her husband was gone to the war. . . . We had to help with the little kids in the house like that. . . . They were really a pain. Just think, when we were seven, eight years old, playing outside, then my mother would call us in to take care of our little nephews. [One of them] was fourteen months old and cried a lot. She'd say, "Come put the baby to sleep." I said, "Me, I'm last in line—I don't have babies but I have to take care of one." (E29)

Two of the women interviewed lived with boarders, but their presence does not seem to have presented any major problems. According to one of the women:

> To start with, my mother put beds in the double parlour and they slept two to a bed. In those days, it didn't make any difference. . . . That is, people worked things out easily enough—there wasn't a problem as long as they were eating all right. (E16)

Their contribution to the family budget did not, however, slow the children's entry into the job market.

The phenomenon of the broken home was not a rare one in this period because death often carried off the parents when they were very young or illness prevented them from fulfilling their parental role.[8] Two of the informants were raised by their grandparents, one after the death of both her parents, the other because her widowed father had to earn his living and could not take care of her and her sister from whom, moreover, she would be separated at an early age. The youngest child of a family of seven was raised in part by her sister, who was fifteen years older, because her mother was too ill to care for her when she was born. For reasons she was not told, the eldest child of another family was sent to an aunt who was living in Ontario, where she went to primary school. She only saw her family every two weeks during the school year and in the summer during vacation. In order to be able to work, a widow had to place her three daughters in convents outside of Montreal, where the board was cheaper;

between the age of seven and fourteen years old, this informant lived there during the school year and often even during summer vacations, separated from her mother whom she saw only two or three times a year. Three other women lost their mothers when they were between the ages of fifteen and twenty. When she was thirteen, another came to live with one of her sisters who was working in Montreal as her parents had stayed in the country. Finally, within a matter of months, one of the informants lost her mother and then her grandmother, who had taken over; the family was forced to scatter and she found herself, at the age of fourteen, boarding with friends of her family and forced to work to support herself.

Thus, in eleven out of thirty cases, the women interviewed lost either their father or their mother before reaching adulthood, or, for various reasons, did not grow up with their natural parents. If we take into account these "broken" families and those who were living either with relatives or as boarders, we can observe that only fourteen lived in an intact "nuclear" family until they married. Thus it would appear that the model family centred on the couple and their children did not correspond to the reality experienced by the majority of women of this generation, at least before they were married.

School

For the majority of the women interviewed, their schooling represented only a brief stage preceding their assignment to domestic tasks or their entry into the job market. If most of them did learn the elements of reading, writing, and arithmetic, only five of them finished school. On average, they left school around the age of thirteen, that is, even before they had reached the legal age to work;[9] by the time they reached the age of fourteen, twenty-one of the women interviewed, or more than two-thirds, had either already quit school or were just about to do so. If it is true that the economic constraints on the family represented a genuine obstacle to education, we must also stress that quitting school was generally accepted as automatic, often without the parents even having to ask. "We didn't go any further," was what many of the informants said. Even if school tended to be abandoned as soon as possible, it could sometimes serve as a substitute for families who were experiencing some difficulties. Thus, several of the women interviewed boarded in a convent for a year or two, because of the illness or death of their parents. In rural areas, distance was a factor in choosing boarding as a solution that would allow one or more children to continue in school, if the family was able to pay the fees. But more often, the fact that institutions providing education beyond the primary grades might be far away encouraged early school-leaving.

Quitting school around the age of eleven or twelve was often preceded by irregular attendance, generally because the child was needed at home. "I couldn't [go to school]. I always had the kids on my back" (E18), as one of them said. "[My mother] made us miss school a lot to babysit" (E2), another stated. In rural regions, this obligation, together with bad weather and work on the farm, combined to reduce regular school attendance to a minimum. "We hardly went at all in winter—the roads were too bad.... I didn't go half the time" (E3). In general, all this absenteeism had the effect of discouraging any interest in studying and quitting school was therefore viewed with indifference or at least with no particular regret, even though certain of the respondents admitted to having enjoyed school. The eldest in large families were evidently more likely to be taken out of school very young, but, as we have already seen, the younger members of a family had a tendency to interrupt their studies quickly if their elder brothers and sisters had not finished school. In this case, quitting school could become a personal decision, as this recollection attests: "I got too many bad grades because of my handwriting.... That's why I left school. I told my mother I'd rather go to work than to school" (E8). In general, we do not encounter much of a difference in the level of schooling among the children of the same family; the youngest may have had less need to work but the climate in the family often meant that very few developed the kind of interest that would be necessary to finish a course of studies.

Only two of those who left school before the age of fourteen asserted that they would have liked to continue, an ambition which they passed on to their own children. But more often, the decision to quit school, whether imposed by circumstances or by parents, was viewed with a certain fatalism, as we see in the account by this informant:

> In those days, we didn't react the way they do now; there wasn't any rebellion. I couldn't go board. I would've liked to. I couldn't—I had to help out at home. So, that was the end of that—that was all there was to it. I didn't hold it against anyone—not my parents or the children who were coming up behind me. It wasn't their fault. In those days, you accepted sorrows like you accepted joys. You didn't rebel against your parents. (E20)

With the exception of one informant who went to work as a domestic, the women who quit school at eleven or twelve did so to help their mothers at home for a few years before going to work for wages. On the other hand, leaving school after the age of thirteen coincided with taking a job. Around fourteen or fifteen, this transition represented a normal and generally well-accepted step.

Working Experience

The years at work before marriage, more than the few years they passed in the classroom, represented an important stage in the lives of the informants. Whether at home or in the factory, the majority contributed to the family economy at a very young age and several of these women spent more time at a machine or a loom than at a school desk. "I had to do something to earn my keep" (E12), one explained. This sentiment that everyone ought to take on as early as possible a portion of one's upkeep by going to work was still widespread among families that had recently entered the working class.

Domestic, Factory Hand or Salesgirl?

With the exception of three informants who lived on farms until their marriage and a fourth who was raised by her grandparents in relative comfort, all the women in this sample held paid employment. Ten of the twenty-six girls who went to work first spent some months and sometimes several years helping their mothers with the housework. But all of them who lived in the city or even near a factory area worked for wages. In fact, their recollections indicate that the participation of girls in the labour force had become the norm in working-class families (and even in some farm families) at the beginning of the twentieth century.[10] The progress of industrialization both in Montreal and in the province, as well as changes in the job market would have brought about a greater participation of girls in the labour market.

Generally speaking, provisions of legislation concerning child labour were widely known and respected; just one informant began work at the age of twelve as a domestic, while three others were working behind shop counters, part-time, at the age of thirteen. In certain families, the need for additional income obliged the children to perform small jobs for the neighbours in return for a little money while they were still in school (errands, babysitting, and the like). But these small jobs seem hardly commonplace, at least among girls, and more often, they waited until they were fourteen before looking around for a steady job. By that age, half of the twenty-six women were working, while three more began work during their fifteenth year. Among those who went to work after the age of fifteen, seven delayed their entry into the job market in order to help their mothers for several years, while the delayed entrance is explained for three others by their remaining at school longer.

The family, which determined when the child went to work, often acted as an agent when it came time to find a job.[11] Therefore, it commonly fell to the mother to place her daughters as domestics. In some cases, she would even use the classified ads: "Mama got us jobs as maids. She put an ad in the newspaper and people came to see us; they came to our house so that they could find out what kind of people we were. We packed up our bits and pieces and went to their houses" (E2).

Apprenticing a child, though rarer, was also organized by the mother, who always decided what trade her daughter was going to take up. This is the way that two of the informants became a milliner and a chocolate-maker, while three others were apprenticed as hat-makers. What these latter three have to say, however, makes it clear that fairly often they did servants' work at the cost of their training and only one went on to take up the trade. "The woman was supposed to show me how to make hats, but she didn't. She had me washing the shop windows, sweeping, and cleaning" (E16). But even if they did get good training, the conditions were often only fair:

> She showed me the trade. Those were the days when we shaped our hats on wire forms.... She showed me how to line the hats, then put on ribbons, do the fancy-work. Then I had to stay there Friday nights. She gave me fifty cents for the week and my supper on Friday. She was what you call a head seamstress, she made models and samples. She made supper for the two of us. You know what she made? You know those nineteen-ounce cans of creamed corn? The two of us ate that with some bread. That was our supper! They were mean in those days. They made everybody work for nothing. But we were so happy just to be working.... As for me ... I used to walk to save my big fifty cents so I could give it to my mother. (E16)

Those whose elder sisters preceded them at work had an easier route to finding a job. In this connection, we should observe that the ghettoization of female employment seems clearly to have been in play since the informants almost never mention the presence of a brother in their place of work. One exception is worthy of note, however. In this case, the informant and her family were recruited by an agent to emigrate to Montreal to work in a textile factory.[12]

Lacking an elder sister, an aunt, a cousin, or a friend might act as go-between. The classified ads were seldom used, since even without contacts, finding a job presented little difficulty. "In those days, we just went and asked if they needed help. It wasn't like now.... You had to go see the owner of the plant—he was the manager. You had to go through him" (E20). "I was the one who went to ask for a job. In those days we went to find jobs on our own. But it wasn't as hard as it is now to find a job" (E8). Most of the informants used these informal means to get hired.

Very often they were hired on the spot on the basis of a quick glance on the part of the employer. In any event, he wasn't taking much of a risk because teaching the work to the new employee fell to the part of the "senior" woman who would show her how the machines operated. After a couple of hours or a couple of days, rarely for more than a week, the new hand would have to fend for herself and if she couldn't, she risked being fired. A number of the informants insisted on the quickness at which they learned and turned out the work, an essential quality given the speed of the machines and the piecework system, the most widespread method of payment.[13] Rather than complaining about the pace, their comments reflect their pride in having been able to adapt to working conditions which demanded speed and precision.

With bureaucratic formalities reduced to a minimum, it was also easy enough to find a new job if pay raises did not come along quickly enough or if the employer turned out to be too demanding. Of course, the majority of the respondents worked during the 1920s, a period of relative prosperity. "We would walk out at noon and then an hour later, start up somewhere else" (E21), as one of them said. Actually, the oral accounts allow us to observe a very great mobility in the labour force which manifests itself not only in changing employers but even occupations.

Table 5
Occupations of Informants

Occupations	A[a]	B[b]
Teacher	2	2
Nurse's aid	1	1
Clerk	5	1
Sales clerk	6	1
Skilled labour	2	1
Unskilled labour	14	9
Domestics	7	1

a Number of informants in this occupation.
b Number of informants for whom this was their only occupation.

Looking at this table reveals that it was the factory workers who changed their occupation least often though the majority of them worked for more than one employer. We may note that they worked longer than the other women in the sample; it is among this group that is found the four women who worked for more than ten years before marriage. On the other hand, domestic work, generally detested because of its servile character and because of the extremely long hours which it entailed, is where we observe the greatest mobility, as only one informant worked exclusively as a domestic and she did so for a rather short period of time (one year). As one of the women explained, "We didn't like working in private homes because we couldn't go out. We spent whole weeks with those people" (E2). Domestics' wages were extremely low, between one and five dollars a week, but according to one informant, "What our parents counted was the food. You understand, if you have two working, that's two less to feed" (E2). Most of the time, domestic work represented a transitional occupation between the home and the factory, or the office or shop. These jobs, factory worker, saleswoman or clerk, generally involved a noticeable increase in salary, but what was more appreciated were the working conditions, particularly regular hours and the possibility of contact with other working women. "It was clean, and we weren't bored. It wasn't like in the private homes, where the day was never over. . . . The hell with private homes! We were happy enough—we had our evenings free" (E2).

In this connection, it must be stressed that it was not simply the household tasks or the conditions inherent in this kind of work that put them off, but also, and most particularly, the context in which they arose. Beyond the isolation, the arbitrary employers, the long hours, and the array of tasks demanded of them, what they detested above all else was the idea of being "in service to" someone else, of playing the subordinate's role in a highly personalized relationship.[14] This factor would explain why women did not express the same sentiments regarding the household tasks they performed for their own families, as we shall see later on.

At the other end of the scale, a career as a teacher represented one of the principal openings for young women in rural areas where the school commissioners were not very demanding in terms of their training:

> In those days, they didn't expect normal school. We had our diploma, the first diploma, not the higher diploma, and that allowed us to teach. . . . You know, it was almost automatic because there wasn't much for girls to do aside from teaching. You had to be satisfied with going out to clean or being a maid. To us, this didn't offer us girls anything—we'd had enough of kids at home. (E19)

Thus, the restricted range of possible jobs for young women, not to speak of the distaste they evinced in regard to working as maids, directed a number of them to choose factory work or teaching.

One informant worked as a stenotypist; she took a private course, paid for by her unmarried aunt, who lived with the family. "Mama could not pay for it what with the cost of keeping up the house, so my aunt said to me—she had read about it in the paper—'If you want, if you're interested, I'll pay for your course'" (E15). The other informants who worked as office clerks or employees did not have any particular training; one of them first worked as a sales clerk before being "transferred to the office" where she did the accounts; another was a domestic before being employed checking the washing in a laundry. Finally, we must point out that one of them was a victim of sexual harassment on the part of three successive employers, which led her to abandon this sort of employment to become a milliner.[15]

Despite difficult working conditions and low wages, most often they appreciated their work experience: "For me, it was like going to a wedding, working there" (E29). Not everyone expressed such enthusiasm, but most retained clear memories of this period in their lives that they liked to talk about. The atmosphere and the relationships with other women at work were generally good, but it was rare that friendships born in the workplace went outside the factory walls and only a few mention leisure-time activities shared with their workmates. Leaving work, which occurred shortly before marriage, generally put an end to these short-lived friendships: "There were some who got married while I was there, but then they disappeared—we didn't see them any more" (E23). Only two informants preserved friendships from that period of their life. It appears that married life provided few opportunities for women to pursue personal relationships. After they left the factory, their lives became redirected as a function of their new role as wife and mother and the responsibilities that it entailed. As we shall see, these new obligations were so absorbing that they would hardly have time for themselves. After they married, their social circle would shrink to women of their immediate family (and sometimes a neighbour or two), who were also married and mothers.

Despite this complete, if sometimes only temporary, break with the workplace, all could still describe, with effect and often with pride, the details of the different operations they performed as part of their job in the factory or the office. Others could recall, sometimes with emotion, the children they took care of or the generosity of a "madame" who treated them "like one of the family." In general, they had few complaints about bosses or foremen, even when they were demanding. In any case, the absence of unions meant that they either had to adapt themselves or quit. According to the narratives, none of them had had contact with a union and they had little to say on the subject: "We didn't talk about that in our day" (E7); "We never heard about them" (E8); "We didn't talk about it—we only had the boss" (E11).

The obligation to contribute to the family finances on the other hand excited a mass of reflections, often very different from one another, especially among the fifteen informants who gave their entire wage to their parents until marriage. In the majority of cases, they would give their pay to their mother and "you mustn't open the envelope," several specified. One of them recalled the resentment that she felt during this period. "Myself, when I was fifteen, I was rebelling. I said to myself, we raise the kids. If they're not able to support four, why make five? I realized later that it was how it was then, that it was a mortal sin to use birth control" (E6).

Most, however, recognized that their contribution was essential and displayed a resigned understanding in this regard. "They needed the money. We gave them our wages. Of course, we kept a few pennies" (E19). Several of them justified this practice by the fact that the parents supported them and by the fact that they didn't have much opportunity to spend their money. "We were well dressed, well fed, we didn't lack anything. It isn't like today, we didn't have so many things to do in our free time" (E11).

Most of the time, out of all of her salary, the young woman got twenty-five or fifty cents, sometimes a dollar, rarely more. Much of this money was spent on transportation; evenings at the movies at ten or fifteen cents a time, as well as life insurance premiums, or buying silk stockings or other personal expenses ate up the rest. One way of getting a little more money than the parents allotted, a rather common practice, it appears, was to erase the amount of money written on the envelope and replace it with a lower sum, pocketing the difference. "That was stealing! That was stealing from your parents. We weren't used to that kind of thing!" (E23) one informant indignantly remarked. So, if certain young women allowed themselves to "cheat" in order to achieve a slightly greater degree of financial autonomy, for this informant, as for the majority of her contemporaries, the children's wages belonged to the parents by right and to divert part of the money for your own use was seen as theft. This suggests the degree to which the notion of the family as a labour unit in which the needs and desires of the individuals that comprise it are not taken into account was still firmly fixed in working-class families of the first or second generation. It goes without saying that none of our informants admitted to having pulled this particular trick!

It is important to point out that boys did not benefit from much greater latitude than the girls when they were among the oldest in the family. As they got older, however, they could keep a larger part of their wages more often than the girls could.[16] As one informant remarked, "They kept a little more—if they were taking a girl out, that cost them more. In those days, girls didn't pay for anything" (E19).

Contributing to the family income did not bring about much of a change in the child's status in the family or grant her greater autonomy. As one informant explained, "I hadn't grown up in their eyes. Oh, no! I started [to work] when I was barely sixteen. I was old enough to work, but I wasn't old enough to have a boyfriend" (E15). Because of their poverty, the parents in fact had no other choice than to count on the revenue provided by their children's labour; they had to maintain a certain degree of authority in order to require them to contribute to the family upkeep.

When several children were working or when the family had fewer dependents, it was then possible to keep one's salary and contribute to the family by paying board. This mode of functioning, which permitted a greater financial autonomy, seems to have been greatly appreciated by those who experienced it. "There were lots of families where they gave all their pay—for myself, I liked it much better this way . . . if I couldn't buy myself something to wear, I wouldn't take it out on my parents" (E29). A number of the informants began by turning over their pay but as they got older or as their salaries rose, paid board that ranged between three and ten dollars a week. At that point, the young worker became wholly responsible for her personal expenses; one of the informants shared the cost of the telephone bill with her sisters because it was principally used to receive phone calls from their boyfriends, at least according to their parents. Their savings also had to go toward a trousseau for their marriage and to pay for the cost of their outfit, and sometimes even for the wedding and the reception. Thus the financial autonomy enjoyed by those who retained a part of their salary was accompanied by obligations which meant that very few were able to save up a little nest egg that would last until they married.

Learning Domestic Work

Generally speaking, girls began to learn domestic work when they started school, though some of them developed particular skills even younger than that, as a respondent recalls with pride: "I started knitting before I went to school" (E4). In rural areas, the children had to milk the cows before going to school in the morning. They worked in the garden and in the farmyard and helped out with a whole host of tasks:

> She [my mother] planted flax—we shredded it into tow. Afterwards we would spin it into weft for the loom. That's what we did in the summer. In winter, we prepared our weaving for the vacation. We spun wool in the winter to weave, to make into wool blankets, even skirts.... Us girls did all that. We spun scented grass and sold that in Odanak to the Indians who made baskets out of it.... My mother would go there to sell it. Then my mother could get a lot of goods with that, with the money. (E22)

Girls also had to help their mothers with the various tasks associated with making bread, preserves, jam, and other foods. Making soap and candles as well as clothing were jobs in addition to the usual household tasks of cooking, laundry, and cleaning. The workday, which began early, extended until late in the evening as the women spun, wove, or knitted by the light of a kerosene lamp.

In town, the range of tasks was more restricted but girls started doing work around the house very young as a rule. When they were of school age, girls were doing the daily housework (sweeping, dusting, washing the floors), accompanying their mothers to the grocery or the market, setting the table and doing the supper dishes and sometimes those of the noon meal before returning to school. Some of them in this period began to accomplish more complicated tasks:

> I was back from the convent school and then I sewed on the machine. I pieced quilts.... I always helped Mama with the dishes. We had a ton of dishes! I helped her do the cooking on the weekends. And then there was the laundry—in those days, we didn't have the machines you have now. I used the washboard to help my mother. A glass board. You scrubbed. I wasn't very old when I was using a washboard.... I was doing the housework since I was no bigger than that. (E20)

Watching the babies and sometimes even taking care of them was also part of their responsibilities, as the following remark attests: "When you're a big family, it's the first one who picks up the baby that changes its diaper. You can't wait for Mama because she's doing something else.... When I got married, my youngest brother was a year and a half old—when I stopped having to wash diapers, I was forty" (E6).

A number of women assert that they were able to keep house competently by the time they were twelve or thirteen. Those who had mothers who worked outside the home or were ill had to put into practice very early the skills they had learned: "I was twelve then [when my mother went to work for a few months]," an informant recalled. "I took care of the house" (E6). Another remembered: "I was thirteen when she went to work and I found myself taking care of the three youngest boys.... I kept house—I was used to it, I'd always helped out" (E25). If a number of them took great pride in what they had done, some regretted that their childhood had eluded them. "I grew up very young" (E6), one of them stated, summing up their feelings.

Their fathers and brothers participated in the housework to the degree that it involved some physical strength or took place outside (taking out the ashes or the garbage, splitting wood, bringing in water, shovelling snow, and the like). But these tasks, especially in the country, could just as well be performed by the women. "We didn't always wait around for the men" (E3), and "That wasn't always men's work" (E4), were comments that cropped up often. In some families, both rural and urban, the boys were called upon to perform some "women's work" around the house, but as soon as the girls could take over, their contribution ceased. In one informant's home, "on Fridays and Saturdays, my mother went to sell at the market ... and then the rest of us on Saturdays had to do the housework. Two of the boys we got to wash the kitchen floor.... The boys did the dishes and made their beds in the mornings" (E21). But this level of participation by boys was quite exceptional and the following quotation corresponds more closely to what we more frequently heard: "Little boys were like little kings. Very few homes made the boys work. They couldn't be touched. If there was something to be done, the girls did it. The boys worked for money—delivering groceries" (E5).

Having a job meant less time for housework. In the evenings and on Saturdays, young working women nevertheless helped with the housework, and did the shopping and the dishes, but rarely the cooking or the washing. For this reason, certain of the respondents who had quit school in order to take a job right away claimed that their knowledge of cooking and sewing was rather limited and went so far as to swear that they had not felt really ready to keep house at the time of their marriage. "I got married without knowing how to do anything" (E23), said one of them;

another related, "I told him [her future husband] that since I was working, I didn't know how to cook" (E15). A third agreed, "When I got married, I'd never sewed or cooked" (E24).[17]

Learning how to do housework could thus also be limited to the performance of simple skills that did not demand the kind of technique or knowledge associated with cooking or sewing. In part, their jobs prevented the young women from being more available, but according to a number of informants, their mothers did not seem especially anxious to teach them how to sew and saw the kitchen as their own domain where they did not tolerate any intrusion. Were they motivated by lack of time, fear of waste, or by pride in their position as mistress of the house who wanted to stay in control of these two important aspects of their work? Their motives were not always clear, but the following remarks reflect the lack of training experienced by some of the informants: "I used to ask my mother to show me how to sew and she'd say, yes, yes, I'll show you. . . . She never did show me" (E15). Another said, "Mama could sew but she never let me near her sewing machine. Never, because she could do it—that's what she told me" (E7). Another had a similar recollection: "I couldn't touch the machine. . . . She didn't want us to be involved with anything to do with food. We could look, but touching—no" (E27); yet another: "That [cooking] she didn't want me to do. That was for her; me, I learned to cook after I got married" (E8). Additionally, the division of work among various girls in the family could mean that some of the girls developed certain skills while others did not. Thus, in one family, the three older sisters shared responsibility for cooking, cleaning, and sewing, each taking charge of one area. "If there was time to make pies and cakes, then I was there. But my oldest sister, she was the one who did the sewing—she sewed on the buttons and did the mending for my little brothers. . . . When I got married, I didn't know how to sew" (E19).

The following table shows the different modes of learning the two most complex household tasks as well as at what point they were learned:

This table shows that if the majority of the informants learned the rudiments of cooking and sewing from their mothers, how and when these two important elements of modern domestic labour were learned varied more than we might have thought. Thus, one-third of the women in the sample learned how to cook after they were married, whether on their own or from the mother-in-law, when the young couple were living with his parents. One learned from her employer when she was a domestic (recorded as "work" in Table 6).[18]

Table 6
Learning Domestic Work

When learned	How learned	Cooking	Sewing
Before marriage	Mother (or substitute)	19	11
	Training	0	1
	Work	1	2
After marriage	Mother-in-law	4	0
	Mother	0	2
	Organization	0	1
	Friend/neighbour	0	2
	Self	6	4
Never learned		0	7

When it came to dressmaking, the respondents note that, unlike cooking, they sometimes turned for advice to friends or neighbours. Having worked as a domestic or as a dressmaker also provided good training. An informant who never had a paid job spent time as an apprentice to a dressmaker in a neighbouring village:

> I spent a year in M with a woman who took on apprentices. She had us doing hems and she showed us how to sew. That's how I learned how to sew. Because my mother was good, she could sew well, but she told me, "I can't show you everything. I don't know how to make clothes. You'll be better off if you go out to learn." I was there a year to learn.... I lived in the woman's home. This woman was the sister of our old school teacher and she did dressmaking for everyone in M. That's how I learned.... We had to bring our own food. She gave us a bed, but we had to bring our own covers. If I didn't have something to eat, my father gave me a few bucks and I would buy what I needed.... There were two of us—she always had two apprentices.... She was always in demand as a sewing teacher. (E17)

School does not appear to have played a large role in the teaching of sewing, nor, for the most part, of cooking either. In fact, none of the women we interviewed attended homemaking schools and very few learned basic cooking at school; at the most, they were taught to mend and to knit. The cost and the space needed for the equipment to teach these subjects probably explains why so few of the schools in the public sector offered them.

Even more striking is the relatively high number of women who did not know how to sew when they got married—sixteen out of thirty—although a very large majority of their mothers did sew. Seven of them never learned while nine others had to learn as the constraints of a very tight budget left them no option. Abandoning instruction in sewing, which was, up until then, an important part of domestic labour, represents the clearest indication of the kind of transformations in housework that was occurring in this period.

———

*T*he view we get from the analysis of the first stage of the life cycle of these informants allows us to observe that their socialization, centred on the roles of wife and mother to which they were destined, was also punctuated by experiences that might contradict these objectives. In fact, most working-class families could not do without the financial contribution of their daughters, fostering their entry into the job market, sometimes to the detriment of their training as future housewives. But as wage work was imposed because of the priority given to the family economy, without regard to individual needs and aspirations, it contributed to reinforce the sense of duty and the values of devotion and self-effacement that girls were expected to develop in preparation for their future marriage. The poverty in which they grew up represents another factor that demands our attention, because the women would evaluate the difficulties they encountered during the Depression in the light of their living conditions as children and young women.

Chapter 3

Beyond Romance: Courtship and Marriage

"Then you were happy—you got married and you thought you were going to heaven." (E2)

Marriage represented a critical stage in the life of women of this generation. Even if, by virtue of the Civil Code, the young woman only left her father's authority to pass to the guardianship of her husband, marriage marked a new stage in the life cycle which was emphasized by the religious ceremony and the celebrations which accompanied it. In marriage, the young woman took her partner's name, swore to honour and obey him, left her parents for a new home, and expected to engage in sexual activity, which was now sanctioned to the degree that it would allow her to become a mother, the only condition which conferred on women genuine adult status.

One of the effects of the Depression was the postponement or even cancellation of many marriages; this effect did not appear in the present sample.[1] This group consisted of eighteen women who were married between 1919 and 1929 (five of them in 1929), ten women married between 1930 and 1932, and two married in 1934 and 1935. Thus twelve of them were married after the Depression had begun, but with the exception of one woman, who delayed her marriage for three years because fiancé was unemployed, only one couple, married in the autumn of 1929, was worried about the economic climate to the point that they investigated the likelihood of the husband's losing his job and chose a closer, and

---

therefore cheaper, destination for their honeymoon. It should be noted that they were the couple who were the best off in the sample and thus had the most to lose. As we shall see, this indifference on the part of the other couples indicates clearly that men and women of modest circumstances did not hope for ideal conditions before being wed.

Courtship

Going to work around the age of fourteen marked the beginning of meetings and outings with boys. Generally, however, it was not before the age of sixteen or even eighteen that parents would permit their daughter to entertain her suitor in the evening, a symbol of the serious dating that preceded a trip to the altar. In order to reduce the risk of premarital sex, they sought to reduce the length of time that the young people might go steady, something that was not supposed to occur before the suitor was ready to start a family.

These acquaintances commonly were made within a rather narrow circle of people. In the majority of matches, the informants met their husbands through their families, friends, or neighbours, most often through a combination of the three: "I knew his sister, she lived near us and I went over there a lot. One fine day, he came when I was there" (E8); "When I decided to get married, it was to a nice boy who happened to be a friend of my brother. He lived in our street. He was a friend of the family" (E15).

Five of the informants, however, met their husband at their place of work,[2] while six others made the acquaintance by chance while walking about the neighbourhood[3] or when at the movies, thus without any introduction. Thus young women met young men predominantly through family and immediate neighbours, but their horizons were enlarged as they went to work and as they engaged in new kinds of leisure activities, like the movies. Automobile outings for the luckiest,[4] ice-skating on the public rinks in winter, picnics on Saint Helen's Island, then reached by boat, and outdoor concerts in parks in the summer, as well as dance parties in friends' homes or in municipal halls are among the various activities that urban young people enjoyed, sometimes in flagrant violation of the dictates of the Church. The following recollection provides a good description of the sort of youth many experienced before they married:

> in the evenings, we'd go out, that was to walk around, eh? We took walks—
> we went from St. Henri to Verdun. There was a dance hall on the water.
> That's where we went to dance. The priest were against it but . . . it's funny
> to tell you this, but the boys in our day, it wasn't life like it is today, they

respected us. There were all-night parties. They arranged them with the families. It would start around nine o'clock and go on till six o'clock Mass the next morning! We would dance! And none of the boys would try to kiss us. They weren't our boyfriends—we were all just friends. When we met each other to go dancing, it wasn't like it is now. . . . We had a lot of fun, but it was decent. [Those boys] all lived right around us. We all lived in the same neighbourhood. We'd meet each other at the Corona Theatre on Notre Dame Street. We knew their families. (E29)

If some of the women interviewed claimed to have had a number of "beaux," most of them went steady only with their husband. Actually, ten of them had had two serious suitors, but only two of them chose to break off with their first boyfriend themselves, one because the young man made "dishonest" propositions to her and the other because her fiancé had expressed his intention to go on giving his pay to his mother after they were married. But more often, it was the young man who broke things off, which he might do rather brutally, seeing that it would be enough for him simply to stop coming by every week without any other explanation. On the other hand, if his visits remained regular and the young woman agreed to entertain him, then the couple were almost obliged to continue in the direction of marriage. Dating etiquette, which mandated that girls could not demonstrate any interest without transgressing the norms of behaviour suitable to their sex, limited their freedom of choice to boys who were interested in them, and explains why they were reluctant to break up with their boyfriends out of fear of being left "on the shelf." If she could always refuse the attentions of a suitor, the young girl was still the one who was chosen rather than the one who chose.[5] The following recollection is a good illustration of this situation:

His brothers came and bought a farm at S. Then he came to pay a visit to his brothers—when he was at their place, he would come by every evening. . . . Finally, well, he said, "If you want to, we could get married." I said, "I don't know, give me time to think about it." Because there was another boy who came from the town—he only came in the summers to spend his vacation with his uncle. And he often came to our house because my father knew them well. His aunt told him, "She's a pretty girl and she can keep a good house," then . . . anyway, I decided to marry my husband. And that put an end to my romances. (E17)

Uncertain about the intentions of the young man from the city whom she clearly preferred but who did not seem interested in her, despite his aunt's hints, this informant finally chose to accept the marriage proposal of another suitor. Her conclusion ("and that put an end to my romances") underlines the absence of romantic sentiment that characterized certain marriages, which were based more on mutual respect or a certain pragmatism.

Even if parents were generally content to exercise a discreet and indirect surveillance over the unmarried couple, they rarely found themselves alone with one another, so important was it to preserve the young woman's virginity, whether or not she was of age. This concern would even grow with industrialization and the appearance of new places for young people to meet away from traditional family settings, since it became more difficult to exercise control over the young.[6] On dates, the parents made sure that the couple was accompanied by a brother, a sister, other adults, or, if necessary, their friends: "In our house, I was never allowed to go out all by ourselves. My brother was always along as chaperone.... You know, we had chaperones in those days"(E19). On visits to the young woman's home, which were a feature of serious courtship, the young couple rarely found themselves alone in the parlour. If it were to happen, the likelihood that a family member might interrupt at any time was generally enough to guarantee exemplary behaviour. The fear of later being blamed for her conduct—so embedded was the notion that only the woman sinned if she engaged in sexual activities outside of marriage—or worse yet, of being abandoned for not remaining "pure" until the wedding night was generally enough to see to it that the girls would demand that their fiancés behave themselves properly,[7] as this informant explains in guarded language:

> You must always respect yourself, that's the main thing.... If you respect
> yourself, then he'll respect you for your whole life. Because there are plenty
> of men, when the woman ... later, when things go bad, they'll shove it in
> your face. I said to myself, he'll never shove it my face.... Then later he
> told me too, if you'd been a woman "like that" I would never have married
> you.... no, you should never have anything to reproach yourself for. I got
> married and I called him Monsieur C. and he called me Mademoiselle B.
> You're going to say that it's ridiculous, but that's what it was like in those
> days. (E28)

In the case of long engagements, however, it sometimes required a great deal of willpower to resist "temptation," as another respondent explained:

> It was about time we got married—how many times did we almost go
> wrong. Even though it was very strict, there were always ways, right? And I
> could not give in to temptation. In those days, for us, you could go to hell.
> It was a mortal sin.... And, of course, some did get pregnant. (E24)

Actually, the watchfulness of companions and self-control did not prevent all premarital sex. Despite the prohibitions, amorous urges sometimes overcame morals or the fear of losing, all at once, one's virtue, reputation, and fiancé. Thus two of the thirty informants became pregnant before marriage. In both cases, the couples became involved when they were very young, a circumstance which prolonged the period of abstinence.[8]

> When I was eighteen, my mother let him come to the house—before that we used to meet on the sly. . . . He would come to the lane behind the house with his bicycle and whistle. . . . We met each other when we were fifteen and gave in at eighteen or nineteen because the longer it went on, the more passionate we felt. At the end of the day, I was pregnant when I was twenty and got married when I was four or five months gone. (E13)

Despite the "sin" she had committed, her parents proved rather understanding: "Mama put her arms around me and hugged me and said, 'All right, then, you'll get married. We have to make things right.' No one ever criticized me" (E13). Their situation was effectively "regularized" since in both instances, the young man agreed to acknowledge paternity and marry the young woman, thus avoiding the necessity for her to spend time in Miséricorde Hospital and to give up her child to its orphanage, as well as having her reputation and that of her family forever tarnished. It must be pointed out that the father-in-law of one of them did suggest an abortion: "My father-in-law heard about it and wanted me to get an abortion. I said no—if I was having a baby I would keep it—I wouldn't have an abortion" (E13). The marriage, precipitated by the situation, took place discreetly—there were few guests, the wedding dress camouflaged the bride's "condition," and they made a brief honeymoon trip to preserve appearances.

In addition to exercising fairly strict supervision, the parents generally expressed their approval or disapproval regarding the choice of mate. If in most cases the range of social occasions made it likely that girls would meet young men from families that were already acceptable, still it could happen that parents might intervene and demand that a relationship be broken off if the suitor or his family did not seem "good enough" to them, or if he did not seem serious enough to get married, or because another candidate appeared more suitable. Four of the informants had to break off with their fiancés for one or another of these reasons. Two of them later met another young man who met with unanimous approval, a third married the candidate her parents preferred, which turned out to be a disastrous choice, while the fourth reunited with the one she loved and married him over the objections of her mother, who did not attend her wedding and with whom she remained on bad terms for fifteen years. Without mounting a formal opposition, some parents expressed reservations about a marriage which they considered hasty because they thought their daughter too young or the engagement too short. "Mama told me, 'You don't know him, you haven't had the time to get used to him'"(E8), said one informant who had gone out with her future husband for only four months.

On average, the couples went out with one another for a little more than two years before getting married, but there are large variations from one couple to another; in thirteen cases out of thirty, they dated for less than two years and in six of these cases, for less than a year. On the other hand, a third of the informants dated their husbands for more than four years before going to the altar. These long engagements were less the function of economic difficulties than of the extreme youth of the couples, which required that they wait for a longer period of time before being wed. They were often interrupted by breaks imposed either by circumstances or the parents:

> We had a number of dates, I suppose. In the winter, we went in groups—we went skating with my brothers. We did that all winter. . . . After Christmas, then the retreats began in February, the parish retreats—the priests preached from the pulpit [how] the boys had all the sins in the world. Then Mama said, "No more boyfriends. If you don't tell them, then I'll tell them myself." So then . . . I told my [future] husband, "Mama says that we're too young to go out together during the retreats. . . ." When the retreats came along, the boyfriends took off! That's how it went for three years. . . . That meant he must have been the one for me because anyone else would never have come back. (E15)

In one case, however, marriage was delayed for three years because the fiancé had lost his job due to the Depression, while in another, the woman explained her long engagement by the low salary her fiancé was earning and the hold his mother had over him:

> We didn't have any money. Engagements lasted a long time in those days because the pay was so low. And then, they had a mother who took all their money. She'd say, "Give me your money and when you get married, I'll outfit you." In those days, it wasn't like today, the children gave in to everything. (E11)

In general, the couple's economic situation did not seem to be the primary influence on the decision to marry. As we will later see, the majority of them in any event were in a rather shaky economic position at the time of their marriage.

On average, the women in the sample were 21.4 years old and the men 24.9 at marriage. In fact eighteen of the women married before the legal age of twenty-one. Of these women, three were sixteen, seventeen, and eighteen, and eight were nineteen. Likewise, the great majority of the men were younger than twenty-five when they married. Given that the sample is composed of survivors of this period, it is possible that it is formed in part of people married younger than the average for their generation.[9] On the other hand, these figures are in accord with those Lucia Ferretti found for the working-class parish of Sainte Brigide at the turn of the century,[10] confirming the role played by social class in determining age at marriage. Because they did not have to conform to the conditions prevailing in rural regions, where they would have to wait until they owned land if they did not inherit the family farm, or of the middle class, where sons first had to acquire a profession, working-class men had the possibility of marrying at a younger age, that is, as soon as they had a reasonably steady job.[11] This condition represented a kind of minimum standard—among the husbands of the women interviewed, some had savings and were earning wages sufficient to assure the decent support of their families. For the majority, however, their low wages excluded one or the other of these possibilities—in these circumstances, it was pointless to delay marriage indefinitely.

The ways and places that young people became acquainted, centred as they were on family and neighbourhood, fostered a very considerable geographical and social endogamy. In twenty-two out of thirty cases, the couples in fact came from the same district, the same locality, or from a neighbouring district or village. As well, although it might happen that the in-laws were better off, it was unusual for marriage to allow one of the partners to rise to a higher social station; thus in sixteen cases, the father and the father-in-law of the informants had similar trades or jobs. Where differences in job status existed, these rarely reflected marked differences in income or living standards between the two families. This similarity in social affiliation is confirmed when we examine the status of the partners themselves: we may note that seventeen of the couples were earning similar salaries, while two couples were the sons and daughters of farmers and were still working on the farm when they got married. Five factory workers married white-collar workers or small businessmen (shopkeeper, taxicab proprietor) while four office workers married manual labourers. Their level of schooling was also comparable, although four of the informants were clearly better educated than their partners, including the two teachers. We should observe, however, that, whether they were of equal or inferior schooling to their husbands, it would appear that the women read more than the men, perhaps because supervising their children's homework permitted them better to retain the basic skills they had learned in their brief education.

Finding a "Good Husband"

Given the low wages and unenviable status of the spinster in the society of that time, marriage involved an undeniably utilitarian aspect for women—it was through marriage that they could best assure their economic survival. But if that was to happen, they had to find a "good husband."

The "good husband" that every young woman hoped to meet was defined most of all by what he was *not* rather than by what was expected of him: "He should *not* run around after women, he should *not* be a drinker, he should *not* hang out in taverns. That's what a man . . . stay at home, then go to work. A good man. A little strict, maybe, but a good husband" (E2). In essence, if not in this exact formulation (not drinking, staying at home, being a good worker), this is the description to which the informants return time and time again to depict their ideal husband or to justify their choice of mate. If some of the informants mention physical appearance or talk about "falling in love," the primacy accorded to these first criteria more than to anything else is evidence of a certain pragmatism induced by a fear of finding oneself dependent upon a partner more concerned with exercising his prerogatives as head of the house than with assuming the obligations of the position. In a society that refused to recognize divorce and in which the Civil Code extended full authority to the father of the household, the wife, who was required to submit herself to his will, indeed risked finding herself without a livelihood and practically without recourse in cases of non-support or conjugal violence. As one of them observed, "In those days, the man was lord in his house" (E9). The condition of economic dependence and submission in which married women were placed inspired them to choose a man who would willingly and faithfully assume his role as provider without abusing the rights conferred on him by the Civil Code. Considering the narrow range of choice of husband available to some of these women and the absence of discussion between the future husband and wife, finding the ideal husband became a real stroke of luck, as one informant explained:

I had a man made out of gold. But then I was lucky because in those days, I have to say our eyes and ears were stopped up when we got married—we didn't know anything about it. We were just not informed—we could have been in real trouble. . . . I'm aware that there are sometimes signs that give a hint but when we don't know any more than that. . . . I was really lucky. (E15)

Very few of the couples actually discussed questions like managing the budget, educating the children (let alone how many of them) or any other sort of future plan. In order to explain this way of embarking upon a life together, several referred to the lack of marriage preparation courses to guide them;[12] "In those days, there was nothing like that being done. Then, it was the same for everyone. You think that's funny, eh? We got married, we didn't think about the future" (E29).

This lack of communication, typical of a family organization based on paternal authority and the complementary roles of provider/housewife might mean that the young woman remained unaware of her fiancé's old love affairs for some time. "He had been going out with the same girl for four years (when he started to court me) and I didn't know about it. I found out after we were married" (E8). Another recalled, "My husband was a widower, but I didn't even know it. He told me a couple of months after [they started going out] that he was a widower" (E2). For some, this state of ignorance extended even to the financial situation of the future husband. "In those days, you didn't know how much money your husband had. It wasn't like now—we didn't know anything when it came to money and we didn't ask. We didn't know what our husbands had" (E2). One of the informants was even deceived by her fiancé: "He didn't have anything! He showed my father a bank book with a thousand dollars in it, but he didn't have a cent!" (E27).

As another remarked, such discussion hardly seemed necessary to couples who had nothing or next to nothing: "He didn't have anything and neither did I. There was nothing to talk about. That's how we got married in those days" (E22). In fact, expectations were clearly laid out and the division of responsibilities, seen as complementary and indispensable to each other, was established from the beginning: the man would go to work and bring home his pay; for her part, the woman would take care of the house and the children.[13] As the territory and the role of each was determined in this way, it was hardly necessary to discuss the modalities of the future life of the pair, especially since the decision-making power, in theory at least, if not in practice, was delegated to the head of the family.[14]

The acceptance of the apparent immutability of these social roles is especially perceptible in the unwritten rule that women cease work upon marriage. This question did not become the subject of discussion for the overwhelming majority of these couples, since it was obvious to both partners that marriage signalled the end of paid work for the wife, who would be henceforth occupied with taking care of the house and the children. This social norm was considered as a rule that it was impossible to break, as it also embodied the husband's desires:

> I worked for six years in my life because there was no question of going to work after you got married. Your husband would really tear his hair out! Oh no! It wasn't allowed in those days. (E15)

> Married women weren't allowed to work in those days. My husband did not marry me for me to support him. And it was the same for my brothers-in-law. Nobody went to work—it just didn't happen in those days.... No married woman worked.... It wasn't done. Men had their pride. They didn't want their wives working. (E23)

> When you got married in those days, there was no question of going on working. And for the married man it would have been a disgrace if his wife kept on working. (E29)

These oral histories highlight the importance that men attributed to the fact of "supporting" their wives—it was a matter of "pride," of "honour," that is, of social status. If they were supporting a woman at home it meant that they were adequately fulfilling their role as provider; additionally, it was proof that they did not belong to the poorest of social classes.[15] The recollections of another informant who tried to convince her fiancé, without success, of the advantages that might derive from a double salary conveys this idea well:

> I talked about it with my husband, but there was no question.... One of us had to give in—I gave in instead. I would have liked to go on working, but I saw that his pride would have taken such a huge blow that I had to make a choice. People took a dim view of women working. It meant that the husband was not able to support his wife, that he wasn't able to earn enough money. (E10)

In fact, only one informant did retain her job for a year following her marriage in order to finish paying for a washer and a sewing machine that had been bought on credit.

Thus the dictates of domestic ideology were successful in imposing the idea that paid work for married women was unsuitable because it betrayed great poverty. Custom and the internal rules of businesses for their part persuaded women that for all practical purposes, they were forbidden to work. For some, indeed, transgressing the behavioural norm was equivalent to breaking the law:[16] "Married women didn't have the right to go to work.... There was too much unemployment—they preferred to hire heads of families" (E6).

The clergy also placed itself in opposition to the employment of married women, but, oddly, the informants did not seem to be aware of it though they were, for example, perfectly in touch with the positions taken by the Church regarding contraception. Several reasons might explain this lack of knowledge. It is possible that this prohibition was either disseminated less widely or was limited to channels less accessible to working-class women.[17] It should be stressed that, unlike contraception, the Church's view on married women's working was not a question of dogma; rather, it was one of a number of questions of temporal order on which the Church took a position. While taking a position on married women's working for wages in other forums, during the *"Semaines sociales,"* in the pamphlets produced by the *École social populaire*, or during the congress of Catholic trade unions, for example, the Church was perhaps more insistent about the prohibition of contraception among its parishioners, judging that this would, at the same time, limit the presence of married Quebec women on the job market.[18] It must also be said that the birth rate had been constantly declining in Quebec since the nineteenth century while relatively few married women worked outside the home, at least until the 1950s, if we may trust the census figures. Under these conditions, the Church might have chosen to concentrate on disseminating its prohibitions against birth control, knowing that its proscriptions in this area were being less well obeyed.

But if the majority of informants quit their jobs when they got married, many of them stated that some of their fellow workers were married though hiding their matrimonial status from the employer out of fear of being fired: "Of course, many women were married—they were working in secret. I knew some of them—they went on working under their maiden name" (E6). This evidence tends to confirm that the number of married women who were working was probably higher than the official statistics would lead us to believe.[19] It should be pointed out that the informants did not criticize these women. Rather they saw what they did as representing a personal choice, one they respected even if it violated a norm to which they themselves conformed.

By and large, as it was a sign of entry into marriage and thus to a superior status, the women were happy to leave their jobs. If some of them admitted to being bored in the course of the first months of married life, the preparations for the arrival of a baby rapidly came to fill up the days that might have seemed a bit long at the beginning. As we shall see in a future chapter, this obligation to renounce their jobs did not altogether extend to other kinds of paid work that they could carry on within the home, inside the framework of their regular domestic duties and sheltered from prying eyes, thus preserving the husband's pride and the hierarchy of roles within the household.[20]

The Wedding Day

All the informants very clearly recalled the smallest details of their wedding day, right down to the weather. Even those, indeed, whose marriages were not the happiest did not have to be pressed to recount the events of the day and describe their outfit. If, however, this day remained memorable, it was less because it was so magnificent an occasion than because it conferred a new social status on the bride. For the majority of couples, in fact, the straightened circumstances imposed by their socio-economic situation did not permit them to lavish large sums on the wedding, or to adopt the new wedding customs which were becoming widely observed among more well-to-do classes.

Thus the proposal most often took the place of an engagement party, as the couple hardly had the means to multiply the festivities. The same economic considerations governed the bride's choice of outfit. For some years, the white wedding dress, symbol of purity and virginity, and the veil had been becoming more and more identified as appropriate wedding attire. The demands of this costume, devoted solely to a single event, however, implied a certain degree of financial comfort, as it cost a great deal and could not easily be adapted to other occasions. For this reason, most of the informants preferred a pastel or neutral colour for the dress and, where necessary, the going-away outfit, which they bought or had made. "You were supposed to get married in white, but I said, hah! I'll never put a white gown on again. I'd rather have a grey dress that I can wear more than once" (E17). Thus, even for this very special occasion, the women were first of all concerned with the practicality of their purchases, which they intended to get the best use out of. Only three of the informants conformed to the new fashion of the white wedding, though eight of them wore a veil rather than a hat. Of these, three belonged to the

Children of Mary, which furnished the young bride with a veil in addition
to organ music and a special service at the Lady Altar.[21]

The money the couple had at their disposal also affected the wedding
day itself, generally held at the beginning of the week. Most often, this
began with a modest religious service that involved a minimum of pomp
and that was conducted in the presence of the immediate family to whom
might be added some of the relatives. If some of the informants had a
"big" wedding with bouquets and maids of honour, most had to be content with a "small" wedding, with no organ or red carpet, followed by a
modest reception to which only the brothers and sisters were invited. The
simplicity of the events of the day is explained by the modest means of
the bride's family, the early hour of the day at which the service took
place, the fact that it was a workday, and by the immediate departure of
the bride and groom on their honeymoon journey.

Although very few of the women were married in white, more than
two-thirds of the couples followed the custom of the honeymoon, which
was borrowed from our neighbours to the south. In most cases, however,
the groom had only a few days of unpaid holiday and had little money to
devote to the enterprise. Thus the couple most often went to relatives
who lived in the country in Quebec or the United States, a circumstance
that hardly provided the sort of privacy that the honeymoon was supposed to be for. The mother of the bride in one case even accompanied
the happy couple! Despite everything, it would seem, at least in urban
areas, that the honeymoon was a custom so firmly established that it was
on its way to becoming an obligation that one could not shirk without
revealing a state of abject poverty. That is why two couples, in order to
preserve appearances, pretended to take the train to some other destination but got out at Saint Hubert and returned home secretly the same
evening.[22]

Setting Up Housekeeping

A review of the various possessions the couple had when they married will
permit us to get a clearer view of their economic situation and put into
some sort of perspective the impact the Depression might have had on
their standard of living. Savings aside, they might have owned furniture, a
car or other property belonging generally to the husband, as well as the
bride's trousseau.

The Trousseau

In a study of the trousseau in France, Agnès Fine observes that, regardless of its contents and its value, the trousseau represented an essential in women's lives; through the first half of the twentieth century, at least, it seemed altogether inconceivable to be married without the provision of a trousseau.[23] But while in the sixteenth century it involved the furniture of the bride's bedroom, bit by bit the trousseau was reduced to linen, especially to sheets. According to the author, however, the meaning of the trousseau remains the same: "The bride provides the nuptial chamber. . . . It is the room, the bed, the sheets where the new couple will have sexual relations."[24]

Under the impact of industrialization and urbanization, the meaning and tradition of the trousseau seem to have lost their force. Perhaps we should also consider how and to what degree transporting this custom to North America might have altered it. Nevertheless, one fact remains—the trousseau represented an important element of the marriage at the beginning of the century. This is what the oral witness of most of the informants makes plain and, indeed, only three of them lacked a trousseau. A few of them, married in the countryside, were even given bedroom furniture, as in the tradition reported by Agnès Fine: "I had my bedroom set. In our family it was Papa who gave it to us—he provided our bedroom set. There was a dresser and a chest of drawers, a vanity table and a bed, with the mattress and pillows—everything that went with it" (E17).

In the majority of cases, however, the trousseau was confined to household linen, though for some informants, the term also referred to the clothing, underwear, and nightdresses that they wore on their wedding day.[25] I had my trousseau for myself, to get married in, but I didn't have a trousseau for the house" (E23). This trousseau was generally collected over a number of years, starting when the young woman left school and sometimes even earlier than that. It was often made from purchased yard goods, though occasionally the material was woven on the farm. The fashion of embroidery was still quite widespread, as almost half the women in the sample embroidered the tablecloths, sheets, and pillowcases that made up their trousseau. In the poorest families, they bought unbleached cotton and used sugar sacks as well, which they bleached before sewing and embroidering them. The coarse cloth might also come from the factory that employed a member of the family. It is impossible to know if this material was given away by the companies or if it was spirited off by the employees. The latter hypothesis seems the more probable.

The trousseau often represented the only property that belonged to the young woman herself, a fact which could take on special significance if she was going to live with her husband's family. But unlike the custom Agnès Fine remarks upon, the women in the sample did not try to preserve their trousseaus untouched. In fact, the trousseau was made of sturdy material, in the expectation of a long and constant use. In this sense, it represented an important contribution to the family property because it obviated the need to buy household linen for some years to come. "I had all my linen. I didn't have to buy anything for maybe ten years. And that helped a lot. Now that's wealth, eh? Those beautiful sets of sheets" (E24). Once they were worn, the sheets and tablecloths could be cut down to fit a child's bed or converted into dust cloths. If once there had been a sexual signification associated with the trousseau of which a few hints still remained, for the urban working class, it was viewed much more as an important economic contribution made by girls and their mothers who invested time and money in the making and accumulation of items which would become a significant part of the young married couple's possessions.

Savings and Personal Property

Once the wedding had been paid for (that is, the clothing, the service, and the honeymoon), barely more than half of the couples possessed savings which, in some cases, were from the young woman's nest egg. Even then, the amounts saved up would not have been sufficient to support the couple for more than a week or two in the event of unemployment.[26] In these circumstances, it is certainly not surprising that the majority of couples first went to live with other members of their family, most frequently with the husband's parents, precisely in order to avoid the expenses connected with setting up a home of their own.

Some couples already had some furniture when they got married. Four girls brought their bedroom furniture with them,[27] while two couples had acquired a dining-room suite. A widower had retained the furnishings from his first marriage, another just the bedroom furniture. Quite often, when the couple lived with the parents, these provided the bedroom furnishings, which the young people could take with them when they left.

By the time they were finally settled, whether immediately after their marriage or some months later, the majority of couples furnished two or three rooms: the bedroom, the kitchen, including an icebox and a coal or wood stove, and, in more than two-thirds of the group, the living room, usually including a sofa bed, in the expectation of children. Rather frequently, this last room was sacrificed, either because the rented flat contained only two rooms or because buying living-room furniture was beyond the couple's means.

Of the nine couples who bought their furniture on time, six were living with the husband's family, which suggests that sharing expenses in the early months of marriage did not necessarily allow the young couple to save up the sum needed to set up housekeeping. Rather than relying on credit, more than half the couples bought their furniture used. Three couples furnished their first home with donations from members of their families, while seven others bought all new furniture, paying cash.[28] Between these two extremes there are a variety of situations involving a combination of gifts and cash or credit purchases of new or used furniture. In general, we observe a level of poverty which limited the quantity and quality of the furniture and accessories the couples could acquire— few of them could permit themselves a carpet, occasional tables, or other decorative items. Only eight couples acquired a washing machine, which meant that, at the beginning of their marriage, at least, the majority of the women scrubbed clothes by hand, at the washboard, in a tub or in the bath, if the flat had one. Finally, seven couples had a sewing machine, but in five instances this was one they inherited or they were given, either because the informant's mother had died or because she no longer used it. We should observe that the acquisition of a sewing machine often came before the purchase of a washing machine, because it was the better investment since it permitted clothing to be made at home, at a considerable saving.

All the small utensils and appliances that the couple received as gifts should be added to the inventory of goods they owned at the beginning of their marriage. Most of the informants stressed the utility of the gifts that came from their families. If most received dishes, pots and pans, and trays of all sorts, and sometimes household linen, those in luck were given electric appliances (toasters, irons) and silverware.

With few exceptions, the trousseau, the savings, the furniture and the wedding presents constituted the entire wealth of these households. For the woman who was about to take charge of the house, these goods both represented the tools of her trade and would affect the way in which she would carry out her household tasks, a subject that we will examine in greater detail in a later chapter.

The First Home

For most of these couples, the first months of their life together, far from being intimate, were passed in the midst of one or the other of their families. One couple who came from the country went to live for six months in a room in the house of someone they did not know; four couples lived with the grandparents, or with the sister or the brother of the bride, but the majority, thirteen couples out of eighteen, lived with the husband's family. This patrilocality should probably be interpreted as smacking of a tradition which goes back to the pre-industrial period, when the young woman went to live on the land her husband would inherit; moreover, four of these couples were living in rural areas when they got married. In the urban setting, this practice emphasized the role of provider which was extended to the husband's family. This period could also be considered as a transitional period in which the bride was initiated into the way her husband and his family liked to live.

The insecure economic situation not only of the couple, but sometimes of the husband's family, most often explains why these shared living quarters presented themselves as an inherent condition of marriage: "It was agreed that I would stay with his mother—he didn't talk about it much—he put his cards on the table and that was that" (E2). Two of the women interviewed referred specifically to their fathers-in-law being out of a job to explain this decision. A consequence of the Depression indeed was to accentuate the economic dependence of certain parents on their children:

> Only my husband was working, and then my sister-in-law. . . . Since my father-in-law was out of work and my husband, if he married and set up house on his own, would have deprived them of an income, my mother-in-law said, "If you want to stay with us. . . ." She had four rooms and she gave up the back bedroom to us." (E16)

If the young couple was to "benefit" from their own room, often the only place in the flat that permitted a modicum of privacy, the other members of the family had to cram together, particularly at bedtime. Thus, one informant lived with her husband, his son by a previous marriage, her mother-in-law, two sisters-in-law and a brother-in-law in a four-room flat. This case, though extreme, is not unique, and it likewise happened that the living room had to be given over to the newlyweds. In conditions like these, it is not surprising that the arrival of the first-born child gave the signal for them to leave. In fact, the majority of couples, ten of eighteen, lived with their in-laws for a year or less, the time required for the young woman to become pregnant and perhaps give birth to her first baby. Only four couples continued to live with their families in the first year following the birth of their child.

The financial arrangements that parents and children came to were different, depending on the needs and the economic situation of both parties. Most frequently, the newlyweds, who had smaller incomes, paid a weekly sum for room and board. But sometimes they would share the costs or even take over the rent, electricity, and heat, with the parents supplying only their food. As their contribution, one informant worked for her mother-in-law, who had a boarding house:

> When we got married, his mother was running a large boarding house. . . . We stayed there with the other boarders. I lived with my in-laws for two years. We had a bedroom and a beautiful bedroom set. And we were saving money by staying there. I helped her out—she had to do all the cooking. There was a meal at noon and thirty-five people came to eat. It cost thirty-five cents a meal. They ate well. . . . I didn't do the cooking—I waited on table. . . . There were two tables, placed end to end. Before the people got there, I had to lay the table, set out the places. I was the one who did all the serving. Oh, my God! That was really work. And in those days, there weren't any dishwashers! I was the dishwasher—I was earning my keep. She didn't pay me anything, but I was earning my keep. As soon as we got a little money together, after two years, we were out of there. (E11)

Another also helped her mother-in-law who did the washing and ironing for her neighbours. In general, however, the daughters-in-law only helped with the daily housekeeping, which they did together. The majority of the women interviewed conformed to the way their mothers-in-law did things without objecting and tried to maintain good relations despite any disagreements which were bound to surface. Some of them also benefited from their stay by learning how to cook. "I learned to cook after I got married because I was living with his parents and his mother was a real cordon bleu chef. That meant that I learned to cook from her" (E8). Even when both women got along well, the daughter-in-law was usually happy to leave to set up housekeeping with her husband on their own. "I was glad. I was the happiest person" (E2).

Thus, the custom of shared living arrangements seemed to have been alive and well in the urban working-class setting.[29] This situation is explained in part by the newlywed couples' lack of savings and their inadequate income (and sometimes that of the parents). But if they lived together for economic reasons, it is also true that several couples finally moved out on their own without having saved up a nest egg sufficient for them to set up housekeeping. Thus sharing a home did not seem to be the result solely of economic considerations—tradition must also be taken into account in their choice. More than marriage itself, the arrival of the first child symbolized the foundation of a new family and truly involved the establishment of a separate household. This coincidence between the birth of the first child and family autonomy means that the majority of couples would not experience an intimate relation of just two persons until old age, if, indeed, both partners survived until then.

———

*F*or women, marriage meant, in principle, that they more or less put themselves henceforth in their husbands' hands in order to ensure their support. Consequently, courtship was not free from economic considerations when we look at it from the woman's point of view. Her choice of partner was based on practical considerations which could easily overwhelm amorous sentiments. Those for whom the two coincided were generally thought to be lucky because the passive role women played in courtship limited their choice, which could turn out to be cruelly disappointing.

Because of the socio-economic background of most of the couples, material considerations also influenced the style of the rituals involved with the marriage service and wedding reception. Despite all the symbolism associated with the event and the importance which it held for women particularly, the marriage was rarely celebrated with any sort of splendour. One got married according to one's means and, as Lucia Ferretti observes, "the wedding appeared ... less as a celebration than as a bureaucratic formality."[30] Indeed, at every stage of the couple's relationship, from courtship to marriage, to the first years of married life, we observe the influence of the poverty of their background, which often existed well before the Depression. Finally, we must add that marriage for these couples had as its primary objective the establishment of a new family. Therefore, hardly any time would go by before the arrival of the first child. This is the subject that will occupy the next chapter.

─────── *Chapter 4* ───────

Motherhood

"Life was having children." (E24)

T he reproduction of human beings is at the heart of all endeavours in the private sphere. Bringing children into the world and taking care of them represents the principal element in domestic labour. It not only consumes the most time and affects the quantity of housework, but in a much more fundamental way, it is principally this responsibility, attributed exclusively to women, that has come to justify the existence of a separate domestic sphere, set apart from the marketplace, and the assignment of the wife/mother (and, by necessity, child-rearer) to this sphere and to the activities that it entails. Motherhood, the foundation of modern domestic labour, has occupied the greatest part of the lives of the women interviewed.

In this period, as we know, clerical and medical discourse associated marriage and sexuality very narrowly with procreation and most often reduced women to their biological capacity to bear children.[1] Exalted again and again, motherhood represented at once the primary reason for marriage, the "natural" and inescapable destiny of women, their unique vocation, the condition essential to their full physiological and psychological development, a noble duty, when it was not seen as a "blessed bondage,"[2] that women could avoid only by defying their fundamental nature and endangering their physical and moral health. Thus the use of contraception was not only formally prohibited by the Church, but cer-

Notes to Chapter 4 are on pp. 201-204.

tain physicians warned that it could have dangerous effects. Among the numerous evils that lay in wait for women who sought to limit their families were: "More and more neuropathic women, premature ageing, uterine fibroids, certain organic scleroses, total neurasthenia, nervous imbalances, [and] uterine cancer caused by more than one chemical irritant used habitually."[3]

Acceptance of and blind submission to this sort of discourse was not altogether invariable. If all the women we interviewed did consider motherhood the principal reason for marriage and sexual activity, once the first child, however ardently desired, appeared, the halo of romanticism surrounding maternity often began to fade. Abruptly brought into contact with the physical realities of pregnancy and childbirth, seized by the daily responsibilities of the child's care and upbringing without always having the means at their disposal to carry them out, most of the women wished to space out their pregnancies and several couples did not hesitate to use means to prevent them.

Sexuality and Contraception

Generally, the women knew nothing about sex when they got married. As girls, they were not warned about the arrival of their menses and received no explanation once their periods started except that it would happen every month and that they ought not to talk about it with anyone. The details of the sexual act, associated as it was with sin, were never described and thus remained a mystery until the wedding night, which sometimes had quite a surprise in store for them: "I never thought it would be like that" (E7), said one of the informants, summing up the general feeling. Even as teenagers, most of them had not been advised about their mother's pregnancies or the imminent arrival of a new baby. When the mother went into labour, they would be shooed out along with the other children and if they no longer believed in the "Indians" who were supposed to have brought the baby, "we never did know the real truth" (E20), as one of them said. The secrecy that surrounded these events hardly encouraged them to ask questions. Modesty, shyness, or fear of committing a sin, all of which were inherently associated with sexual matters, kept them from satisfying their curiosity by asking friends or women at work who, in any case, knew very little more than they did. Those who were born on farms were not any better informed because they had generally been kept well away from animals who were breeding or giving birth.[4] If they had never changed a little brother's diaper, they would have had no idea of masculine anatomy.[5] "When I got married, I was completely stupid," one of them said. "But in any event, I managed like everybody else.... No, it's true ... I was married at twenty-three and I tell you, I didn't know what a man was" (E28). In these circumstances, it is hardly astonishing that once they got pregnant, some of them wondered how the child would be born. "When my first baby was about to come into the world ... three months before he was born I asked my neighbour where he would come out.... She had a good laugh at me for that" (E6). Her naivety is not unique; at least two of the other informants admitted to having asked the same question.

> Men were not as ignorant of sexual matters and they undertook to initiate their wives: I was completely dumb. I didn't know anything. I didn't know how "to buy" a baby[6] when we got married. My mother never told us anything about all that. She was embarrassed to talk about such things with us. He told me on our wedding trip what was about to happen to me. I didn't know. I wasn't afraid. He was sensitive about it. If I hadn't wanted to do it, he would happily have waited. (E12)

The husband's attitude in these first moments of intimacy determined the view that these women would have of sex. But if some of them referred to their husband's "sensitivity," for most of them sex became a "duty" from which they derived no pleasure. Even if not all of them broached the subject directly, many of them complained indirectly about their husbands' sexual appetite, which to them seemed insatiable, or expressed a certain comfort in having a husband who was not too demanding in this regard,[7] which leads us to suspect that, one way or the other, sexual relations were for them a real chore.

Thus, while motherhood might be considered woman's primal vocation and the primary purpose for marriage, most of the informants were kept in ignorance of the biological realties bound up with it and the question only rarely was discussed by the partners, at least before marriage. A kind of fatalism, which can be attributed as much to ignorance of contraceptive practices as to the religious context of the period, characterizes the attitude of almost half the couples: "There wasn't anything, you never heard of anything that would prevent a baby.... You'd often think, if I only had something.... Some had ways that they talked about, but I only learned about them later" (E3); "Birth control was out of the question. It was the law of the Church. You had to have babies." (E29)

Nevertheless, despite Church teachings, which were widely disseminated during the annual parish retreats and familiar to everyone, fifteen of the couples tried to limit the size of their families, though, it must be said, with limited success. In almost every case, they came to this decision after marriage and the birth of one or more of their children, as their sexual intimacy aided their discussion of the subject.[8] Unless they were under the care of a physician, resorting to contraceptive methods or devices appeared aimed less at preventing all further births than at delaying the arrival of a new baby for as long as possible. The workload involved in a large family, the couple's financial situation, and the desire to raise and pay enough attention to each of the children were among the reasons most frequently provided. The following quotation illustrates the variety of reasons at the heart of such a decision very well:

> I told the good Lord to send me children, but that I did not want them to suffer later. Large families always have problems. Someone is always overlooked in a big family, even if it isn't meant. So I said, we're going to avoid that. That's what the two of us decided. Because my husband made such-and-such a salary, and I said, I wanted to see that they were educated. That's what I was missing. I really suffered because I couldn't finish school. . . . So I said, my kids, if they want, they're going to get an education, they're going to study and I'm going to help them. And that's what I did. You have to plan. I said, I'd rather have a small family and be able to give them what they need. It was their education that I was thinking about for later. (E16)

The economic climate particular to the 1930s certainly exercised a decisive influence on some of the couples; in fact, the majority of those who used contraception were either living on home relief for a greater or lesser period of time or were suffering from reduced incomes. Despite all that, as we have just seen, few of the women used exclusively economic reasons to explain their decision. Furthermore, other couples who experienced similar economic difficulties did not think it right to limit the size of their families, which tends to demonstrate that low incomes do not always constitute a sufficient incentive for birth control.[9] The internalization of religious values, the rural origins of the couple, and a large number of children in their original families constitute a number of the factors which could have led them to have large families despite an uncertain economic situation. Thus, the five women in the sample who had more than eight children either came originally from the countryside or from families of more than eight children. One of them, who had sixteen pregnancies and brought eleven children into the world despite an income which was largely inadequate, said, "I thought that's the way it always was, since I came from a big family" (E22). On the other hand, the reverse is not always true: not all of those who came from large families had a lot of children. How the women viewed their mothers' experiences of motherhood also had a role to play.[10] As one woman who came from a family of eleven commented, "I didn't want to have a big family. I didn't want to bring up eleven like my mother. I thought she'd had enough problems. I didn't want to follow in her footsteps" (E19). Finally, it must be emphasized that those couples whose relationship was based exclusively on the husband's authority and in which there was an absence of any discussion between the partners were clearly less likely to control their fertility, taking into account the necessary cooperation which such control demands.

According to their testimony, these women most often originated the decision to limit the size of the family. "After the third, I said it's time to take a little 'break'. We can't manage—we'll never make it" (E23). "After I had my little girl, the oldest one . . . I said, 'Well, that's that for a while.' Then my husband said, 'There's always a way to be careful' " (E19). However, as the last comment suggests, the methods used, a condom in three and withdrawal in eight of the fifteen cases,[11] required women to depend upon their husbands. The Ogino-Knauss (rhythm) method, based on fluctuations on the menstrual cycle and used by the other couples, equally required the husband's cooperation.

Before their marriage, the women were altogether ignorant of these various ways to limit family size; it was the husband who knew about condoms when the couples used them and it was the doctor who explained the rhythm method—the only one acceptable to the Church[12] —while not every doctor was willing to reveal information of this kind, even to women whom they had told not to have more children because of their many miscarriages.[13] As for the couples themselves, despite their married status, they were too embarrassed to ask for explanations of this method they had heard about: "We had too much modesty to go to the doctor and ask how it worked" (E6). Moreover, although they knew well enough that their recommendations to limit family size flew directly in the face of Church teachings, the doctors did not seem particularly interested in reassuring their patients on this score: "The doctors, you know, didn't say what they thought about the clergy or all that—they left it up to you. . . . I felt I was being pulled from one side to the other" (E15). Caught between contradictory instructions emanating from the two authorities they had been taught to respect, the women found themselves in an especially cruel dilemma when the doctor recommended sterilization:

> Every year there was a new baby. I had seven of them. If I had listened to the doctor, I wouldn't have had seven, I would have had five. He wanted to operate on me, but the priests in those days said it was a sin to be operated

on. So that meant I had seven and the last two were crippled. . . . In those days, you weren't supposed to be operated on. [The priests] would say, "It's better to die than to have the operation." We were here in order to procreate. But when I saw that I was beginning to bring children into the world who weren't well, I said, that's the end! And I had myself operated on. (E12)

Unlike the condom and the rhythm method, withdrawal had the advantage of requiring neither special knowledge nor expense to use. As one informant explained, the practice was "simply natural" (E5) and the decision was only the couple's business. All these considerations probably explain why this method was the most widely used although it was the least reliable.

In the religious climate of the time, the decision to use contraception (or to undergo a hysterectomy) represented a genuine moral dilemma. Even when women were convinced of the logic of their decision and fully conscious that the intransigence of the Church and the priests verged on absolute contempt for women's health and even for their lives, they felt nevertheless that they were breaking the rules of the Church and continued to confess their sin:

It was cruel when you went to confession. It was not a small thing to say that you had used birth control. But I had to confess it. . . . the priests would scold us. . . . We would tell them, "The doctor said that I mustn't have any more children." They didn't care—the baby would live even if the mother died. That's all they had to say to us. It wasn't right." (E5)

For the Church's part, in fact, no motive, not even a medical one, could justify the use of mechanical contraceptive methods. Abstinence and the rhythm method, which in short allowed the determination of periods of abstinence during the menstrual cycle, were the only permitted means. Because the rhythm method required explanations which were hard to come by, it was not widely used. Most of the couples therefore used contraceptive methods forbidden by the Church and almost all of the women involved found they were refused absolution at one time or another.

Rather than meet with such a refusal or abandon the Church altogether—which would have been clearly impossible as a result of the importance of religion as a social behavioural standard—some of the women chose to practice their religion only halfway, in part so as to be a good example to their children, but staying away from confession and communion. Others knew how to find a confessor who would make concessions; according to one informant, the Franciscans were particularly tolerant and the news got around. "Everyone went there. They were a little less.... But the parish priest, you couldn't get away with anything with him" (E20). The next comment is a good illustration of the different strategies used by couples in order to receive absolution:

> I remember going to confession so I could make my Easter duty, to go to church, and my husband said, "I'll go ahead of you."... He'd go in, confess, and come out and give me a signal not to go in if he hadn't got it [absolution].... Oh, yes, they refused to give us absolution!... One time, we tried three priests. Finally we hit upon one... I don't know, maybe he was tired, it was late, he must have been hungry and he must have wanted to get out of that blessed confessional box—anyway, he ran us through quite quickly. I don't even know if he heard my confession. We managed to whisper as much as we could—just in case. (E10)

If the confessional allowed the priest to exercise a direct and individual control over women's sexual lives and fertility, the annual retreats, which men and women attended separately, represented a choice medium through which to spread the message and castigate the recalcitrants before a large audience. The newspapers voluntarily reprinted the sermons given by prestigious preachers invited by the richer parishes, facilitating the wider distribution of these directives, so no one could claim not to have heard of them.[14] These annual retreats, during which women were recalled to their duty in fiery rhetoric, were often successful in reawakening guilt in even the most hardened. Some of them nevertheless managed to relieve their guilt, at least in part, by telling themselves that they were respecting the spirit of Church regulation. The Church, in fact, had always condemned the use of contraception, linking it with the desire on the part of women to free themselves of their family responsibilities in order to benefit from a greater freedom. When that was not the motive, then breaking the Church's commandment appeared less serious:

> Oh, yes, madame, I was refused absolution, yes, indeed, that happened to me. I didn't repent because I was using my head. In my opinion, the priests were there to inform us, but they weren't there to raise our kids. And in those days, it wasn't easy. So if we wanted to look out for our kids' welfare, we had to use our heads. I would have gone along [with the priest] if I had been doing it for my own pleasure, you know, to be freer. No, on the contrary, I was always at home.... You know... women always felt guilty because in those days, they had those retreats and when you went to the retreat—I went to them all—you were going to go to hell.... It shook you up, let me tell you. And afterwards, you went back to normal, but you thought about all that. But I always said to myself, it is the good Lord who will be the judge. If I'm guilty, then something will happen. (E16)

It should be noted that even if it was the men who actually employed contraceptive methods, it was the women who felt the guilt and who were blamed. Men seemed to have a much more elastic conscience and, in order to be left in peace, did not hesitate simply to hide the facts from their confessor. One husband recommended that if his wife wanted absolution, she not tell "what we do in our own bed" (E6). Another felt fully justified in limiting the size of his family in the light of his income: "My husband said, I'm the one who earns the money. It doesn't make sense to live like the animals, neither better or worse" (E5). This attitude on the part of men can be linked to several factors. In the first place, their socialization was less focussed on obedience to the standards of behaviour than that of women and they were generally allowed a greater latitude and freedom of will. Thus they were used to exercising their authority. Certain kinds of behaviour were tolerated in men, even when they were forbidden by the Church, like sexual activity outside of marriage. Moreover, it was certainly easier for men to justify their decision to limit the size of their family as their earning capacity was mathematically demonstrable. More children meant more work for women but the amount of extra labour entailed was less easy to quantify.

Thus, regardless of the religious climate of the period and the guilt which it engendered, more than half of the fertile couples in the sample (fifteen out of twenty-eight) chose to control the size of their families for a number of reasons. This number would tend to suggest that the women of that generation were less submissive to the Catholic Church than is generally thought, at least in urban areas.[15] The number of sermons preached on the subject, moreover, indicates that the Church was well aware that its directives were not always being observed.

Except on medical advice, the use of contraception was intended more to space out new arrivals after the first few births than to prevent them altogether to accord with a pre-established ideal family size. All of these couples in fact wanted to start a family and all of the women wanted several children, which is hardly surprising in view of their socialization and the social value placed on motherhood. Even among couples who used contraceptive methods, the number of pregnancies and of children is still quite high compared to our present standards.[16] Thus nine of the women who admitted to contraceptive use had had at least five pregnancies and six had had five or more children, none of whom were necessarily "accidents." The use of unsure methods or the failure to utilize them correctly, however, did mean that some of them had more pregnancies or more children than they had planned on: "My last, he's my little Ogino" (E24), one informant explained, with a certain degree of humour. For the same reason, contraception did not always contribute to the shortening of the period of family increase that still took up the major part of these women's lives.[17] "After twelve years," explained one of the informants, who had had five children, "I had my little girl, and then five years later, I had another one.... They were accidents.... They didn't have the pill in those days.... After I had them, I was glad I did, but when I first got pregnant, I wasn't thrilled" (E23). Nevertheless, those who used birth control methods had, on average, two fewer children than the others and completed their families in four years less, as the following table indicates:

Table 7
Average Number of Pregnancies and Children and the Years between the First and Last Child According to Use of Contraception

Couples	Pregnancies	Children	Years
No contraception (13)	7.5	6	16
Contraception (15)	5.4	4	12.4
Fertile couples (28)	6.3	5	13.8

As we can see, these women, whether they used birth control or not, had fewer children on average than the myth of the large family[18] would have endowed them with. Of the twenty-eight fertile women in the sample, only five had more than eight children and of those, three had more than ten. Most often, in eleven of twenty-eight instances, they had between three and five children and six of them had fewer than three. These women had, therefore, on average, two fewer children than their mothers had.

Motherhood

While the Catholic Church tried to maintain its ban on contraception, physicians increasingly were invading the fields of obstetrics and child care. Indeed, from the end of the nineteenth century, scientific discoveries in the area of health had provided a new occasion for the medical profession to rely on recent knowledge to impose itself on the population and especially on women. To doctors, the high infant mortality rate was in itself a sufficient reason to justify their intervention more.[19] Women who failed to consult them and who preferred to bottle-feed were roundly condemned and held responsible for the death of their offspring.

Although the women interviewed were strongly encouraged to see their doctors, their lack of money did not always allow them to avail themselves frequently or directly of medical advice. That is why most of them made use of the three kinds of health services that had been created around the First World War and that acted as a kind of go-between for the doctor. These were the visiting nurse service of the Metropolitan Life Insurance Company, the *Goutte de Lait*, and *Assistance maternelle*. As they were frequently mentioned in the course of the interviews, it is useful to provide a brief discussion of the origins, objectives, and services offered by the three organizations.

Because Metropolitan Life charged premiums as low as five cents a week and because they sent an agent weekly to the home to collect, the company had been successful from the turn of the century in attracting a clientele among working-class families. In 1909, the company created a visiting nurse service for their policy holders who were ill and for their pregnant wives. During the seventh month of pregnancy, the nurse would come to explain to the expectant mother how to prepare to give birth at home in the most hygienic and sterile conditions possible in order to avoid any infection or complication. After the delivery, she would come during the nine-day period of confinement then observed in order to take care of her patients and bathe the mother and the infant, teach the young mother how to give her baby a bath, and prepare her breasts if she were nursing.[20]

Complementing this service, *Goutte de Lait* (well-baby clinic) provided free medical consultations throughout the early years of the child's life. Created in 1901, the first *Goutte de Lait* clinics were primarily intended to promote breast-feeding and to distribute safe milk to those who were not able to nurse. After 1913, they multiplied along parish lines and became real clinics for newborns and young babies. The organization also offered prenatal classes where women learned how to care for and feed their children and at the same time received advice on hygiene in general.[21]

Finally, for the most deprived, there was *Assistance maternelle*, which began activity in 1913, created for their express benefit by Caroline Leclerc Hamilton. This organization both made home visits (most often to make sure that their beneficiaries were indeed in dire poverty) and provided free medical advice and assistance for mothers and layettes for babies. The organization had a clinic of several beds for giving birth and occasionally paid the cost of a hospital delivery.[22] In 1924, *Assistance maternelle* aided 824 mothers whose cases had been brought to its attention, often through the agency of other charitable organizations like Saint

Vincent de Paul, and distributed 374 layettes.[23] During 1932, one of the hardest years of the Depression, the organization helped 4,194 mothers and furnished more than two thousand layettes.[24]

More than doctors, whose fees were a severe strain on the family budget, it was the nurses and volunteers of these three organizations who instilled in the women interviewed the new standards defined by medicine in the areas of childbirth and care of the newborn. In fact twenty-seven of the twenty-eight fertile women in the sample used the services of the *Goutte de Lait* clinics while twelve also received visits from the Metropolitan Life nurses and three were aided by *Assistance maternelle*.

Expecting

"Once I got married, then the babies started to come" (E2). As one informant explained, the first child often arrived barely nine or ten months after the wedding, rarely as much as a year and a half. As they wanted to have a family, most of them were happy to find they were pregnant after a couple of months or even weeks of married life. Evidence of a second pregnancy, which often occurred shortly after the birth of the first child, was not always as heartily welcomed. The experience of a particularly difficult first labour, for example, could give rise to feelings of panic: "After that, when I saw I was starting another one, I cried. I'd had so much misfortune" (E2), said one informant, who had lost her first-born. "With the girls, I was happy, they were the first," said another, referring to her twins, "but the others, I loved them, but I was so sick, I was close to death each time. That meant I was afraid of having my baby each time I found I was expecting" (E29). Difficult economic conditions, inadequate income or unemployment due to the Depression also meant that the arrival of another baby was dreaded. "He was working up until 1933. . . . After that there wasn't any more construction. And the little ones kept coming every year. That was really hard. They have to eat, eh? But when the man isn't working—" (E12).

As one of the informants observed, the feelings of despondency or even rejection that accompanied repeated pregnancies might be shared by the husband as well:

> You know sometimes, you have children, it's not what you'd like. It's the same for a man. For woman, the more children, the more work she has. It's the same for a man—the more there are, the more money he has to bring home, the more he has to provide and he has to work. He wouldn't have to

worry so much otherwise. . . . If I had listened to my husband, I would have
had two or three . . . maybe he was discouraged. (E2)

Thus, men and women both dreaded the successive arrival of numerous
babies. Repetitive pregnancies and deliveries represented a heavy burden
for women who saw their strength and health undermined while their
work grew. For men, additional children meant an increase in their economic responsibilities.

Preparing for the Birth

To get ready for the birth, most of the women did not consult a doctor
until around the sixth or seventh month. According to one informant,
when the mother felt the baby move, then she knew that she should see
the doctor shortly. If everything was unfolding normally, they would not
go back to the doctor until they went into labour. Some of them had
never met the doctor until the last moment; in contrast, others saw a doctor several times throughout their entire pregnancy. These were either the
best off or the poorest among the women, those whom *Assistance maternelle* took into its care.

> They gave us a large flannel blanket, two sheets, some pillowcases and they
> gave us linen for the new baby. . . . We were followed up by them—we had
> to go, you know, once a week. . . . They gave me a bassinet, they gave me
> some bottles. . . . We would go to the *Assistance maternelle* in the afternoon.
> We'd have a snack, the doctor was there, and the nurses gave us advice—it
> was just like today with the prenatal courses. . . . I had to have a lot of milk,
> so they had Poupart Dairy leave me two quarts free. I wasn't the one who
> paid, they did. Then, when the babies were here . . . we went there and they
> gave us cod-liver oil and drops to put in their ears if we needed them. You
> know, they kept an eye on the babies until they were six months old. (E25)

Several informants made use of the prenatal clinics offered at the
Gouttes de Lait. "Every Wednesday, the doctor held a *Goutte de Lait*. He
taught us. Wednesdays were for women who were expecting. They
showed us how to make a layette and how to organize our work [so it
wouldn't be too much]" (E21). One of the women also recalled going to
get a pamphlet the organization was distributing without charge. Finally,
more than a third of the women had the benefit of advice from the
Metropolitan Life visiting nurses. According to their reminiscences, the
nurses seemed to stress cleanliness and antiseptic bed linen and articles for
the birth.

From the seventh to the ninth month, she would come once a week to show us how to make mattress pads for the bed for the delivery. She had us take newspaper, sterilize it in the oven, then buy some cheesecloth. She had us alternate the paper and the cheesecloth and sew it all together with big needles. She had us make big ones and little ones. (E15)

We got a little tray ready with everything we would need for the baby. . . . We had very clean jars with lids for boiled water. And for the cord, the bellybutton, we had real linen cloths—we cut them into squares with a hole in the middle for the cord to pass through. Then we wrapped all of it in a clean sheet and put it in a hot oven to be sterilized. After that, we wrapped it in another clean sheet—and put the whole thing on the little tray. When the nurse came [in the days following delivery], she had the things we'd prepared, she had a basin of water that had been boiled to give us our bath. (E29)

According to the oral histories collected, the extent of the preparations appeared to vary, as did the frequency of visits before the delivery. In any event, it is clear that these preparations were more elaborate than those undertaken by the women who were content to make a few pads out of old sheets stuffed with newspaper as their mother or mother-in-law advised. As the informant just quoted stated, "In my mother's day, there wasn't anything of the kind. . . . The nurses showed us everything. . . . I have to say we really worked in those days when we were having a baby because we weren't rich!" (E29). Making all the necessary items consumed a great deal of time, but most of the women who were aided nevertheless appreciated the service, especially because the nurses provided follow-up care during the eight or nine days of confinement following the birth. For those who had trouble finding help or advice, there is no doubt that the visiting nurse service provided precious support.

Giving Birth

The Metropolitan Life nurses did not aid the doctor during a delivery. A few of the informants were able to pay for a private nurse but the majority had to rely on the support and help of their mothers or, where the young couple was still sharing living quarters with the husband's family, of their mothers-in-law. A sister or a neighbour might also substitute for the mother when she was deceased or lived too far away. Even if Quebec no longer trained midwives after the end of the nineteenth century,[25] the women often used the term to describe the women who helped them in childbirth. "I always had Mama come and be my midwife" (E27).

Whether he just happened to be at home at the crucial time or whether he had been sent for on purpose, the husband in more than a third of the cases was present for at least one birth, supporting his wife or even taking an active part in different stages of the process. "My husband held my shoulders" (E2), one related, while another said, "He was the one who gave me the chloroform to put me to sleep" (E4). Other men, however, expressed strong feelings of helplessness and fear when their wives were in pain and preferred to wait in the next room or even flee the house. "He would take the children to my mother's, and he wouldn't come back home—he couldn't—he was a sensitive man. He wasn't able to watch me suffer. He was good for making them but not for watching them come" (E12). Even if he preferred to leave the house or, if he did stay, could not always make himself useful (one informant's husband took the chloroform himself that had been meant for his wife!), the partner was still not automatically excluded as would be the case for hospital deliveries until the 1970s. Rather, the presence or absence of the husband seemed to be a question of personal choice, a function of both his inclinations and the state of the relationship with his wife. These oral narratives tend to confirm the findings of an American study that husbands were more frequently present at the birth during the nineteenth century, when the obstetrician came onto the scene, their presence coinciding with the emergence of new feelings about the relationship between husbands and wives and with children. The reduction in the size of the family, which made each birth a rarer and thus more precious event than had been previously the case, would also have contributed to a closeness between the partners at this crucial moment.[26]

Childbirth, even if it took place in the privacy of the bedroom, nevertheless had become "medicalized"; in addition to striving to reproduce a sterile environment worthy of a hospital, the oral histories commonly mention the frequent use of anaesthesia (ether and chloroform) and often, as a result, of forceps. Thus, during her first delivery, one informant was too drowsy from the ether administered by the doctor to push, so he had to use the forceps, almost pulling the baby's head off in the process. "He was a butcher," she said. "If we'd had a competent doctor, the baby might have been saved" (E16).

Almost a third of the women, especially those who had their babies after 1940, delivered at least one of them in a hospital.[27] Opinions about this experience were somewhat divided: if for some the hospital offered the advantages of safety and of rest following delivery, others asserted that childbirth was no less painful in the hospital and that the period of bedrest could be stressful due to worry about the children who were left at home. "My mother-in-law was looking after my children. I was more worried about them because she was so old" (E2).

In fact, the majority of these women said that they would not have used the services of a midwife exclusively, as often their mothers had done, because they thought it too risky. It would appear that the medical campaign on the incompetence of the midwife had had its effect. Their confidence in modern medical technique did not always prevent them from severely judging the practices and competence of certain obstetricans. Thus several women remarked that, despite their fees, which ranged between ten and twenty-five dollars, sums that might represent a week's wages, the doctor would show up at the last minute while a nurse followed the progress of labour. Rather often as well, whether or not a nurse was present, he only certified the birth, leaving "chores" like bathing the baby to one of the women, a nurse, a midwife, or someone else, who had come to help the woman giving birth.

Despite the claims of the medical profession, doubt often was cast on the competence and effectiveness of these practitioners in relation to the very high rate of infant mortality of the period. "In those days, women would have fifteen or sixteen children because they would lose five, six, or even more. That's how the babies died—the doctors didn't know a thing" (E29). Several also reported having cured their babies themselves, using traditional remedies, after they had followed their doctors' advice in vain. In at least two cases, premature babies were saved thanks to the treatment provided by a mother-in-law or a neighbour. "The old women said that this child would not live. My mother-in-law was the one who saved him. He didn't have any fingernails, he didn't look good. She put him to bed in his bassinet and surrounded him with bottles of hot water," one informant recounted. According to another, paregoric, then widely used, was even dangerous for babies. "They slept so deeply you would have thought they were dead" (E5). Whether founded or not, these charges reveal that there was no general agreement yet about medicine and the medical profession and that women were relatively critical of the intrusion of these "experts" into the areas of obstetrics and child-rearing. Despite the medical campaign which sought to charge women with the responsibility for infant mortality, the latter generally considered it to be an inevitable phenomenon, considering the state of the evolution of medicine, thus tossing the ball back to those who would make them feel guilty.

This critical attitude is also reflected in the small proportion of women who nursed their babies and in the comments collected in connection with the service rendered by *Goutte de Lait*. Thus, despite numerous exhortations in favour of breast-feeding, the only effective means of combatting infant mortality according to the "experts," half of the women did not breast-feed at all, and of those who did, several stopped after the first month.[28] Lack of milk, but also the numerous inconveniences associated with this practice explain why women did not nurse more often or for longer periods of time. The enormous demands made by nursing on the mother's time, the impossibility of her being able to accomplish other tasks at the same time as breast-feeding, even the isolation in which nursing had to take place so as not to offend modesty, meant that a number of the women left off, especially when their other children demanded their time and attention. The majority of these women knew that breast-feeding could delay a new pregnancy and those who nursed for long periods generally did so for this reason.

A very large majority of the women we interviewed took their children to the *Gouttes de Lait*. Here the children were examined, weighed, and vaccinated; their young mothers were given nutritional advice and told how to take care of their babies. The fact that almost all in the study used the service does not mean that every woman was uniformly happy with it. For various reasons, some of the women definitely appreciated it, especially for their first children. "I found that it helped young women who didn't know anything, like me" (E15), one of them stated. Another added, "It was the only chance we had to weigh our babies" (E13). On the other hand, several also emphasized that the service involved various, and not inconsiderable, drawbacks. One informant explained, "I didn't like going there that much because when you went, the temperature was different for the baby—they took all his clothes off. There were babies there with colds, with whooping cough . . ." (E20). Even without the risk of infection, several informants also remarked that it became difficult to get to the clinics after the second or third child. "But after that, the third one, I didn't go to the *Gouttes de Lait* anymore. I had to take all three of them with me" (E23). Although it seems to represent an exception, the recollections of one of the women interviewed provides us a glimpse of the conflicts that could arise between the mother and the volunteers about what was appropriate care for the new baby:

> Me, I never liked to go to the *Goutte de Lait*. No. The *Goutte de Lait* used to tell us, "All right, don't give this to your baby or he'll die—don't give that to your baby or he'll get sick. Give him this, don't give him that." They made babies sick that way. In my case, I took my children there. Then [the nurse] didn't want me to feed them solid food before they were nine

months old. The baby was crying day and night. No matter how much I nursed him I couldn't fill him up just on milk. So then I started to give him solid food. When she found that out, she told me not to come back to the *Goutte de Lait* because I was an unnatural mother who didn't want to raise her children. (E25)

Furthermore, after a couple of pregnancies, mothers developed a certain expertise when it came to the diagnosis and treatment of common children's ailments.

When the children were sick, we were the ones who took care of them. We knew what they had, all the kids had it. For measles, we knew to keep the room dark—we learned that ourselves, listening to other women talk. I had two sisters older [than] me, watching what they did, you learned automatically, I suppose. (E23)

It is important to note that the clinics only screened children; in case of illness, they were referred to the family doctor.[29] The women preferred to go directly to the doctor, if they were not caring for the child themselves. Since the *Gouttes de Lait* did not treat the more serious medical problems, a number of the women did not see the need to make regular visits which ate into precious time for their daily routine. Despite the desires of those promoting the service, who insisted on the necessity of regular medical care for every child, very few of the women went regularly to the *Gouttes de Lait* with every one of their children.

The Confinement

According to the medical directives of the period, new mothers were supposed to remain in bed for nine days following the birth. Although not every woman followed this prescription to the letter, since some found it excessive, still they needed to rest before they could return to their daily rounds. Slightly more than half of the women in our sample had either a private nurse or a visiting nurse from Metropolitan Life to provide medical follow-up during the period of confinement. Their visits were especially appreciated by inexperienced young mothers who learned from them how to feed and care for their new babies. Some of these women had in fact taken care of their little brothers and sisters, but it was unusual for them to have been entrusted with a newborn and they often felt bewildered following the birth of their first child. Those who either could not pay for a private nurse or who were not insured with Metropolitan Life turned to older and more experienced women—a mother, mother-in-law, sister-in-law, or older sister—who would come to help out after the birth. During their daily visits, these women would take over the various domestic tasks like cooking, cleaning, and laundry that had to be done day after day and which the nurse would not undertake. Even when she was confined to bed, sometimes the new mother would have to lend a hand: "They kept us in bed for nine days. It was awful. I would peel the potatoes in bed. And I would change the littlest ones in bed" (E14). This informant confessed that she had not observed the nine-day customary confinement because, as she said, "When you got up, you had a lot of trouble walking—you were all numb" (E14).

Death, distance, or the care of a still large family meant that only a minority of women in the sample had the benefit of their mother's help. Nor could everyone count on her mother-in-law or the relatives for long periods of time; more than a third, therefore, turned to paid help. These "servants," very often young neighbours who were hired for three or four weeks, received pathetic wages of between two and five dollars, food, and sometimes a bed (that is, they slept on the chesterfield in the living room or shared the children's room), which explains how even the least well off among the informants could afford them. As a result of the Depression, large numbers of young women were available for this kind of work, which would not be the case during the war. "During the Depression, there wasn't any work for girls so the girls hired out to do that [work as servants].... When the war was declared, they started to need girls. A lot of them went to work at Saint Paul l'Ermite where they were making munitions.... That's when it started to be hard to find help" (E10).

A few women could not get any help, whether free or paid, and thus had to turn to their husbands to do the most pressing of the daily tasks. "He wasn't any good at taking care of babies, but he helped me by washing out a few things until I could get out of bed" (E2). This situation sometimes shortened the rest period considerably: "After two or three days, I went back to the housework," a mother of eleven remarked. "I didn't have anyone to help me out" (E22). In the case of large families or where the births had been spaced over a number of years, the eldest daughter would often have the responsibility of helping out her mother after the birth of the last children.

As we can see, professional and paid support complemented and sometimes even substituted for the mutual aid extended by the family to take care of new mothers. Furthermore, we observe a certain specialization in the kind of help afforded. The nurses, who to some degree replaced the midwives, provided care and advice, leaving the domestic chores to the female relatives.[30] The young wives obviously turned to the latter for advice when they could, but because the family could not always come together to provide needed aid, they valued having a nurse at their bedside during the days following the birth. This kind of service forecasts an era yet to come when women would give birth exclusively in the hospital, under the exclusive watch of hospital personnel.

The Care and Discipline of Children

Feeding, clothing, caring for, and raising children demanded from women their total attention and a solid sense of organization. Get up at night to feed the baby or care for an ailing child and be on her feet early in the morning to get the oldest ready for school. Hurry to finish a laundry before they all come back for lunch. Take the littlest one out and do some shopping in the afternoon and come back in time to cook the evening meal. Oversee homework and put the children to bed and then do some sewing in the evening—all of this made up the daily round of tasks and activities that these women had to accomplish often without the space, conveniences, or budget necessary to do the work.

If it is possible to make a list of the daily tasks that come with children, it is harder to sum up the thousand and one activities which their socialization entails and to measure the worry, the sleepless nights, the joys and sorrows their health and their education arouse. While studies of housework have focussed more on the quantity of work that the presence of children creates, it is this other aspect of motherhood that was more often evoked in the course of the interviews. "Work doesn't kill you. Worries and problems do" (E16).

It went without saying that the nurture and education of the children fell, if not exclusively, then first and foremost, on women. As it was unusual for couples still to be sharing the mother-in-law's house after the birth of their first child, most of these mothers found themselves all alone to perform the various tasks that children bring with them. Their husbands were involved to varying degrees, but in any event, these women expected to assume these responsibilities by themselves. "It was just us who raised the children in those days . . . that's what we were used to" (E23).

Fathers would voluntarily look after the children when the mother had to go out to do the shopping, attend church, or, more infrequently, so she could go to the movies to take her mind off things. "I would go out. That would cheer me up a little. One week, I would go out, the next he would" (E5), one informant explained. In general, the men were happy to rock the baby or play with the little ones, but rarely would become involved in their actual care. The tasks that men least often undertook were, in order, giving a bottle or a bath, changing a diaper, taking care of a child who was sick. The reasons the informants most frequently put forward as explanations of their husbands' lack of involvement were their daily absence from home and the fact that women did not work outside the house. "When your husband works long hours every day, he doesn't have time to bring up the kids and help you at the same time" (E24), or "In those days, the wife didn't need so much help—she stayed at home" (E3). This separation of roles was so well established that even when some of the husbands lost their jobs during the Depression, their greater availability would not often translate into increased help, unless they were already used to looking after the children, as a minority of them were:

> My husband was really good. I never had to get up at night for the babies— he would get up. He'd heat the water to warm up the milk to feed them. In the morning, he would get up first and change the baby's diaper and give him a bottle. He would put the baby back to bed for his breakfast and feed the other one. At night, he'd help me bath them. He didn't want me to put them to bed before he got home from work. (E4)

The social division of labour meant that fathers might spend the greater part of the day away from home and thus were rarely available to be involved with the socialization and education of the children, which requires a constant presence. Even if her husband had helped a great deal with the baths and the bottles and the diapers, one informant noted:

> It was me who raised the children practically single-handed because he worked nights. In forty-four years of working, I think he spent only the last ten working in the daytime. When the children were little, I was the one who saw to things. And I wasn't the kind of woman to wait until her husband got home or got out of bed to tell him, "So and so did this, so and so did that." For me punishment should come straight away, and they knew why. He was the kind who never said no and, because he didn't want to say no, he'd say, "Go ask your mother." (E15)

A majority of the women we interviewed agreed that it was less difficult to bring children up properly in that era than today, since respect for authority was still a feature of the parent-child relationship and all methods of education, as yet uninfluenced by psychological theory, sought to instill discipline. Some of the women sometimes regretted that their husbands had not been stricter with the children, leaving them the unhappy job of scolding them:

He never said a word. Sometimes, I'd tell him, "You could get mad once in a while." It meant that I had to be the strictest one—he wasn't strict enough. I would have liked him to be more strict—because it meant that I was always the one who was yelling. I said, "I'm always the one they hate." (E19)

More than their husbands' failure to help with child care or their laxness when it came to discipline, these women seemed to have trouble accepting their lack of sympathy and support when the wives were anxious about the health or future of their children. A number of the women referred to this constant worry, which was the more heavy to bear when it was not shared. In the view of one woman, it was this above everything else that distinguished the mother of a family from a member of a religious order:

I think that the mother of a family deserves more credit than a nun. The nun, she goes to bed at night, she doesn't think about her children. When you are raising a family, and you go to bed, you're happy when the children are little—they're all in bed. But when they're older, then you never have an easy night when you go to bed—they're starting to fall for the boys or the girls. . . . A nun doesn't have to worry about her children. (E2)

It was the women who oversaw their children's schooling and who urged them, the boys especially, to stay in school and acquire a trade, if not a profession, whenever it was possible. The economic situation of the household played a major role in the decision to keep children in school. Therefore, in certain families, only the younger children completed their courses. But even with their economic difficulties, some of the women believed it important that their children stay in school, often because they regretted their own lack of education and passed their hopes on to their children. In order to make this dream a reality, a few even worked after they were married to pay school fees.

Infertility and Mothering

Two of the women in the sample did not have children. Their oral testimony is of particular interest not only because their situation is representative of a not inconsiderable portion of the population,[31] but also because it sheds some light on the experience of childless women.

Given the degree to which motherhood was valued in the period, it is hardly surprising that both of these women express their great disappointment at not having children. One of them even had to put up with her husband's reproaches: "The wife isn't good for anything—she can't make a baby," he would tell her. After nine years of marriage, when the couple had finally decided to adopt a daughter, it was the informant's sister-in-law who went with her to the orphanage to "pick out" a baby, as if even this special kind of maternity was still, for the husband, women's business.

The solution of adoption was not considered by the other couple, who very rapidly found themselves in great demand from all sides. After they had lived for two years with the husband's parents, the young couple moved in with her father, who had recently been widowed. Hardly had he remarried then her father-in-law died; the couple then returned to live with the mother-in-law and an unmarried sister who was to stay with them for thirty-five years. Over the years, the couple successively housed the informant's three sisters who were in temporary difficulties. Furthermore, they raised a niece until she got married. A brother, his wife, and their eleven children also took shelter with them when he had lost his job due to health problems:

> He was on the street with eleven children. We told him, "Come to our house." We didn't have enough beds for everyone.... When they got up in the morning, he and my brother-in-law would say, "It's worse than a battlefield in here—there are dead bodies everywhere." They were sleeping everywhere but in the bathtub. They stayed with us for three months. Then I told my brother, "You have to understand, we can't take care of you for your whole life like this. Try to find a flat." Afterwards, we were sorry—he rented a basement and his baby caught a cold and then died.... There were thirteen extra. The baker was happy when he got to our house—he emptied his van every morning at our place! (E8)

This couple undoubtedly is an extreme case. Less in demand, the other childless informant nevertheless frequently took care of their children when her sisters-in-law were having babies or had to go to the hospital. After having kept one of their nephews from the time he was eleven months old until he was six, in order to relieve his mother, the couple took him back when he was twelve and raised him until his majority. In addition, this informant, who had originally lived with her grandparents, successively took care of her father and her husband's father and mother until their death. Finally, this couple, who did not have a great deal of money, nevertheless paid the grocery bills and bought shoes for their many nieces and nephews in order to help out the parents.

The experience of these two women would suggest that childless women were called upon first to care for destitute parents and to substitute for mothers in difficulty. As they had more time and space, they were left to look after the poor, sick, and elderly in a kind of sharing of mothering among the female relatives. It should also be pointed out that among the women who did have children, three also brought up children from their husbands' first marriages and several raised the children of a son or daughter who was dead, divorced, or destitute. These various experiences demonstrate that neither the birth rate nor the fertility rate closely express reality in regard to women's maternal duties.

---

*T*he inevitable fate of marrying and starting a family appears as something to which all of the women in the sample aspired. This desire for children, which was usually not slow in being realized, was, however, accompanied by an ignorance of sexual matters which might seem paradoxical. At first glance, the use of contraceptive methods by more than half the couples is no less astonishing, despite the hold the Catholic Church had over Quebec society of the day and regardless of the high value placed by social leaders on the ideal of the large family.

The economic crisis which was wreaking havoc at the time when most of these couples were establishing their families seems to have prompted some of them to adopt the ideal of a family smaller in size but better suited to their available means. In the list of motives put forward for limiting family size, the desire to educate the children and to reduce the mother's workload so that she might have enough time for each child invariably appear right next to arguments of a purely economic sort. In this chapter, the interviews have brought out the complexity of motives bound up in such a decision and the importance of such factors as geographical origin and greater or lesser adherence to religious values. Along with the job status of their husbands, to which the women interviewed frequently referred in order to explain family size, their responses reveal the equal importance of how they viewed motherhood, which was often coloured by their own mothers' experience. The physical conditions in which these women fed, clothed, raised, and educated their children will be examined in the following chapters. The impact of the Depression, responsible in part for the reduction in family size, will emerge more clearly as will the strategies utilized in order to cope with all these responsibilities despite what was frequently a difficult economic situation.

Chapter 5 ---

Working for Pay
and Managing the
Household Finances

"My mother-in-law used to laugh at me—she'd say,
if I gave you a nickel, you'd turn it into a dollar."
(E11)

S tudies dealing with the period just before the Depression years of
the 1930s show that, without exception, workers' wages were insufficient to ensure a decent standard of living for an average family.[1] In the
absence of a family wage, children and women as well had to do what they
could through various kinds of work to increase the family income. Even
in a period of relative prosperity, additional pay was as necessary a part of
balancing the household budget as were the wages of the principal earner,
but so was extremely strict management and very careful housekeeping.

Because of unemployment, however, the Great Depression came to
exercise additional pressure on family finances. In these conditions, how
did families ensure their survival? In order to answer this question, the
next three chapters will examine, in order, the role of paid work in the
family economy, that of domestic labour and finally of other means of
support to which the families in the sample turned, including public benefits, private charity, relatives and friends, going into debt, and any other
expedients they may have employed.

In this chapter, we will first of all consider the question of income. It is
important to examine this subject at the outset because income determines the family's standard of life, the quantity of housework as well as
what equipment the women had at their disposal to do it with, and the

---

Notes to Chapter 5 are on pp. 204-206.

degree to which households had to turn to other means of support. We will concern ourselves not only with income deriving from the husband's principal activity, but also with the contributions deriving from the wife's labour, with budget management, and with the impact of unemployment on the household economy and on the sexual division of labour.

A Living Wage

It was generally understood that, after marriage, women would quit their jobs in order to take care of the house and children. In addition to these tasks, the majority would also take over the management of the family finances, which initially comprised the husbands' wages as principal breadwinner. The funds they had to spend would depend on his occupation. In most cases, this factor would also determine whether or not the wives would have to undertake some sort of paid activity in order to make up for a lack of income.

The following table indicates the husbands' occupations just before the beginning of the Depression or at marriage if this occurred after 1929:

Table 8
Husbands' Occupations in 1929
or at Marriage

Status	Number
Self-Employed	
Shopkeepers, tradesmen	3
Waged	
Non-manual workers	6
Manual workers	20
Out of Work	1
Total	30

As we may observe, only one of the husbands, who had been in fact unemployed since the couple was married in 1927, did not have a permanent job at the beginning of the thirties, while three had small businesses (a barber shop, a corner restaurant, two taxicabs). Among the manual workers, eleven were factory workers, while the rest were working in construction (a bricklayer, two labourers), in small businesses (barbershop employee, butcher shop employee, delivery man), and in services (two maintenance workers, one auto mechanic). The non-manual workers included a laboratory technician, a junior manager, two shop assistants, and two office clerks.

According to the unemployment statistics, a number of these occupations were especially vulnerable as the Depression set in. This was particularly true for industrial and construction workers,[2] but in fact almost every one of the couples in the sample was affected one way or the other by the economic crisis. Of the three small businessmen, for example, only the barber was able to retain his business, although he suffered from a decline in revenue as he had to lower his prices by 30 percent, while his clientele also shrank. In 1934, he had to get rid of the second-hand car he had purchased the year before. The other two had to sell up their businesses to avoid bankruptcy. According to their wives' recollections, their failure was the result of their clients' overwhelming demand for credit and the general decline in business:

> When the Depression came, we were obliged to extend too much credit, even though we had to buy for cash. We could have wound up on the street. We had already lost $900 in bad debts. Before we lost everything, we sold up. As for myself, I didn't want to buy on credit—I wouldn't have been able to sleep. . . . There are always people who don't pay. But during the Depression, they always had an excuse. Or they would pay us, but not the whole thing. We lost control over our lives. (E7)

> When I first met [my husband], he owned two taxicabs. And when I got married, in 1929, that's when the crash happened. Then a year later he sold his two cars. He had one man working for him but . . . he had to sell, he wasn't making enough. Marriages in those days—he got paid five dollars for a wedding party. I was happy [when he sold his cabs] I was happier when he had a job and a salary we could count on. He had lots of money in his pockets, but you couldn't count on it . . . he had to make the payments every month. We did not live well. We were doing very well if we managed to have enough to eat all the time. (E29)

Both of them experienced unemployment, and in one case, home relief, before finding a paying job, which one of them kept for the rest of his life, the other until the Depression was over. The fate of these small businessmen was not very far removed from that of elements of the working class on whose members they depended to make a living and from which they had often themselves originated. Without sufficient assets to pay their obligations and wait for better times, fearful of falling into too much debt and losing everything or refusing outright to go into debt at all, large numbers of them would be vulnerable to a major economic crisis like that of the 1930s.

Of the twenty-six who worked for wages, only four escaped any loss of employment or cut in salary. Four others had their workweek cut to one or a couple of days and three, while working the same number of hours, had their wages cut by 20 percent. Seven were without a steady job for more than three years, six others for a period of between one and two years, and the last, and most fortunate, for several months only. Two others—including one whose husband was out of work at the time they were married—had to turn to the Saint Vincent de Paul Society or to relief, but according to their accounts, their husbands' laziness and refusal to provide for the family were to blame rather than lack of jobs during the Depression. All in all, fifteen couples needed governmental aid to survive and two chose to go back to the land as a solution.

With the exception of two informants who were never told, the women remembered very clearly what their husbands were earning when they got married. As they recalled, the level was very low—if two of them were earning as much as thirty-five dollars a week, others made as little as ten and more than half less than twenty dollars a week. According to the data of the federal minister of labour, however, it required $20.18 a week in Quebec in December 1929 and $14.29 a week in December 1933 simply to cover the costs of food, heating, light, and rent for an average family of five.[3] In 1931, the living wage for Canadians was figured at $1050 a year, or about twenty dollars a week, while it would take at least $1500 a year ($28.84 a week) to provide a comfortable standard of living.[4] In this sample, only five men made more than twenty-five dollars a week at the end of the 1920s or at the beginning of the 1930s.[5] The unemployment and short weeks from which more than two-thirds of the respondents' husbands suffered obviously involved a reduction in income and accentuated the financial difficulties they were already experiencing. So, in addition to paying $8.50 in rent directly to the landlord, the Unemployment Relief Commission of Montreal established the sums of $7.15 a week in winter and $6.55 in summer as the amount of aid to be paid to a family of five. These amounts were supposed to cover all other necessities of life (food, heating, clothing) and represented a total of $39.48 and $36.88 a month, depending on the season.[6] Even if we take into account the decline in prices of around 29 percent, according to the data cited previously, these sums represent barely more than half of the $14.49 required in 1933 to cover the basic living expenses of a family of five each week. It seems clear that the families of the unemployed could not survive merely on the grants they received.

Income to Balance the Budget

The inadequacy of workers' wages is already well known. What remains to be documented is the range of other forms of work undertaken by men and women to manage to balance the family budget.[7] Participating in informal economic enterprise was more often left to women because their family and household responsibilities, which, although preventing them from entering the job market, still did allow them a greater flexibility with which to organize their time, so that they were able to engage in different activities in the home.[8] Nevertheless, a considerable number of men were looking for additional income, as the recollections of our informants indicate.[9]

Odd Jobs

Given the inadequacy of their wages, it comes as no surprise to learn that even when they had steady jobs, several of the husbands did other work or made some sort of exchange in order to supplement their incomes, either during or after the Depression. During the Depression years themselves, seven of the husbands looked for ways to increase their incomes.

Thus, a mechanic made money fixing cars after work, while an office worker did different kinds of maintenance at night and on the weekend for the recreation club he worked for. Together with his wife, a woodworker made checkerboards which he disposed of in a draw after his grocer had sold ten dollars worth of ten-cent tickets in his shop, where they were on display. In a flagrant violation of the law forbidding lotteries, one of the husbands sold "hockey cards" at the factory where he worked. Another kept the books for a small grocery on top of his work as a civil servant. The man who owned a corner store retained his sales job while his wife kept the shop during the day and he took over in the evenings. It was, moreover, exactly for this reason that he decided to get married right away: "That's why we got married, so we wouldn't have to pay a store clerk" (E7). Another, who was working for a Montreal department store as a receiving clerk, got permission to run a little snack bar for the use of store employees. He had one woman helping him at lunchtime and he called upon his wife to make certain purchases:

> When he was working, he had the restaurant and at noontime he hired a woman.... It brought in enough. He sold soft drinks, chocolate, gum. There were people who came downstairs to grab a chocolate bar. When he could get hold of some fruit, he bought it. I didn't mind, sometimes he'd call me up and tell me, "Come bring me this or that." I would go and walk down there with the baby in the carriage." (E21)

Clearly the Depression only made it more pressing to turn to all sorts of expedients to make up for shortages in the family income. Before going to the Saint Vincent de Paul Society or the Montreal Unemployment Relief Commission for help, or even while they were receiving benefits,[10] six of the husbands had sought to support their families by undertaking all kinds of activities. Some of the notable stopgaps which the men, newly unemployed, turned to in order to find new sources of income included digging out a cellar with a shovel, washing walls and ceilings, shovelling snow in the affluent districts of the city, reselling breads and cakes bought directly from a commercial bakery at the end of the day when the unsold merchandise was returned, peddling the remainders of blocks of ice or bootlegging alcohol which the man made in his shed (and hid in the baby carriage for delivery), and opening a little "restaurant" at home. The informants also report other activities or deals carried out by different members of their acquaintance, suggesting that this phenomenon was very common. For example, a brother-in-law went hunting and sold the game he had killed and butchered, a neighbour cultivated eight garden plots on land furnished free by the city and sold the vegetables, and so on.

To this list should be added the different jobs that the men accepted on a temporary and often part-time basis before they found permanent employment. In the majority of cases, indeed, their years of unemployment were interspersed with periods when they had jobs (not counting the public works that some of them were required to do), which brought, along with a supplementary income, just enough hope to support the next period of joblessness. These odd jobs and other forms of paid activity did not always mean that their wives could avoid having to find ways to earn money.

Working in Your "Spare Time"

We generally tend to think of women in this period as homemakers and this is largely how they appear in the census figures. In the sample collected here, however, only six did not engage in any paid activity after they were married. Among those who did contribute to the family income, six began work after 1939, when it was easier for them to free themselves of family responsibilities and at a time when paid work for married women, if not altogether acceptable, was in any event more tolerated. One of the others decided to go to work in a munitions factory at the beginning of the war in order to recoup the family finances that had been sapped by the six years that her husband, a bricklayer, had been almost constantly out of work.

Among the women who worked for pay during the decade of the 1930s, five had jobs outside the house, while the thirteen others worked at home in one or several paid capacities. Needlework of various sorts—dressmaking, embroidery, beading, smocking, knitting—represented the most common kind of work, with eight of the informants engaging in it either for companies or independently. Another worked for two years for her mother-in-law, who was keeping a rooming house, in exchange for room and board for herself and her husband, while six let rooms or took in boarders.[11] In four cases, the lodgers were parents or friends of the family, who would sometimes put up with living conditions that a stranger might have had more difficulty accepting, like sharing a sofa bed in the living room with one of the sons of the family or sleeping on a folding cot set up for the night in the hall leading to the kitchen. Taking in roomers or boarders in fact involved a small investment that not all were able to make. A flat with an extra room was required and it was necessary to get hold of an extra bed, a set of sheets and some blankets, none of which could be managed by the poorest and largest families. A study conducted by the federal government into the Canadian family concluded:

> It is clear that the families who take in lodgers are not those who are living in uncomfortable living quarters or with limited facilities. . . . It would appear that taking in lodgers is more a source of revenue for the more prosperous class of wage earners than for the poorest class and that this practice cannot be turned to as a way of relieving poverty.[12]

Two informants took in washing and hired themselves out as cleaning women,[13] while three others ran a little business. One of these first managed her husband's business until he was forced to sell. After being out of work for several months, she sought work as a private dressmaker from the owner of the concern where she had worked before her marriage. He, however, preferred to employ her husband as a private chauffeur on a permanent basis, while hiring her as a maid when he needed extra help, for parties and so on. Another woman invested an insurance payment that she received following an accident in a little "restaurant" which she ran with her husband for a short period while he was out of work:

> I think we started with about fifty dollars worth of stock. Nothing much—a little candy, a few cigarettes, a little of this, a little of that. Nothing much. We lasted about a year. Yes indeed! Five cents for a Coke! There were a lot who didn't have the five cents to buy it. (E26)

An informant, widowed in 1930, also decided to open a little restaurant. She rented out a room as well to different relatives and also did dressmaking for her neighbours. Despite all her efforts, the income she derived from these three occupations was not enough to support her children. After exhausting the life insurance payment from which she paid her rent, she had to contemplate, with some reluctance, the solution of remarrying:

> When you see you have no more money. . . . The Depression was starting. When you were selling only five or ten cents worth a day, you're not making much. . . . You start thinking about a lot of things. You say, my children what are they going to do? Soon I'll have no more money. That'll be it. You say, OK, I'll get married. . . . If I'd had a pension . . . I would have kept my restaurant. I wouldn't have remarried. For a while, I wanted to go to Ontario. If I'd known anyone there I would've gone because they paid widows a pension there. (E3)

This extract highlights the economic importance of marriage for women. As fate would have it, the second husband lost his job a month before they were married and the couple finally decided to go back to the country to live.

Finally, the third woman sold her baking while she was living in the country for a time in hopes of improving the health of her paralyzed daughter:

> I said to my husband, "Do you know, I'd like to make pies and cakes. I think I can sell them on Sundays." Yes, indeed, that's what I started to do, madame. . . . I never had enough of them! I sold out. My husband said, "You'd do better with a store." Well, I said, "If only I could." We had a kind of little shed, it was about as big as my hand and we used to put the wood in there. It was not exactly a good store. But he made me a counter and I put it in there. On Saturdays, I would have to spend my whole day making pies and cakes! I would make them on Saturday, I would make my pastry, my cakes. (E17)

This informant was not the only one to make money from her culinary talents. Another of the women, who also cleaned houses and did dressmaking, made baked beans and maple butter (out of black-market brown sugar) during the war that her husband sold for twenty-five cents a container at the grocery where he was working. "I made them in my spare time, all by myself," she said. Sewing and cooking, traditional feminine accomplishments and two important elements in the domestic labour of women, could be easily transformed into paid work. These strategies are a tribute to the resourcefulness of these women who sought to take advantage of the skills they had mastered so well and demonstrate as well that the line between the marketplace and the unpaid economy was, for them, a slender one indeed.

The work that married women did for pay was thus indeed far from being inessential, even if it was, for the most part, accomplished at home, unseen and unrecorded.[14] When we look at the list, the first thing that strikes us is precisely the variety of things that women were doing, often several at the same time, especially those who had always worked at home. As one respondent, who also worked cleaning houses, explained: "I did alterations, hemmed dresses, took up slips, and did mending. Then there was ironing. There was a little woman . . . she always brought me [her washing] on Monday morning. I would do a small wash for a dollar or seventy-five cents, whatever I could pick up. I always did those things" (E16). Another related:

> We didn't have enough money. I used to smock baby clothes. Then I had my boarder who gave me six bucks a week. That helped a little, my husband was making ten dollars a week. . . . I was always doing some kind of sewing to make money. I was sewing for practically thirty years. (E13)

Clearly, it was economic necessity that motivated the women who decided to earn a little money. Some did not look for ways to improve their level of income, however, despite their husbands' inadequate wages, while others, whose husbands were doing better or who had smaller families, nevertheless did work, often for specific purposes, like paying off a debt or educating their children. In other words, the notion of what was necessary to assure the well-being of a family varied from woman to woman according to individual standards. The amount of the husbands' income was therefore not the sole factor that came into play when a woman decided to work, although in a majority of cases, it was the determining one.[15] As we shall see later on, their husbands' opposition meant that certain women did not go to work, regardless of their financial difficulties.

In general, the majority of the women who contributed to the family income during the 1930s had begun working even before their husbands were laid off or had their wages cut:

> He was making ten dollars a week. We couldn't manage on that. I started to work. I sewed for everybody, I knitted, and I did everything to make ends meet. . . . I did dressmaking, knitted for everybody, made little dresses—I knitted socks and mittens, I braided rugs—fifteen cents for mittens, thirty-five cents for socks, a dollar and a quarter for a braided rug. It wasn't a fortune. Although for me, it helped me a lot. (E22)

According to their recollections, only three informants began to work specifically because their husbands were out of work. On the other hand, nine of the husbands lost their jobs for periods ranging from several

months to several years without there being any question of their wives
going to work. A number of reasons were brought forward to explain
what might appear as a paradox:

> I thought, but who would I leave the kids with? There wasn't any daycare.
> You were taking a chance leaving kids with a neighbour. . . . There wasn't
> any point in trying to get work to do at home, because there wasn't any. Or
> if there was, then it paid practically nothing. . . . You couldn't have stayed
> on relief. . . . I felt it was better if my husband did odd jobs here and there.
> (E25)

The number of dependent children as well as the husbands' opposition
comes up constantly in the oral histories, revealing a considerable ambiva-
lence: "I would have liked to go to work," one of them maintained, "but he
didn't want me to. Anyway, the children were too little, I couldn't leave
them. In those days, you didn't leave your babies with someone else"
(E20). Another was sure that she would not have been able to find work:

> There wasn't any more work for girls than there was for men in those
> days. . . . And I'd never had a job,[16] let me tell you I'd have had a lot of trou-
> ble finding work too. Later on, when I was older, I figured things out. Then
> I was too timid. Maybe if I had more guts I could have found myself some
> kind of job. But my mother-in-law had never worked outside the house.
> Myself, I felt I had to be like her. (E19)

Underneath these arguments, one detects a certain reluctance, as much
on the women's part as on their husbands', to bring about a reversal in
roles that would be incompatible with defined and accepted social norms.
The presence of young children especially represented a major obstacle to
women's working for pay, even if the out-of-work father would have been
available to take care of them. The majority of the women also were posi-
tive that there was no work for women without actually having looked for
any. In fact, in the nine cases where the wife had never made any financial
contribution to the family, the sexual division of labour was so rigidly
ingrained that it prevailed over the need to find additional income.

Otherwise, when we look more closely at the five women who did
work outside the home before 1939, we realize that two of them worked
for less than a year, while another was employed only part time. Only two
became the principal family breadwinner—one for a period of four
years—and only one of the two husbands had totally stopped working at
the time. Moreover, neither had more than two children and these were
cared for by someone other than their husbands even when he was free to
do it.

The women who were already doing paid work at home before their husbands became unemployed continued their work and even increased their efforts whenever possible; as a result of the Depression, however, many of the private dressmakers lost a part of their clientele. But no one of this group ever entertained the notion of replacing their work at home with work outside it: "I sewed for other people for housekeeping money during the Depression. I was a big help to my husband—he was doing what he could and so was I," one respondent said. But when she was asked if she ever thought about getting a paying job, she answered, "My husband wouldn't have allowed it, no. He said that a wife . . . we could only go out by the day,[17] there wasn't any other work" (E5). Just like the men whose wives made no financial contribution to the household before they were unemployed, those who accepted their wives working at home for pay would never have stood for her finding a job outside the home. This reversal of roles would have been a direct threat to their superior position as head of the household and would have represented too sharp a blow to their pride which had already been fairly well shaken by failure to fulfil this role adequately. It would seem that the family model of bread-winner/homemaker was so entrenched that even extreme poverty was insufficient to dislodge it.[18]

In general, and in an altogether astonishing way, the women had more trouble recalling their own incomes than their husbands' wages. Two factors may explain this phenomenon. On the one hand, the relative lack of importance that they accorded to the money they made, which they regarded as a secondary income, hardly aided recollection. On the other, the amounts they got varied enormously, depending on their clientele (if they were self-employed, for example), or the amount of work they could do when they were paid by the piece. "It was an extra. It didn't give me a steady income" (E22), as one of them said. The proportion of women's earnings in the total household income is therefore almost impossible to establish. From the information we have, we observe, however, that these earnings varied from three to ten dollars a week and that, in certain cases, they might represent up to 50 percent of the husband's wages. One thing is certain—the money they earned went toward the needs of the household and not those of the women, as they paid the rent and bought groceries and clothes for the children. The following is a representative statement from the histories: "It didn't pay a helluva lot, but it was only that it gave me a little something at the end of the week. . . . When [my husband] didn't have enough, then I was the one who paid, I would put it toward the rent or to buying clothes for the kids" (E17).

Less commonly, as we have already pointed out, the sums were accumulated with an eye to paying for the children's schooling. "With that money, I was able to send two to high school," one informant proudly declared. But this form of savings was only possible in smaller or better-off families, where the husband's paycheque was enough to cover basic expenses. In most cases, the wife's earnings were used to pay for part of the rent or the groceries. This contribution could, moreover, make the difference between living below or just a little above the poverty line.

Managing the Budget and Women's Economic Power

Regardless of any additional revenues, the income of these households remained generally very low. Making ends meet was a real feat and one which confronted most of the women in this sample. According to a tradition that was deeply rooted in the working class in Quebec as well as elsewhere, it was most often the wife who was had the responsibility of administering the family budget.[19] How money was handled between husband and wife could, however, take on different forms, revealing power relations within the family.

In half of the families in the sample, the husband turned over his entire pay to his wife, who gave him an allowance for his personal expenses. The practice was prevalent throughout the working class, especially among those who earned the least, thus tending to confirm the hypothesis that holds that it represented, for men, a way of avoiding the challenge of managing on wages insufficient to support a family.[20] Quite frequently, these men did not even know what the household financial situation was, as they had no interest in the subject:

> I was always the one who handled the budget because my husband was not good at it. He would always say, "You take care of it." Like with the insurance and so on. He would never know how the insurance got paid and all. It wasn't his problem." (E19)

Even if they only rarely interfered once the money was given to their wives and did not demand a precise accounting of expenses, this way of handling money did not necessarily mean that they had given up all their economic power. Some of them, for example, expected that there would always be something left over to supply their need for extra cash. "That's why he gave me the wallet, he knew I would take care of it and when he asked me for five dollars, he knew I would have it. I always had it. If I'd said, "I don't have it," he wouldn't have liked that. You learn these things once you get married" (E2). Others threatened to take over the family finances where they were badly managed. "My husband told me, I am going to give you my pay. But if I see you're wasting it, then I'll keep it and take care of things myself" (E5). Whether they were completely detached from household matters or managed to retain a certain degree of control by insisting on their own demands or floating the possibility of interfering in the management of the money, these men did not have as their first concern balancing the budget.

In nine families, the husbands exercised a greater degree of power over how the money was used. Some of them kept the amount they wanted for their expenses (tobacco, transportation, etc.) and gave the rest to their wives, while others gave over only the amounts required to pay part or all of the running expenses. The two following recollections illustrate these different modes of operation. "When Friday night came around, he kept his expenses and the rest I had. I was the one who took care of everything. I was the one who paid the rent, the lights, I was the one who saw to everything" (E8). "He gave me the money to meet our expenses. But it was my husband who handled the purse strings and he knew how to manage. He didn't drink" (E29). This way of handling money appears most often among the families where the husband was earning a higher wage, but also where the husband had his own business or where part of his income came from tips or commissions. As these situations resulted in variable incomes, the wives we interviewed did not know precisely how much their husbands earned. Such was the case for another informant, married to a barber:

> I never knew exactly how much he made, never. Because they made tips. Anyway, he had to keep them to pay for everything—cleaning his outfits, his tools, he was the one paid for those things. He had to be sure to have enough. But I always had enough for the household expenses. (E24)

This practice of keeping the extras also occurred in connection with other kinds of activities, not always entirely legal, that brought in money, as we see here:

> He would come home and give me all of his pay. There wasn't any lottery in those days, but he sold hockey cards and he sold a lot of them. The guy who ran the whole thing would bring him the complete series and he would sell them at the plant. So he made money that way. It wasn't an enormous amount, but for his expenses. . . . Because a man, he needs money in his pocket. . . . That money was his. I was lucky that he made that money because I didn't have to give him a cent. (E11)

Wiser because of the experience of her mother, who had had to solve by herself the problems arising from an inadequate family income, one informant insisted that this task be shared: "When I got married, I said that the money had to be dealt with by both of us. That way, it's not always the same one who has to worry. . . . I said that we both had to handle it. We had the best system. We talked about it before we got married" (E6). This way of managing was, however, only adopted by three of the couples in the sample.

At the opposite extreme, three participants, married to workers, never had any money at all in their possession, their husbands taking over paying all the bills, including the groceries. Philosophically, one of them said, "I said to myself, if anything happens, I won't get the blame" (E30). She insisted, however, on the fact that her husband had "always fed her" very well, suggesting that he had therefore fulfilled his obligations toward her. In this regard she was, nevertheless, better off than another woman, whose husband drank and played cards:

> I didn't have anything to manage, he wouldn't give me money. You know, there were men in those days. . . . I didn't know he was playing cards. He was drinking, too, when he played. I knew, I found out all about it a little while later. He would pay some of the rent and the food. At first, he was the one who bought the food. He didn't want me to buy just anything. He only bought what was strictly necessary. . . . I used to cry a lot. I asked my mother, "Is this what marriage is?" (E18)

This last example, although it might seem unrepresentative, is nevertheless not unique and allows us a glimpse of how far the economic dependence of women could go. This situation has, moreover, much in common with that of two other of the women whose husbands, who also had drinking problems, only worked now and then, both during the Depression and after it. One of them, pathologically jealous, refused even to allow his wife to work to support the family. All in all, seven of the husbands were in the habit of drinking regularly, often to excess. In at least four cases, the money they spent on their addiction deprived their families of the minimum they need to live and forced their wives to rely on their own paid work or on charitable organizations, the government, or their relatives to get by. In three other cases, the informants stated that their husbands had prevented the family from improving its economic condition. Excessive drinking, apparently quite common as it affected more than 20 percent of the husbands in the sample, had grave consequences for the standard of living of these families. Their behaviour also shows with total clarity that the pay envelope belonged by right to the husband

and that he could dispose of it virtually as he chose. It was, furthermore, because so many men were given to drink that the Dorion Commission had agreed to recommend changes to the Civil Code in this connection.[21]

Refusal to support was clearly against the law, but it was difficult for wives to launch proceedings and these often proved ineffective. One of the informants brought her husband to court on three occasions. As she herself said, the spouses who were found guilty were liable to a month in jail, which would not have given their wives any greater means of supporting the family decently, in fact, quite the contrary: "when the judge saw him the third time, he told him, 'if you come before me one more time . . . there won't be any more talking. . . . I won't listen to your wife and you'll go inside.' Inside! What good would that have done me?" (E27).

When we raised the question of their management, the majority of the women, especially those who held the purse strings, were quick to say that they were not wasteful, that they always tried to get all they could out of everything they had, and that they managed on the money they had at their disposal. "We always got by on what he made," one of them said. "We never went into debt" (E4). In fact, making ends meet without complaining about having too little money seemed to be a mark of a good homemaker and a good wife. On the one hand, it was a way of showing that their housekeeping and managerial skills were advanced enough to compensate for a lack of income; on the other, by being undemanding, the women also avoided placing their husbands' breadwinning capabilities into question, thus preserving their dignity. For both these reasons, they were generally very proud of having successfully coped on their own with balancing the budget. In the end, however, some of them realized the drawbacks of a system which rested the entire weight of this responsibility on their shoulders while opening the door to their husbands' complaints:

> In the beginning, I didn't mind because I was a good manager. But what happened was that he didn't actually do the shopping anymore and he didn't know what things cost. He'd fuss about the prices. It was all right at the beginning. But afterwards when our expenses got bigger, he didn't know what things cost and he'd say, "That cost an awful lot! Where is the money going?" Then you feel guilty, you say, "My God! Am I wasting your money? Am I a bad housekeeper? You feel guilty and it's not your fault. (E16)

This guilt is linked to the fact that the women felt that the money was not theirs but belonged to their husbands, even when the men did not go out of their way to make them feel that way. The sense that they were

spending someone else's money also explains why they so seldom complained of being short of money and why they generally did not feel they
had the right to intervene on the subject of their husbands' work, even
when the possibility of better-paying jobs existed.[22] One informant,
whose husband worked as a machinist in a textile factory, said of his pay:

> We had to be careful—he didn't make a lot of money. He could have made
> more, as other factories were paying better. But he was so used to working
> there, he'd been there for years . . . he loved where he worked. I never told
> my husband what to do because it's important to have a man who's working
> and who loves his job." (E11)

Some of them even had qualms about asking for money, relying on
their husbands' goodwill: "I had a cup—he'd leave me money in it. Every
day he'd leave me some. It embarrassed me to ask him for money. I didn't
like it—he was the one who left it for me" (E4). The status of breadwinner also conferred certain privileges which, as we have seen, were demonstrated not only in the habit of some of the husbands of keeping back part
of their earnings for drink, but also in the custom of some of the wives of
reserving the best of the food for their husbands: "I was always careful
that he got served first," one of them said, "and always the best piece of
meat. Sometimes, I thought it was unfair" (E2). If the purchase of furniture was generally decided by both of them, the husband generally got
what he wanted when it came time to think about more important expenditures. Thus, one respondent had to accept her husband's decision to
buy a house, which they lost during the Depression: "I was never fussy
about buying houses in the city. I didn't like the idea. But it was my husband's money and that's what he wanted. It was his money and no one
could say anything about it" (E17). Another woman, in contrast, would
have preferred to invest in a house rather than borrowing to buy an automobile: "My husband wanted to have a car. I wanted a car too but it
would have been better to buy a house, but my husband didn't think of
that" (E2).

Giving over the pay envelope to the wife, whether in whole or in part,
was far from representing a form of power for the women, something of
which they were, for the most part, perfectly aware.[23] On the contrary,
these oral histories tend rather to refute the thesis that holds that the
domestic sphere represents an area of power or of counter-power for
women because it is there that they exercise control.[24] At first sight, it
would seem logical that women who were in charge of making purchases
should be left with the money to do so. Too often, however, this practice

allowed the husband to get away cheaply from a permanent headache, all the while maintaining the illusion that he was adequately fulfilling his role as breadwinner. If disaster overtook the family finances, he could always place the blame on his wife's bad management. She herself would tend to take the blame and to say as little as possible about the difficulties she was facing because she felt that her homemaking skills were at stake.

Making Ends Meet

As we have just seen, most often it was the wives who took on the responsibility for managing the household budget and who had to plan for what it was spent on. Without question, the most critical aspect of women's domestic labour was their making ends meet on an income that was generally insufficient, as the welfare of the whole family depended on their ability to make do on the money they had available. Checking prices, buying only what was strictly necessary, wasting nothing, not going into debt were constand bywords in their oral histories: "I never wasted anything"(E1); "Every cent counted" (E2); "You had to count the pennies all the time" (E5). One respondent explained just how she managed to get along despite her large family and a desperately low income: "Only I never had my hair done, never bought lipstick, never bought a stick of gum. Never make an unnecessary expense, eh? Never, ever, ever. I never went to the movies—I didn't know anything about it" (E22).

Looking back, all of these women were surprised themselves to observe that they had managed to get by on so little. When asked what she had done to manage, one of them answered, "I can't tell you. All I can say is that God was with me. I never went into debt. When I wanted to have a little something, I had the money saved up. . . . How did I do it? I don't know" (E22). "For a while," said another, "I had to work miracles" (E2). A third maintained, "Don't ask me how I did it. I don't know" (E28).

In fact, as they described in detail how they managed, it became evident that these women had a very strict set of priorities that they tried to observe, even when the intervals between paydays sometimes made their task complicated. This was particularly true of those whose husbands were paid twice a month, which sometimes required them to get through three weekends on one pay.

First of all, they had to pay the irreducible expenses like electricity and rent, the last of which the landlord generally collected at the door, encouraging promptness. "Rent and electricity, those are the first things to put on the budget" (E5). "The rent money was the first thing of all. I would rather skip eating" (E14). Thus, the rent and the electricity were seen as "debts" that they made a point of honour of paying regularly. Once these obligations were met, the remainder of the money went to pay for food, for wood or coal for the stove, and, in last place, the expenses connected to clothing, transportation, insurance, and if there were a few pennies left, to recreation.

If we look in detail at each line of these budgets, we note that the women tried first of all to find a place to live with a rent that was no more than their husbands' weekly salary. Given the smallness of their wages, this meant that the living quarters open to them were often of very poor quality or too cramped for the size of their families.

Once the family was housed, it was next necessary to think about feeding it. According to data furnished by the *Labour Gazette*, feeding a family of five cost on average $11.02 in December 1929 and $6.72 in December 1933; these figures indicate that for these two years, food represented 54 percent and 46 percent respectively of basic expenses.[25] Despite this reduction, food represented an important item in the budget. In order to meet their families' needs without putting too great a strain on the household finances, these housewives performed feats of ingenuity both in buying and preparing food for the table. They chose the cheaper cuts of meat and avoided purchasing prepared foods that were too expensive. "We never bought anything already made" (E2), as one of them said. Tinned products were largely confined to tomatoes, corn, salmon, peas, and beans for the majority of the women. Fresh fruit, with the exception of apples and bananas, appeared only rarely on the menu, and in general, they contented themselves with a rather narrow range of vegetables: potatoes, carrots, turnips, and onions making the most frequent appearance on the table.[26] The tiny sums paid by home relief would further reduce the quality and variety of food consumed. As one informant noted, "We bought potatoes. In those days, potatoes didn't take too much out of your pocket. . . . They cost less than anything else, so you could eat more of them. It was a way of filling yourself up without it costing too much" (E19).

The importance of food, as a basic need that had to be satisfied, and the difficulties that might accompany the task of feeding the family appeared spontaneously in the comments that were collected on this subject. Quite frequently, indeed, the informants insisted on saying that despite all their financial difficulties, and despite the Depression, their families, the children in particular, never lacked for food, which implies that nourishing the family was a constant worry. "To want for food, that was the worst possible thing. I would rather not have had clothes on my back. Eating was enough" (E2). "We always ate our three meals a day" (E14). Not missing a meal did not, however, necessarily mean that the food was the best quality or that the menus were well balanced, as some of the women were well aware. "We always ate, maybe not as well as we might—but we always ate" (E23). "I used to put all kinds of things together to make one big dish. We couldn't eat steak, but we never, ever suffered because of a meal" (E28). For others, "not having food" meant literally not having something to eat, without regard to the quality of the meal: "We often had mustard spread on bread. But we always had something to eat" (E19). Another informant said, "We were never really destitute during the Depression. We always had something to eat" (E8); her comments express the idea that it is the total absence of all food that was often associated with genuine poverty. That is to say, their desires, even at the level of satisfying their basic needs, remained very modest.

Among these needs, spending on clothing came in last place and was often reduced to the minimum. The husband and the older sons almost always wore store-bought clothes while the clothing of the other children was made at home, either from new material or, more frequently, remade out of old garments donated by relatives. In order to cut costs, the youngest children wore hand-me-down clothes and even shoes when their father was handy at replacing soles. Those who were less talented at sewing would buy their clothes from Saint Vincent de Paul and the Salvation Army or from pedlars who would charge interest for spreading out the payments.

What with the husband, who had to go out every day to work and the children, who had to be decently dressed for school, the women, who spent more of their time at home, found their needs being met well after those of everyone else. Their wardrobe was limited to a couple of cheap cotton housedresses and one or two better dresses that were suitable for the rare occasions that they went out: "At home, with the kids, we wore cotton housedresses. We never put pretty dresses on our backs. We had cheap cotton housedresses with an apron over them. On Sundays, we wore a good dress. When we went out, we dressed up" (E11). One of them, who for fifteen years wore the same winter coat she had bought the year she got married, explained, "After I took care of my children and my husband, there wasn't anything left for me. So I wore other people's stuff that I fixed up for myself. I wore other people's clothes for a long time" (E16). Another recounted, "I remember when we had the restaurant, I had just two dresses—wash the dress, iron the dress. Day after day—wash the dress, iron the dress. . . . Me, who hates to iron!" (E26).

In the majority of families in the sample, virtually the entire budget was devoted to basic necessities, and that was even before the effects of the Depression made themselves felt. Because of job losses and wage cuts the crisis often required them to make cuts in their essential outlays— housing, food, clothing, and heating—despite the reduction in prices that the Depression brought about. The women did not, by the way, comment on this price reduction, probably because it coincided with the growth in the size of their families. In order to maintain at least a minimum quality of life, the women would utilize even more energetically those various strategies with which they were familiar or which they were forced to adopt—increasing their work in the home to supplement their income, but also packing the family into a smaller flat, keeping a closer watch over the budget, buying less and buying cheaper, inventing yet more economical recipes, calling more on relatives when possible. These last strategies will be examined in greater detail in the next two chapters.

------

*E*xamining the incomes of the families in the sample, the sources of this money, and how it was managed has allowed us to observe that the breadwinner/housewife model did not correspond to the reality experienced by the majority of the families under consideration, as eighteen of them were dependent for their survival on the combined incomes of the two partners, in the 1930s alone. The Depression is not, however, altogether responsible for husbands' working two jobs or wives' working for pay, as the majority of these households (fifteen out of eighteen) depended on various sources of income even before unemployment deprived them of the wages of their principal breadwinner. Rather than changing the nature of the remunerative activities that women engaged in, since they, for the most part, continued to turn to work in the home, the Depression caused housewives to intensify their efforts. In fact, the sexual division of labour was rooted so deeply that just one woman was in the position of chief family breadwinner during the period of her husband's joblessness.

The overwhelming majority of these women was responsible for making the purchases and paying the running expenses of the household. Because they were required to translate their husbands' wages into goods for their family's consumption and because where they lived was often the place where they also worked for pay, there was no clear distinction for these women between the public and the private sphere.[27] The interconnection between different forms of work which were carried out in the two spheres was especially visible during the Depression while the importance of their role as housewife and administrator only grew in proportion to the degree that unemployment deprived them of their normal sources of income.[28]

To guarantee the well-being of their family while buying the least they could at the best possible price sums up the challenge faced daily by the majority of these housewives. Regardless of the additional income they could raise from their paid activities, there is no doubt that they would not have met it without extremely careful household management. As one informant explained, "I never went without food or clothes. But if I hadn't sewed and bought cheap, I would have gone without" (E3). This is the area we will examine in the next chapter.

Chapter 6

Housework

"*I was quite a success in my life as a housewife.*"
(E5)

ousework, by which we mean the various tasks required to feed, clothe, and care for a family, undoubtedly represents the most substantial element of women's domestic labour. Unlike the kinds of care and worry associated with motherhood, for example, household tasks are indeed easier to conform to what we generally see as "work," because the time they take to accomplish can be measured and because they lead to the production of specifics (meals, clothing) that are also quantifiable. As we were able to observe in the previous chapter, household tasks furthermore are easily transformed into paid activities or a job, which accentuates the parallel.

Since the middle of the nineteenth century, this form of work has undergone numerous transformations, as much in the sort of tasks that had to be done as in the kinds of tools available to do them. Industrialization in fact permitted a growing number of urban housewives to buy certain manufactured articles instead of making them at home: bread and a few other basic commodities; soap, yard goods and, to a certain extent, clothing were among the products that would henceforth be purchased by the majority of these women, at least from time to time. Electricity and running water, which were generally available in working-class districts in the second decade of this century, were certainly the two innovations that

Notes to Chapter 6 are on pp. 206-10.

had the greatest effect on how they did their work. Finally, from the beginning of the twentieth century, housework became the object of a series of pronouncements aimed at rationalizing its execution in conformance with the new scientific and hygienic standards that were beginning to appear. From the 1920s onward, it would also begin to be invested with an emotional charge that would make it into a "labour of love."

Despite all these transformations, it was still the fact that, for the women interviewed, the family represented more an area of production than of consumption, and that would be true until at least the 1940s. In fact, their insufficient incomes meant that the majority of them had no other choice than to produce the most goods and services possible while devoting what little money they had to those expenses that were essential and unavoidable. In this sense, what they produced represented a crucial contribution to the economy of the household, as this production met the needs that their cash income would never have stretched to satisfy. Moreover, it encompassed such a range of products that when the Depression arrived, it was difficult for them to add new tasks to those that they were already doing. Unlike middle-class women, who could substitute their own labour for the purchase of consumer goods during the Depression, the majority of the women in this sample had not as yet attained mass consumption and thus could not return to practices that they had never abandoned. The Depression, however, did have the effect of expanding their workload while making it more difficult to carry out those tasks they were already doing or increasing the frequency with which they had to be done.

Women's Space and Workplace

The new gender division of roles brought about by industrialization went hand in hand with a spatial segregation for activities appropriate to each sex. Bit by bit, after the middle of the nineteenth century, the urban dwelling becomes the space specifically for domestic labour and the place where in the future only women work. The domestic workspace, however, reaches beyond the narrow confines of the home to extend to all those places where some part of housework is carried out:[1] shops, school, medical clinics and the like. The conditions in which these housewives had to live and work therefore depended, in part at the very least, on the degree to which their housing provided healthy conveniences, on the general layout of these lodgings, and on the range of services available in the districts in which this housing was situated.

The Neighbourhood

During the 1920s and 1930s, the women we interviewed lived in various working-class districts in southwest Montreal and the east end of the city, in Verdun, and in certain newer areas like Rosemont, Villeray, and the Plateau Mont-Royal. Except for Verdun and the Villeray and Plateau districts, which were almost exclusively residential, the older areas were developed at the same time as industrialization and, at the beginning of the Second World War, still exhibited characteristics left over from the nineteenth century. First of all, these districts, situated along the Lachine Canal and Notre Dame Street to the east, always contained within their limits a mix of industrial, commercial, and residential areas. Even if these last were separate, the air one breathed was polluted by the factory chimneys that dispensed black soot everywhere. On the other hand, the proximity of workplaces and businesses allowed the men to get to work on foot or by a short streetcar ride and the women to do their shopping without having to traipse long distances.[2] The informants, furthermore, underscored these advantages as only one of them brought up the drawbacks connected to the industrial environment in Saint-Henri, where she lived for just one year as a result of her husband's changing jobs. Because she had not been born in the district, she was perhaps more able to recognize these inconveniences that had become invisible to the other informants, who had been used to them for a long time:

> It was quite dirty and full of smoke, with all the cars passing and the factories. . . . You would do the wash and then you had to hurry and get the clothes in before noon, [because] when the [factory] whistles blew, all that coal dust would fall all over our clothes—all those little black polka dots. . . . And of course the children, they were always dirty—they were all covered in soot. I would send them out dressed in white by the front door and let them in by the back and they would be all black. I would have to wash them. . . . And remember, there was a park just across from our house—people said we lived in the nicest part of the neighbourhood! (E21)

The residential areas of Montreal's working-class districts, whether old or new, typically lacked green spaces and contained the highest concentration of population and the least adequate housing. These districts, built to accommodate a rapidly growing working-class population, featured streets lined with two- and three-storey attached houses that held from two to six flats. The oldest of these dated to about 1860—built close to the sidewalk and having neither front yard or balcony, they had interior staircases and sometimes portes-cochères that led to other housing situated at the back of the rear yard.[3] The exterior staircases, which along with rear laneways would become characteristic of the Montreal urban landscape, made their appearance around 1900. These lanes were particularly lively. They were at once playgrounds for the children and passageways for pedlars and for the coal and wood delivery men who could thus reach the rear sheds where the fuel was stored—and represented the quintessential area of urban socializing for the women and children of the working-class neighbourhoods.

While the urban working-class district at the beginning of the century was often polluted and over-populated, it was not transformed during the day into an exclusively female zone, in contrast to the modern suburb. Morning, noon, and night, it was criss-crossed by children on their way to school, by men and young people going to work, and by numerous deliverymen, itinerant salesmen, and pedlars offering their wares door-to-door or shouting them in the street. These neighbourhood bonds, which merged, as often as not, with those of kinship, also contributed to the intense life of the district and helped to keep its housewives from the isolation that was frequently deplored in the period after the war.[4]

Housing

The working-class districts in Montreal where the informants lived during the Depression had been built in the late nineteenth and early twentieth century, when building standards were not overly demanding. Each of these neighbourhoods, of course, contained its better-off areas where the local elite lived, such as the streets surrounding Georges Étienne Cartier Park in Saint Henri or the eastern part of de Maisonneuve, also called Viauville, but by and large the amount of money these households had to spend on rent, between twelve and eighteen dollars a month, kept them out of the better and larger flats.[5] In the majority of cases, these women had to be satisfied with a four- or five-room flat on the second or third floor, as the occupant-owners commonly kept the first floor, roomier and giving onto the yard, for themselves.

Whether this housing was old or new, the buildings generally filled the whole width of the lot and were attached on both sides. To allow each of the rooms a bit of light, most of these flats had a double room at the front although in some of the older ones, the centre room had no window at all.[6] In addition to the absence of natural light and ventilation, these long, narrow flats often had but one room that could offer a modicum of privacy. This was, however, kept for the children, who went to bed early, while their parents had to be satisfied with the room off the parlour, which was simply curtained off.

More often than not, the lack of adequate insulation meant that, especially in the third-floor flat directly under the roof, the tenants sweltered in summer and froze in winter and had to pay considerably more for their heat, which generally came from a stove in the kitchen at the far end of the flat.[7] In these conditions it was very difficult, if not impossible, to distribute heat evenly through the entire flat. For the women, these circumstances meant that they did their work in badly lit and poorly ventilated rooms, in uncomfortable temperatures—conditions strongly reminiscent of the factory floor.

All of the housing inhabited by the informants in the survey was connected to the municipal water mains and had electricity. The hot water heater was not, however, included in the rent and had to be bought or rented by the tenants. Still, the kitchen had to be large enough for one of these boilers and the flat had to be connected to the gas lines which fuelled them. In any event, because of their minimal incomes, most of the informants were not able to afford this luxury—in fact, only three of them had always owned a water heater and just seven more had rented one shortly before the Second World War. These boilers did not work automatically. They had to be lit each time before hot water was desired. Certain kinds were attached to the stove and only worked if the stove was lit, something that was hardly practical in summer. In order to save money or time, the hot water reservoir was often used only for the weekly baths and laundry, which meant that the housewives who had one still continued to heat water on top of the stove to do the dishes or other household tasks that required smaller amounts of water. "The gas was expensive. You had to save on everything" (E19), said one informant. Another explained, "It didn't work automatically like today—it was easier to put a kettle on to do the dishes. We heated the boiler more for the laundry or for a bath" (E15).

Though all of the flats had a flush toilet, in several cases this had been added after the house was built and installed in one of the rooms where it was walled off by a flimsy wooden partition.[8] Only fourteen of the informants had always lived in accommodations that boasted a bathtub, while seven more had to wait until after the war to achieve a flat with this convenience. Unless she had a hot water boiler already, the housewife had somehow to heat the water the family needed to wash themselves. The absence of a bathtub, as well as the fact that there was almost never a sink in the lavatory, meant that housewives had to rely solely on the kitchen sink, at which the family got washed, meals were prepared, and dishes and laundry done. This sole source of running water was in heavy demand on washdays and complicated women's work. In certain flats, the kitchen sink was so tiny that they had to wash the dishes on the kitchen table in a basin while others possessed large washtubs that were more useful but that took up a lot of space in the small rooms. The absence of counters and storage space did not make the women's work easier, either. In short, these facilities were far from the functional kitchens recommended by the "experts" and from which better-off housewives were beginning to benefit.[9]

Finally, most of the old flats had softwood floors that had to be scrubbed with a brush and "lessis" (soap ends), a particularly hard job.[10] This is why several of the informants spontaneously remarked on the presence of hardwood floors in some of the flats they had lived in. "One place I had was ever so beautiful—hardwood floors and everything" (E29). Lacking these, and if they could afford to, buying linoleum flooring made cleaning the floor much easier.

Lack of money also meant that families often had to sacrifice the parlour to make an extra bedroom. Having neither room nor money, twelve of the women in the sample thus waited several years before acquiring the furniture for this room. Whether they bought it when they were first married or some years later, most of them preferred to get a more versatile sofa bed than a chesterfield. The parlour, even if it was furnished, was thus often transformed into a bedroom by night and was not reserved for a single function, which was a sign of a greater degree of financial comfort. Nevertheless, the youngest child often slept in the parents' room until quite an advanced age, while the children's rooms, and even their beds, were always shared. Some members of the family might have to sleep in the kitchen or the hallway on a folding bed. This crowding and the use of extra beds (folding beds, sofa beds) that had to be put up and taken down daily and the several kinds of activities that took place in each room increased and complicated the work of the housewife who was anxious to have a tidy house.[11] Keeping order was not made easier when the number of persons per room exceeded a critical number, since space to store things was especially lacking. Hooks put up behind the bedroom doors and in the hallway near the entrance did their best to make up for an absence of wardrobes. Large appliances like wringer washers and sewing machines were squeezed in with some difficulty, generally winding up in the kitchen. The space available in some flats was so tight that the idea of buying such equipment could hardly be entertained. The shed, situated behind the building, where coal and wood was stored and an outside cupboard installed along the partition that separated the rear balconies of the attached houses added to the storage space. Among other uses, perishable food could be stored in this cupboard during cold weather.

The costs of moving to new accommodations could severely strain an already tight budget. A popular saying of the time, indeed, asserted that "three moves equals one fire."[12] Nevertheless, at least half of the women in the sample moved at least every year or two from the time they were married until the end of the thirties. There are a number of explanations for these frequent moves. Commonly, when a young couple first set up housekeeping on their own, they often picked a two- or three-room flat, which was initially cheaper but which would prove too small after the birth of the second or third child—after a few years, they would have to find something larger. The poor quality of the flats—inadequate insulation, presence of vermin, absence of certain amenities, too-small rooms—would encourage regular moves thereafter. If the head of the family took a new job, this might also be a reason to move, as the men generally preferred to be able to walk to work to save on transportation and to come home to eat their noon meal.

In view of the very low wages, the slightest rise in rent also might force a family to move. "I sure have moved in my life! When I think about it. . . . If the landlord raised the rent a dollar a month, we moved. It was too much, we couldn't pay it" (E29). The Depression of course contributed to increasing the frequency of these moves, since half of the women we interviewed had to shift to cheaper accommodations, in other words, to a smaller, less comfortable, and often less well-equipped flat, thus giving up what little comfort and convenience they had previously had.[13] If the entire family suffered from the deterioration in their housing conditions, it was the women, for whom the home was the place where they at once both lived and worked, who were the most affected.

For women, moving to new accommodations represented an increase in their work as well. Not only did they have to find the new flat and pack and unpack the family's belongings, but they also had to clean it from top to bottom and, if they had the money, repaint or repaper, run up new curtains, and so on. In order to reduce costs, they often called upon their relatives to help out and, if possible, got a contribution from the landlord:

so I took another place, but it was so dirty! I cleaned the flat. The landlord gave us wallpaper and he gave us paint, we had to do it all ourselves. . . . We worked like crazy but it didn't cost us anything. When you moved, you rented a truck—if you had a relative with a truck then he'd come help you move and it didn't cost anything. That's why we moved so often. (E29)

Ownership would permit important renovations that would effectively improve the conditions in which the homemakers did their work[14] —refitting the kitchen, adding a bathtub, hooking up to the gas lines, or doing electrical work. But few couples were able to treat themselves to such luxuries. In fact, only four of them owned a house before the war.[15] Two of them had inherited, while the other two could make the purchase thanks to the absurdly low cost of some properties:

We bought ourselves a little house. . . . We paid two hundred dollars for it, just for the taxes. . . . It had four rooms. The inside was finished in BC fir, varnished wood, both the ceilings and the walls. We had a toilet but no bath. There were four nice rooms. The front of the house was clapboard and there was only one balcony that didn't have a railing. The other three sides of the house were made out of Coca-Cola signs! Well, all kinds of tin signs that had been painted over. (E6)

The Depression in fact brought about the bankruptcy of many small owners who were stuck with tenants who could not pay the rent or who themselves were out of work and thus could not keep up the mortgage payments or pay their taxes. This exceptional situation meant that certain families could buy houses for a song. But it also meant that others lost everything they had. This is what happened to one couple who had bought property thanks to an inheritance shortly before the Depression began. It would seem, indeed, that this last situation was the more frequent and that the Depression did not encourage property acquisition since in Montreal, in 1941, only 11.5% owned their own homes compared with 15% ten years earlier.[16]

Finally, we should also remark that another couple was able to afford a good quality flat because some landlords, in desperation, were ready to lower their rents rather than see their flats go empty:

I got married in 1932, so the Depression wasn't over yet. The Crash had happened but the hard times were still with us. There weren't any jobs, the houses were empty. . . . In January, we took . . . the streetcar up to Jean Talon—it was Isabeau then. . . . All north of Saint Denis there, the second and third floors were all for rent. There was practically a for rent sign on every other house. That's where we rented in January, but we didn't have to start paying until we moved in in April. The landlord was very happy that

we'd rented it. At eighteen dollars a month. The most beautiful flat I ever
had—I had hardwood floors, double doors separating the dining room from
the kitchen, walnut coloured. It was all enamelled—the woodwork, all of
that. It was beautiful—four rooms with a bathroom and a nice cold pantry.
(E15)

The instances when women and their families could benefit from
improved housing because of the Depression were, however, rare. As was
remarked earlier, the Depression was more likely to raise the number of
relocations and reduce the number of small owners. Due to the uncertain
economic situation, these were unlikely to be motivated to undertake
major renovations that could have improved the living conditions of their
tenants. Indeed, the number of renovation permits noticeably diminished
during the Depression as did the number of new housing starts.[17] Nor did
the war encourage the construction of domestic housing, so that by the
end of the 1940s Montreal families were in the grip of an unprecedented
housing crisis. By postponing home building and by limiting home
improvements to middle-class owners, the Depression, in addition to
increasing the number of removals, also held back the improvement of the
workplace of housewives of the poorest classes.[18]

Implements of Work

A majority of household appliances, like the washing machine, the vac-
uum cleaner and the dishwasher, were patented in the United States in the
course of the nineteenth century, very often by women.[19] But it was not
until the beginning of the twentieth century that they became available on
the market, often to meet the needs of hotels and restaurants and several
more decades would have to pass before they would be adapted for use in
the home and homemakers could buy them.[20] Certain small appliances,
like the electric iron or the electric toaster, became more rapidly available.
In general, however, the high cost of the new large appliances as well as
lack of space or the absence of the utilities needed to run them (inadequate electrical wiring, no gas connection) meant that working-class
housewives had to do their work without modern equipment until at least
the Second World War. An examination of the tools available to the
women in our sample will allow us to determine which of them could be
found in the majority of houses and to consider their advantages and disadvantages for the housewife.

Among the appliances which offered more disadvantages than advantages were the wood, coal or combination stoves (wood and coal, gas and
coal) used by more than two-thirds of the women interviewed during the

1930s. Their surfaces were not entirely enamelled and thus required considerable upkeep if they were not to rust. Another of their considerable disadvantages was that they gave off an intense but local heat, which did not manage to spread the full length of the flat but which did overheat the kitchen, especially in the summer during mealtimes or on laundry day. In addition, these stoves had to be continually fed and they produced ashes which had to be thrown away after they were sifted to retrieve lumps of coal ("clinkers") that had not burnt down. Most of the informants had no regrets that this drudgery disappeared when they bought their first gas range:

> Then I screened the ashes! . . . In the beginning, we sifted them with a screen, we would put a sack underneath. Later on, my husband had bought a sheet metal rocker—there was a screen on top and a handle on each end, then you dumped the ashes in, they fell into the rocker, then the bits that weren't completely burnt stayed on top. (E28)

Considering the astronomical cost of electric refrigerators,[21] it is hardly surprising that only one of the informants possessed one at the time of her marriage. Two others had bought an enamelled icebox, but all the others had to make do with a wooden icebox that most of them kept until the end of the 1940s. Six others did not even have this convenience when they were first married. At any rate, the icebox could keep food for only three or four days and only in small amounts, which was not especially useful to mothers of large families. In addition, one had to keep an eye on the icebox because it was necessary to empty the container that caught the water from the melting ice. Because of lack of space or in order to avoid water damage, some housewives preferred to put the icebox in the shed or on the back balcony. In winter, several also kept food outside, in the icebox or in a cupboard placed at the edge of some balconies. This practice made it possible to save on ice (which cost between seventy-five cents and a dollar fifty a week, depending on how much was bought) as well as saving on the chore of emptying the meltwater.

Electric washing machines, with a metal tub and an electric or manual wringer, began to appear in the 1920s and were, without a doubt, a marked improvement over the washboard or the washing machine that was agitated by hand[22] or by water. But their high price and the amount of space they took up meant that most of the women interviewed waited until they had one or more children before buying one. More than two-thirds scrubbed their washing on a board for a number of years;[23] a few of them did their wash at their mother's or mother-in-law's, or, unusually, borrowed a neighbour's machine. But even when they had a machine, most of them continued to do their daily wash by hand in a tub, at the kitchen sink, or in the bathtub. "You didn't bring out the machine every day to wash the diapers" (E2), as several of the informants explained. That was because these machines were not without their disadvantages, especially when they did not work entirely by electricity. As well, the machine had to be moved to the sink where it obstructed access or took up a large part of the kitchen and it was also necessary to heat up large quantities of water to fill it. Finally, one had to keep a close eye on it to avoid damage, especially with certain models:

> There was an agitator that worked on water power—you hooked up one hose to the tap, the other you left there in the sink so the water was running all the time. You had to watch it—it worked on electricity but you had to be careful that the hose didn't fall out of the sink or there would be damage. And then there was the manual wringer that you had to turn by hand. That was hard on buttons—there was always a button missing. You had to put it through just right. . . . Let me tell you, I was over the moon the first time I got an electric washer and drier. (E8)

The sewing machine was a tool much more important than the washing machine because it allowed the making of clothes and household linen in order to effect appreciable savings.[24] In fact, only five of the women did not have one and most of those who did bought it before they bought a washing machine. Several of the women, especially the youngest in the family, inherited them from their mothers, who had no further use for it after their daughters were married. These were not electric but treadle machines, which meant that a sewing session involved a fairly considerable expense of physical energy. Over the years, however, most of the women had a motor installed, which considerably lightened this particular chore.

The toaster and the iron also were part of the household equipment. These small appliances, more affordable than washers and sewing machines, were often given as wedding presents. Some also took advantage of advertising promotions that offered electric irons and ironing boards as a bonus for buying electric washing machines.[25] But those who got married at the beginning of the twenties, when electric irons were just beginning to appear on the market, or who lived in the countryside when they were first married, used irons that had to be heated on the stove. The electric iron allowed women to iron without having to put up with heat from the stove. It could, however, weigh up to seven pounds, and as it lacked both steam and a thermostat, the housewife had to dampen her ironing with a spray bottle of water and disconnect it when it got too hot.

Altogether, then, there were few conveniences and a narrow range of rather rudimentary tools available to these housewives. The fact that most of these household appliances did not work automatically, along with the restricted space and lack of amenities of their housing, did not make it easy for women to accomplish several tasks at the same time, a possibility that would increase as the housewife became equipped with increasingly sophisticated appliances. It was indeed difficult to wash dishes and clothes at the same time with but a single sink at one's disposal. This meant that the women often had to drop one chore for another more pressing one, creating considerable discontinuity.

The introduction of electricity and plumbing into workers' housing certainly represented two important improvements that separated these women from those of previous generations and from rural women. But in order fully to enjoy all of the advantages that these utilities could provide, the housewife needed the plumbing fixtures (bathtub, water heater, second sink) and the appliances (electric washing machine, gas or electric stove, refrigerator) that few had available to them. One informant, however, who came to Montreal when she married, summed up the advantages of electricity like this: "Back home, even if we didn't have electricity, we had Aladdin lamps. . . . so I didn't find that there was that much of a difference. There would have been the laundry, a washing machine, that would have been the only change" (E22).

None of the women interviewed had to dispose of their appliances because of the Depression, though it did cause them to put off buying certain articles of furniture and equipment. During the 1940s, as their economic situation improved, the majority of them were quick to change their old wood or coal stove for a new, more practical, gas range.[26] It must be observed that these purchases necessarily coincided with the rental of a flat containing the requisite connections, which often rented for a larger amount. All the same, those who did not already have a washing machine bought one during or immediately after the war, while the others traded their old model in on one that functioned completely electrically (both tub and wringer).

Nevertheless, the Depression did temporarily deprive several of the women of their appliances for various reasons. For example, one informant did the laundry for several months in the bathtub because she did not have the money to get her machine fixed. "I had a wooden agitator with a handle in the side and the wringer was broken, which meant I had to do the wash in the bathtub. And it was only something that cost thirty-nine cents. I did the laundry for I think five or six months in the bathtub like that" (E27). In order to save on electricity, another woman used a sad iron her mother lent her that she could heat on the stove. Finally, two informants had their electricity cut off because they could not pay their bills. These cuts seriously complicated their work because they had to put off doing some of it until after dark, when they could reconnect illegally without worrying about inspectors from the company coming by.[27]

Two of the women interviewed went back to live on the land because their husbands were not able to find a job. Without electricity or running water, they had to give up their washing machines and other electric appliances (toaster, iron) and return to making a good number of items at home (bread, soap, preserves and so on) that they had formerly bought. One of these couples bought a little farm that was already in cultivation, but the other had to set up in a "colonization zone," and to undertake the hard work demanded by the clearing and ploughing of a tract of land. These two women had already experienced this kind of life, which made it easier for them to adapt to their new situation. It should be recalled that between 42,000 and 52,000 persons took up land in the colonization zones during the 1930s,[28] so that such would have been the fate of a considerable number of women, many of whom would not have been prepared to deal with changes of this sort.

Organizing Household Tasks

The sexual division of labour within the home meant that housework in general remained the almost exclusive responsibility of women. Moreover, the majority of women in this sample viewed this work as theirs and sought no help with it whatever from their husbands. "When you are married, each one has their own work" (E7). This way of conceptualizing the assignment of tasks and roles within marriage came up on several occasions in the oral histories and shows clearly that these women put their work on the same plane as that of their husbands. In reference to the sharing of housework by young couples, one informant commented:

> When all that began to change, I was really taken aback. For me, a woman who doesn't wash her walls, things like that. . . . well, I said, that's not what a man should be doing, that's women's work. She's the one living in the house. He has his own work, outside. . . . Everything but the ceilings. My husband never wanted me to wash them, or do the painting either—he always did that. He always painted—he painted my house every year. My paint was really good. (E23)

As this recollection suggests, male participation in housework was most often limited to heavy or dirty work—washing walls and ceilings, painting, hanging wallpaper, emptying ashes, taking out the garbage. A few husbands dried the dishes, at least until their daughters were old enough to do it, and washed floors, but in general, the women insisted on doing the housework by themselves. To ask for help was the same as admitting that they were not able to shoulder their responsibilities:

> I was strong enough to do all my work. He didn't help around the house, I have to say. I can't say I ever asked him to. Three rooms, four rooms—it would have been ridiculous to make him do anything. I was quite capable of doing my own work. I had the time. (E22)

Another woman even maintained that men who helped their wives might become the neighbourhood laughingstock:

> The man next door, he helped his wife. So my [husband and brothers] laughed at that guy! They called him the "diaper-washer." That was awful, eh? A man who helped his wife—they made fun of him in those days! ... And we didn't ask them to help us—as far as we were concerned, it was our work. We said, "We don't want to have them in our pots and pans." We were the ones who looked after that. (E29)

The idleness brought about by unemployment did not lead to a greater participation by men in housework.[29] Just as wives did not try to take their husbands' place as principal breadwinner, no more did the men meddle in the housework. If they did lend an occasional hand, it was only to do the jobs they had done previously—going to the store, taking care of the children, washing the floors. According to the respondents, most of the men spent the greater part of their time out of the house, looking for work. Even if they were not home all that much, some of the women found their unusual presence a nuisance: "Oh, sometimes, I'd really get fed up. I used to think, this is not his place. A man's place is to go to work, not to hang around the house" (E19).

In order to get their work done, most of the women had developed a strict schedule. Thus, Mondays and Tuesdays were devoted to washing and ironing as well as the mending. Wednesday was the day for sewing or cooking depending on circumstances, while Thursday and Friday were for the weekly cleaning and shopping. On Saturday, some would take advantage of their husbands' presence to do the baking while he looked after the children. This pattern was generally observed, no matter what happened: "On Mondays, regardless of what kind of day it was, I did the wash. I always did" (E23). A few of the others maintained that they used to have more flexible timetables, even going so far as to make fun of this rather obsessive regularity:

> When I couldn't [maintain the schedule], I didn't give a damn.... It all depended on how I got out of bed in the morning.... If I didn't feel so well, I'd put it off till the next day.... I told myself when to do things. I didn't have anyone breathing down my back. I was the boss. I did what I wanted—as long as the work got done, it was all right. I was never that fussy about things like that. (E12)

This attitude, less common, was found more among those women who had learned their domestic tasks on the farm, where housework followed a different rhythm, or among those who had not experienced the discipline of the factory floor. Factory work, which instilled habits of punctuality (by docking wages if necessary) and taught that the least particle of time should be made profitable, certainly helped to accustom these women to respect precise schedules and to carry out their work according to a virtually unchangeable plan. Several of the women who placed a great importance on their work routine and on a rational allocation of their time, moreover, maintained that their mothers (who had often grown up on the farm and who had never worked in a factory) were less strict in this regard: "My mother would put things off till tomorrow more easily than me. 'If I don't do it today, I'll do it tomorrow.' For me, it was today, never tomorrow" (E2). One of the women in the sample described extremely clearly this new mental attitude, with its overtones of Taylorism, which was to condition the way the majority of the women would complete their household tasks:

> I worked at home just like a regular job. My daughters used to laugh at me.... They'd say, "Mama, you work just like you had a foreman on your back." I did everything to the minute and kept the house spick and span. I had a day to wash my windows. In those days, you washed your windows every week.... I had a day to do the laundry. I did the ironing the same day I did the wash and then I had a day to wash the floors—I had a day for each thing. Saturday was when I cooked. I would make my pastry and I would cook my meats. I had a program like that all the time, every day just like that.... I taught myself how. I really liked to do my work on time. Even so, I was really fussy—I'd say "Oh, this time yesterday I did this and that, and today I haven't done it yet." I worked at home just like a regular job. But I liked that, you understand. (E29)

A heightened concern for cleanliness went along with this discipline. "We had to have everything just so—we kept our houses more spick and span than our parents had" (E2). For some of the women, cleanliness was almost an obsession: "I washed by hand like crazy because the washers we had then didn't get clothes clean enough—so I had to scrub my washing. . . . I did a spring cleaning in the fall as well as the spring—two spring cleanings a year. I never went a year without painting" (E23). Afraid of neglecting her house, one of the women interviewed got jaundice from which she was slow to recover after her first child was born:

> Now I understand that it was because of the incredible stress I was under. I didn't want to neglect my house or my baby. . . . I was running here, there, and everywhere, after the house, the baby, and then my husband, who was working nights—he slept during the day so I had to be careful not to make too much noise. All in all, I see that I must have been under as much stress as you can be. (E15)

Along with the scientific organization of labour, a concern for order and cleanliness were two preoccupations that appeared at the same time as industrialized society.[30] These were associated not merely with hygiene but also with the moral values they served to reinforce—a clean and orderly home at once reflected the presence of an accomplished housewife, preserved the family core from being dispersed, and inculcated in the family members fundamental Christian virtues basic to society.[31] A clean and well-kept home suggested that its occupants, especially the woman responsible for its maintenance, were of high moral character. "Is not to present a clean and orderly dwelling but a way of showing the will to maintain order everywhere and in everything, as the interior of the home reflects the person."[32] In this atmosphere, it is to be expected that the women interviewed were absolutely insistent on their concern for order and cleanliness.

The Cycle of Household Chores

With the passing of days and weeks, the women interviewed performed the same tasks sometimes more, sometimes less, frequently. The laundry, for example, far from being merely a weekly chore, could become a daily one when there were young children.[33] An insufficient supply of diapers, mattress pads, nightgowns, and flannel blankets would make a daily laundry necessary; for women who had several babies, this would mean a number of years of daily washes. "Every morning, you knew there was a boiler full of diapers waiting for you" (E2), one woman recalled. As one informant, who did nevertheless have a machine, pointed out, these "little" washes were done by hand, on a washboard placed in a tub or in the bathtub, and the women often "took advantage" of these sessions to wash out certain articles of clothing. "When I was washing the diapers, I also did some things that were easy to wash" (E6).

As mentioned earlier, most of the women interviewed did not have a washing machine until after the birth of their first, and sometimes second or third, child. Despite this fact, only seven of them used the services of a commercial laundry, most of them on an irregular basis and more frequently toward the end of the decade, and three of these had their own machines. In most cases, only the very large and difficult to launder items, like sheets and towels, were sent to the laundry every two weeks. The rates, by the pound, were not very high—it cost about twenty-five cents to wash the bed linen, towels, and dishcloths. At this price, however, the laundry was not returned dry, but as "wet wash," to the housewife, who had to hang it out before ironing it. Even this minimal cost represented a major obstacle since the family budget was very tight. That is why even those who used this service only did so occasionally, in order to lighten a particularly heavy week. When the husband was out of work, it was obviously impossible to make use of the service.

There were other reasons offered to explain why the women in the sample made so little use of the laundry services. One of them, for example, could never resign herself to sending her washing out of fear of being considered lazy: "Oh, no, I would have done the laundry in the bathtub rather than send it out. I would have been ashamed to send my sheets to the laundry. They would have said, '[She] is really lazy, that one—she doesn't wash her own sheets!' Oh no!" (E17). One informant who used this service several times found the system too complicated and not sufficiently hygienic: "I didn't like it that you had to make a list of everything that you sent and had to keep one copy and give them the other. And then on top of that, people began to say, 'Yes, well, they wash all kinds of stuff there, along with everybody else's wash.' So I stopped sending it out" (E15). Another woman, who never used the service but who had worked in a laundry both before and after her marriage, had similar reservations: "No, first of all, it cost too much.... Then they would lose things. Your wash would go in with everyone else's and that was something I didn't like the idea of very much" (E28). It seems that fear of infection did in fact influence the decision of some of the women, even if there was no proof that this kind of service gave rise to any health problems. The discourse on hygiene fed these rumours and supported the interests of the manufacturers who would rather sell a washing machine to each separate family. It must also be added, however, that ownership of a machine was also seen as an advantage by these women not only because they were loath to use a commercial laundry but because they could thus save money in the long run.[34]

Doing the washing was a lengthy and arduous chore that everyone remembered as a horror. "You started at eight o'clock in the morning and were lucky if you were finished before three. Along the way, you had to feed the kids, mop up, make the beds" (E10). For each load of wash, it was necessary to heat huge quantities of water, empty it into the washtubs or the washing machine, add the soap, bleach, and blueing depending on the load, empty the dirty water into the sink, wring out the clothes, and start all over again.[35] Each load had to be washed and rinsed twice, not to mention that certain items had to be soaked before being laundered. If signs of elevated standards of cleanliness might be detected in all this, it must also be noted that some clothing, especially work overalls, could be very dirty indeed. Other items demanded special treatment—diapers, for example, had to be boiled, as much to get them clean as to conform to a notion of hygiene, while cotton had to be rinsed in blueing to keep it white.

After it was washed, the laundry was hung outside if the weather was fair, or inside if it was raining or too cold. For part of the day, and often until the next morning, the flat was festooned with wash lines. Once it was dry, some items, especially shirts, had to be dipped in starch water and rolled up in towels to stay damp until ironed. Almost everything had to be ironed—sheets, tablecloths, diapers and practically every article of clothing. Shirts, always numerous, were especially hard to do without creasing them. Even if they were not fond of this job, several of the women interviewed said that they went so far as to starch their tablecloths and sheets and iron their tea towels and dishcloths.

Just like the laundry, cleaning the house was something that took place on a weekly and a daily schedule. "After breakfast," one informant explained, "I did the bedrooms. I made the beds and mopped the floor. In those days, we had linoleum everywhere. After that, I did my dusting. That was a regular thing, every day" (E20). This routine, reported by almost every one of the women, was extended at the week's end to include a more thorough cleaning of every room—windows, baseboards, bathroom, and floors all washed. If the floors were softwood, they would have to be scrubbed with a brush and "lessis" in order get them back to golden; linoleum floors, easier to keep up, nevertheless had to be waxed and, as one woman recalled, "In those days, floors had to be done with paste wax. We didn't have liquid wax" (E20).

It was also on Fridays that these housewives did their major shopping. From time to time, they would make an excursion to one of the city markets to buy fresh fruit and vegetables, but most often these purchases would be made at one of the numerous grocer-butcher shops that could be found in the area and that did not require a long journey. Unlike a supermarket, these little concerns offered personalized service in that each of the customers was waited on individually. The informants were quite insistent on this point so as to emphasize the attention they received: "In those days, we didn't wait on ourselves" (E10). Supermarkets, which began to appear in the 1930s, were at first viewed as an aberration because shoppers could take products directly from the shelves. "When they first started, we said, good heavens, they are going to be robbed! Everybody is going to get at everything"(E15). Rather quickly, however, the women observed that self-service had certain advantages, as they sometimes felt uncomfortable rejecting a piece of meat that had been expressly cut for them or an article they had asked the price of.[36] On the other hand, the small grocery stores offered free delivery, which the supermarkets did not necessarily do. Certain grocers even sent a clerk on a daily round of the best customers in order to take their orders. "We didn't have a phone," one of the respondents remarked. After it was taken, the order was then sent to the house. "And we didn't pay for all that," one observed. Indeed, this service was almost indispensable since iceboxes could not keep meat for a whole week and the women could not readily get out to shop with young children in the home.

Groceries were not the only business that delivered. According to one woman, "Eaton's would make a delivery for something like ten cents" (E6). Items like milk, bread, ice, wood, and coal were also delivered at no charge while pedlars hawked their fruits and vegetables, chips, and ice cream in the street. Most of the women regularly used the services of one or more of these merchants and were grateful for them despite certain drawbacks—ice that melted on the staircase, coal men who dirtied the halls, milk that froze before it could be taken in, and the like.

The women in the sample most often turned to local shops, generally concentrated on a nearby commercial street, for almost all their purchases, including yard goods, clothing, household articles, and furniture. They very rarely visited the downtown department stores except for sales or at Christmas. A few of the poorest women got their clothes and furniture from the outlets of the charitable organizations in their parish, like the Saint Vincent de Paul Society. Pedlars sold clothing door-to-door but their prices were usually higher because they sold on credit and only a few of the women interviewed bought from them: "It was the Jews who came to the door selling bed linen, sheets, pillowcases, coats, dresses, everything like that.... It was a lot more expensive, but we were stuck.... They would come to collect from us" (E27).

Thanks both to the variety of products that was delivered to the home and to the nearness of most retail stores, these women spent relatively little of their time shopping or bringing things home. In fact, this last activity was most often undertaken by pedlars or by a young deliveryman employed by the merchant; it would be accurate to say that it was not as yet part of everyday housework.[37]

When it was a question of making purchases involving large sums of money, like furniture and household appliances, husbands more frequently accompanied their wives to the store and some even went on their own. On the other hand, they were rarely involved in buying material or clothing, except for their own, though a majority of them did at least some of the shopping for food. In most cases, this occurred when they were sent to the store now and then by their wives for odds and ends, though almost a third did all of the shopping on a regular basis. This was true for two husbands who worked in a grocery store and who were thus on the spot to bring home supplies and for three others who would not permit their wives to handle the money. These men went so far as to decide on the menus, so as to be sure that their preferences would be respected:

> He was the one who did the shopping, because I had the kids to look after.... I was the one who went to buy clothes and so on, but for things to eat.... he was always the one who went. Sometimes, I'd say, "Buy this or that," but he was always the one who decided. It was OK by me as long as he was happy. That's what I was like.... He told me what to do. (E23)

As is the case in this reminiscence, most of the women used their maternal obligations to justify this division of tasks, which reminds us that child care was the woman's responsibility and that, as a result, their mobility was more circumscribed than that of their husbands.[38]

Most of these women spent several hours a week sewing or mending clothes for their families. More than two-thirds of them made most of their children's clothes, only a third made their own clothes, and none sewed for their husbands. Husbands thus accounted for the greatest part of clothing expenditures, but women, more than children, also wore store-bought clothes.

According to these oral histories, if the women did not make their husband's clothes, it was in part because the men were "too proud" to wear homemade garments, but also because men's clothing required too much work and, if they were to fit properly, greater skill than the women had. As we may recall, most of them had received only a sketchy training in sewing and some of them felt particularly lacking when faced with this task:

> I was not a real, one hundred percent seamstress. I only sewed for my children, for the littlest ones.... I made things for my little guys to start out with because I had two in a row.... I learned, but I had to put my head down on my machine lots of times because I was crying lots of times. I was so discouraged. I didn't know how to go about it and then I was not someone who would ask. (E23)

According to how much money there was, the children's clothes were made out of new material or remade out of their father's old clothes[39] or those of other relatives, which required a lot of work: "those old things . . . that I took apart, turned inside out, washed, ironed, remade. . . . I even made my daughters' coats. I did a lot of work then" (E19). Just like their fathers, the boys graduated to ready-to-wear more quickly than their sisters. "I made all my children's clothes, even the little boys' until they started to wear long pants . . . when they were twelve, but I made my girls' clothes all the time, all the time. . . . I even made the clothes they wore to get married in" (E24).

As for themselves, the women did not go out very much and thus had less need of many clothes. Around the house they wore cotton housedresses that cost so little that they were hardly worth sewing at home. "In the house, I always wore a 'duster' and an apron. But I didn't go out, you know" (E28). The low price of these garments made specifically for housewives (the women interviewed used the English term "duster" for them) allowed them to save precious time to work on clothes for their children who were getting bigger and going to school.

If not all the women sewed, the majority of them mended clothes that were torn or coming apart at the seams—"You put on patches, in those days" (E2), one of them observed—and made sheets, pillowcases, curtains, aprons and the like out of old clothes, cut-price remnants or even from white sugar sacks.

Like knitting, which several of the women did, sewing is a precise undertaking that demands a certain degree of peace and does not improve by being interrupted. This is why the women did their sewing most often at night, when the children were in bed, or in the afternoon, when they were in school or taking a nap. More than any other household task, sewing involved the establishment of broad exchange networks among families and reinforced the bonds among the female relatives; the richer ones gave their used clothes to the poorer ones and mothers and mothers-in-law lent their sewing machines and sometimes took over sewing for their grandchildren.

Within this weekly cycle of housework, there were of course the daily tasks, like preparing meals. Cooking took up a considerable amount of the housewife's day, since virtually all of the women made all the food, from soups to desserts. Two-thirds of them also did some canning, and made their own pickles, jams, spruce beer, dandelion wine, ice cream, and so on. They also had to cut up and mince the meat: "They didn't have all the cuts of meat like nowadays—you got a big piece of meat in those days because the families were so big. If you bought a big piece, ten or twelve pounds, it was cheaper" (E16).

Even if some of them reserved one day a week for cooking, still every day they had to prepare the meat, clean and slice the vegetables and cook or heat up the lot. Preparing meals also involved setting and clearing the table, doing the dishes and the pots, cleaning the stove and sink, and sweeping the kitchen. In fact, many of the women maintained that cooking took up the greater part of their time. "We spent two-thirds of our time preparing meals" (E5). "It's the everyday stuff [that takes up the most time]. When you have a lot of kids, of course you have to do more. Fixing the vegetables. . . . That's what takes the most time" (E17).

The expression "everyday stuff" used by a number of the women indicates the routine aspect of this chore and the simplicity of the meals that they prepared for their families. In general, these were casseroles, stews, hash, boiled dinners, all inexpensive but requiring a long time to cook, especially on a wood stove. In the middle of the afternoon, they had to start thinking about making dinner. The same sort of meat was often eaten for a whole week because the women tried to make the most of their purchases and never to throw anything away. Beef, pork, and veal in turn started as the Sunday roast and then reappeared on the table, prepared in various ways, until Thursday. On Friday, a fast day, there were pancakes, baked beans and fish. Those recipes they did not themselves invent came from their mothers, sisters-in-law, cousins, and neighbours.

Cutting Back on Necessities

All in all, the Depression did not seem to have added new jobs to the housewife's roster of tasks. As we have seen, the majority of them were already using all of their resources and skills to get the most out of what they had. Because they were not consuming anything except essentials, however, the Depression forced them to cut to the bone, which meant that they had constantly to search for alternatives and make important changes in the way they shopped, sewed, and cooked, all of which seriously complicated their household tasks.

Buying as little as possible at the best price was already a way of life for these housewives. As far as actual food purchases went, however, it was often difficult to cut back on quantity. Therefore, the housewives sought new ways to economize by buying lower quality and by stocking up in different ways. Therefore, some of the women began to buy their meat directly from the abattoir rather than from the local grocery, which permitted them to obtain greater quantities at the same price:

> In those days, you could buy twenty-five pounds of meat for ninety-nine cents, I think it was[40] —there were soup bones, all kinds of things—sausage, blood-pudding, not the expensive cuts, you know, but you could get an awful lot for ninety-nine cents.

It was also possible to get cut-rate meat by buying it late on Saturday evening, just before the stores closed;[41] a number of grocers who did not have refrigeration preferred to get rid of their stock rather than risk losing their merchandise by storing it until Monday morning. Finally, one of the informants also bought horsemeat, cheaper than the other kinds.

Some of the women would buy fruits and vegetables that had been reduced because they were wilted, even if it meant taking a little more time to prepare them: "It was a lot of work to make them all right to eat. Sometimes they were starting to go. But if you picked out what was edible" (E5)—

> We would go look for basket of bananas at A's, a grocery not far from us. The kids would look for a basket of overripe bananas for five cents. Sometimes, they weren't edible. Bread, butter, and bananas—that's what they ate. Me too. (E27)

Other women would go to the market to pick up fruits and vegetables that were thrown out at the end of the day by the farmers who had given up all hope of selling them. "My husband would go to Bonsecours market for vegetables. The farmers threw out quite a lot—what was still good, my husband brought home and we ate it. . . . You can't be fussy!" (E25).

As mentioned previously, two-thirds of the women interviewed were in the habit of making pickles and preserves. This activity, however, was not linked to the Depression. On the contrary, a lack of income and the way in which direct relief was dispersed made it difficult to buy the large quantities necessary for their production: "I never canned anything—in the first place, I never had the money to put things up, to buy the jars and everything else you need. I didn't have the money for that" (E12). "We didn't have the money to buy anything. How was I going to buy all the stuff you need to make ketchup, all that kind of thing! They gave us just so much sugar—it takes a lot of sugar to make jam—I didn't make any" (E19). All the same, a single informant tried several times to make bread while she was living on home relief, but it was a long and complicated process, not to mention that her inexperience made it more likely that there would be waste. It was cheaper to go directly to the bakery at the end of the day:

> We would go there at four o'clock in the afternoon when the bread runs came back. We could fill up a whole pillowcase with bread for twenty-five cents. You'd see everybody there—I would see them on the corner, they all had a pillowcase folded up under their arm or some of them had bags. (E20)

Preparing the same amount of food with fewer means and from inferior quality products required a good pinch of ingenuity to create appetizing meals. Sausage, minced meat, spaghetti and noodles appeared very often on the table, prepared in every imaginable way. Dishes in sauce, made with a base of flour and water, were also an economical solution, since they generally did not contain meat: "I made potatoes and white sauce, eggs and white sauce, beans and white sauce, and tinned salmon and white sauce. We ate a lot of paste!" (E25). Desserts were skipped altogether or consisted of "broken biscuits" sold cheaply in bulk or made from recipes that did not ask for expensive ingredients, like the famous "pouding chomeur" (literally, unemployed pudding, poor man's pudding): "If it wasn't going to cost too much, you had to make a cake that didn't take more than one egg" (E25). "I made all my own cakes and I didn't put in any eggs—just a little milk and some baking powder and my cakes were always light" (E29).

Despite all of these strategies, some of the informants simply had to deprive themselves of food so their children could have it:

> I would make a stew, as we called it. . . . I would make it out of spaghetti and whatever stuff was the cheapest and the most nourishing. But that doesn't mean we were well fed. . . . All it meant is that we had something to eat and even then sometimes we had to leave it all for the children. (E27)

On those days when there was hardly anything in the house to eat, the father might disappear around mealtime, saying he was going to look for work, so that his wife and the children could share whatever food there was. One couple often made do with macaroni and butter and sugar spread on bread, while another informant admitted that she had often eaten sugared bread dampened under the faucet. Another explained:

> We often ate mustard sandwiches . . . before the next cheque would come. When we got to the last stretch, we had a little jar of mustard and a few slices of bread and we would say, we're going to have to be happy with that—what do you want, there isn't anything else. . . . My mother-in-law would come and take my little girl. As long as I knew my little girl would have something to eat, it was all right, I knew we'd get by. (E19)

In regard to nourishment, the Depression made the housewives' task more difficult both in terms of getting provisions and devising meals. Even more serious, however, was that it also forced a significant number of them to deprive themselves of food.

During spells of unemployment, buying clothing was the first thing to go. "We didn't have much to wear" (E6), a number of the informants said in essence. Very often, the women, but also their husbands, wore their old clothes year after year in order to preserve their limited resources to clothe their children. Two of the women interviewed who had not previously done any sewing took it up to make clothes for their children specifically on account of the Depression:

> That's when I learned to sew because I used to buy ready-made clothes for my kids in the beginning but later on, I couldn't. . . . You had to make new clothes out of old ones. I would pick them apart to make new out of old. That's what I called it. . . . Everybody gave me clothes—I'd take them apart and make them up for the kids. That's how I learned to sew. I didn't have a machine—I'd go to my mother's to use hers. My husband took care of the kids at night and I went to my mother's to sew. . . . Anyway, my kids were very well dressed—people gave me good stuff, they didn't give me rags. (E12)

In most cases, however, the women who did not know how to sew were more likely to go to the stores run by the Salvation Army or the Saint Vincent de Paul Society.

Finally the costs of heating, electricity, and gas were reduced as far as possible by cutting back on the time they were in use (at night, for example) or by avoiding the use of electric appliances, as we have already seen. Some families turned to fuel picked up along the railway lines or on building sites, or made from cardboard boxes or old newspapers. It was the men who salvaged these materials:

> He'd go out in the morning to look for wood in Saint Lambert. . . . After that, he'd go to the store so he'd have some cardboard. He'd take the cardboard cartons apart, roll them up, and tie them with wire and stack them in the shed to make wood for next winter. Then . . . he'd soak newspapers in water in a basin . . . and make them into balls . . . and then let them dry. There, that was our coal for the winter. (E25)

According to this informant, this kind of fuel increased the risk of fire and required her to "mind the fire" all night long, taking turns with her husband.

Despite the fact that they had to move more frequently, do laundry more often, had greater difficulty in stocking the larder and even suffered deprivation, and constantly had to look for some way to find possible substitutes to satisfy their families' needs, the women interviewed were not unanimous in their view of the effects of the Depression on their household work. Some among them believed that the lack of money did not mean that they had to do much more work. Others agreed that they were forced to do somewhat more, but hastened, however, to add: "Work around the house never bothered me" (E6), and "Yes, but it's just like I told you. It was routine. It didn't make much difference to me. I knew how to manage so we had food on the table" (E29). These statements at once communicate the self-denial of these women faced with their families' needs as well as their pride in being able to confront every situation with no exceptional difficulty. Furthermore, they reveal that the women have a most elastic conception of their time and their capacity for work; even in normal times, the list of household tasks represented a significant number of hours of work in a day that began at dawn with breakfast and the care of the smaller children and continued until late in the evening in front of the sewing machine, whereas their husbands could take a little rest: "You got up in the morning and you never stopped. . . . After supper he [her husband] read his paper—us women, we had the dishes, the kids' homework" (E2).

Several of the women also had to find the time to do work for which they got paid, without, however, neglecting their household responsibilities. Their workday was therefore longer and more broken up, but they asserted that they managed to sort everything out without help and drew a certain satisfaction from having been successful in accommodating everything. One of them, who managed her husband's shop during the day, stated, "I managed.... You can always find some way to work things out.... I don't remember having had much trouble.... I had a lot of energy" (E7). Thus, even though she was continually being interrupted by customers and though she had to put off doing a number of her household tasks like washing and ironing until the evening, when her husband minded the store, this informant did not conclude that her workload was too heavy or too difficult to manage. In fact, although a number of these women were clearly overloaded and frequently working under difficult conditions, most of them agree that at the time it would never have occurred to them to complain:

> To tell you the truth, it was a really, really miserable time. In those days, you didn't think it was so hard, because it was what you had to do. But today, when you think about it all and then what it's like today, what a difference! Take hot water, for example—now all you have to do is turn on the faucet. But then, you had to heat up the water... for the dishes, you had to heat up the water for every meal.... It was really hot in the summer.... For a long time I used to do the laundry in the bathtub on a washboard. Sometimes it would slip—the tub was too wide. The washboard would get away.... And doing sheets... or even long johns.... Sometimes times I just wanted to throw them out! Long johns were a real job. Oh, we had a hard time of it!... Oh! I wouldn't go back to those days. It's not that you want to moan about it when you talk about it now, it's not just to complain... no, no. It's not in order to complain. That was how we lived. (E27)

Still, the women were reluctant to say which job they liked the least. "I liked to do what came along—I'm not the kind of woman who picks and chooses" (E17). "I don't know. It had to be done—I did it. I was happy to do it. I liked it" (E20). "When we were young, we were made to do whatever had to be done in the proper order" (E13). As these comments stress, the sense of duty and the confidence of having performed work that was essential to their families' welfare motivated these women to do their daily work. More than the weight of their chores or the harshness of the conditions in which they were carried out, their oral narratives transmit their pride in being able to assure this well-being despite economic hard times and the Depression.

W hen considered in connection with the overall family economy, housework would appear as the essential counterpart to the wage. Indeed, analyzing various household tasks reveals that those occupying the greatest amount of time were allocated to the production of goods and services directed toward satisfying the basic needs of family members. Production in the home could make up for inadequate family incomes by allowing what money there was to be devoted exclusively to the purchase of goods and services that would otherwise be impossible to obtain. The women themselves, moreover, were aware of the economic importance of their labour, which they thought of in the same way as that of their husbands: "He had his work and I had mine," they were happy to recall, thus putting both kinds of work on equal footing.

In general, the level of consumption on the part of these families was already at a minimum when the Depression occurred. In these conditions, the extra restraints that they had to impose on themselves in the matter of food and housing, among other things, seriously affected the welfare, if not the actual health, of family members and especially impinged on women in regard to their working conditions and their own subsistence. Obviously, the search for makeshifts to allow families to be fed, clothed, and housed despite a loss of income fell to the housewife. As we shall see in the next chapter, the immediate family also played an important role in this regard.

——————— *Chapter 7* ———————

State, Family, Neighbours, and Credit

"In those days, there wasn't any money—everybody was in the same boat." (E28)

The extraordinarily high rate of unemployment during the 1930s forced the government to provide financial support to thousands of households across Canada. The amounts dispensed either as direct relief or in return for public work did not, however, claim to be a substitute for traditional sources of support, like neighbours and relatives, that were already functioning well before the advent of the Depression. The conditions of eligibility for direct relief stipulated, moreover, that the needy first had to turn to their immediate families before asking for state aid. In reality, as we shall see, the support of the institutions of both state and family was required to provide households on assistance with their basic necessities. In this final chapter, we shall examine, in order, the contributions made by these two institutions to the household economy, as well as the role played by neighbours and by going into debt, the feelings that having to turn to these resources could give rise to, and the importance these various strategies could assume during this decade.

Government Assistance

At the beginning of the thirties, unemployment was still regarded as an individual problem caused by some moral failing, like laziness or drunkenness, or, at best, by misfortune. As a faithful proponent of laissez-faire capitalism in economic and social matters, the provincial government of

———————

Notes to Chapter 7 are on pp. 210-12.

Quebec was quite satisfied, from 1921 onwards, to finance private charities, religious communities, or other organizations that ran hospitals and
cared for the needy, orphans, the aged, and the infirm. The Saint Vincent
de Paul Society, which had been deeply rooted in francophone Catholic
Quebec since the nineteenth century, had as its particular vocation the
impoverished who were not in the care of institutions.[1] Operating from a
parish base, this organization was in a position to connect with the entire
francophone population; during the 1920s, for example, it extended aid to
between three and four thousand Montreal families each year.[2] When the
Depression set in, the unemployed turned spontaneously to the parish
branches of the society; like other charitable organizations, it was rapidly
overwhelmed by the demand.

By 1930, the extent of the crisis and of unemployment forced the federal government to react. The Conservative Party, headed by R. B. Bennett and recently elected on a promise to deal with unemployment,
adopted in special session its first Unemployment Relief Act, which ear-
marked sixteen million dollars for public works and four million to be distributed in relief payments. This amount represented only Ottawa's
contribution; in fact, for each dollar spent on public works, the federal
and the provincial governments had to provide twenty-five cents each,
while the municipalities made up the other 50 percent. As for the financ-
ing of direct relief, that was divided equally among the three levels of government. The local governments, traditionally responsible for the
indigent, were thus charged with organizing and dispensing relief
payments,[3] but, in the absence of the competent personnel and adequate
funding necessary to oversee their distribution in most municipalities, this
function was primarily left to private charities.

Until 1933 in Montreal, the Saint Vincent de Paul Society would continue to dispense relief to the Catholic population. The advisory commission on unemployment, created by the municipality, was satisfied to
channel funds through the various Catholic, Jewish, and Protestant organizations while a city council commission on unemployment served as a
placement office to hire men for public works projects.[4] Traditionally,
Saint Vincent de Paul had dispensed mostly goods in kind. With the intervention of the government, this system was replaced by vouchers good
for food and heat; the quantity as well as the variety of products was,
however, controlled. In distributing its aid, the society depended on its
traditional, and rather arbitrary, procedures: the recommendations of the
parish priest or other parish organizations and visits to the home. The

onus on the unemployed to give proof of their religious convictions,[5] the complaints of merchants about the slowness with which they were reimbursed for vouchers, accusations of favouritism on the part of certain shopkeepers who were deprived of the business of beneficiaries, as well as the refusal of the society to provide a list of recipients so that they could be independently verified finally required the city to take over the distribution of relief.

In order to do so, the city established an unemployment commission which laid down new procedures and imposed stricter conditions for admissibility: to be eligible, the claimant had to be fit to work, a resident of Montreal for at least one year (which was soon to become three years), and continue to renew his oath that he was impoverished and unable to obtain help from his family.[6] Following a home investigation and an inquiry to his last employer, the claimant would be given a grant according to the size of his family.[7] If all went well, fewer than three days would elapse between his application and receipt of the first assistance. Thereafter, he was required to go to the distribution office in his district to receive his grant. The beneficiaries were expected to report any paid work they might have had during the previous week. If they had earned less than three dollars, nothing would be deducted from their allowance. Their wives and children were required to declare 50 percent of their earnings.[8] In view of the numerous complaints of small landlords who were facing bankruptcy, the commission also decided to subsidize rents, for which the landlord had to make a claim.

Beginning 1 December 1933, aid was dispensed by cheque. Montreal was one of the few Canadian cities to adopt this system, which ran counter to usual practice. According to the common prejudices of the day, in fact, the unemployed were considered irresponsible, as they were unable to provide adequately for their own needs and those of their families. They were not to be given money directly out of fear that they would waste it on drink or frivolous purchases. But, faced with an ever-increasing number of persons in need, cheques soon came to be seen as the simplest and cheapest solution from an administrative point of view; cheques avoided the need to print vouchers and eliminated the bureaucracy required to redeem them.[9]

The city of Verdun, where a number of the women interviewed lived, established an unemployment commission in 1931. While this body undertook the distribution of aid to English-speaking Protestants, French- and English-speaking Catholics had to apply to Saint Vincent de

Paul, although it was the object of the same criticisms as the society in Montreal. Starting in 1933, Verdun took charge of all relief. Spurred on by the newly elected mayor, Hervé Ferland, the commission initially replaced the vouchers that had been good for a predetermined list of foodstuffs with a system of "open coupons," that permitted families on relief to choose from a broader variety of foods, and finally issued coupons that bore only a cash value, thus allowing mothers of families freely to choose what food they bought.[10] Faced with mounting cases of fraud, Verdun turned to distributing cheques, adopting this system a few months before Montreal. The city, whose scale of aid payments was one of the highest in Quebec,[11] also paid up to 50 percent of the rent for those on relief. Verdun instituted other relatively generous measures, such as distributing oil lamps to those whose electricity had been cut off, providing furniture and clothing, paying electricity bills, and issuing special grants to those who were forced to move, and the like, all of which drew the unemployed to that city from elsewhere; in 1934 alone, a thousand families left Montreal to move to Verdun.[12]

At the beginning of the Depression, the funds allocated by the federal government primarily encouraged hiring the unemployed for municipal and provincial public works. The Unemployment Relief Act of 1930 allocated 80 percent of its funding to public works and only 20 percent to direct relief. The extent of unemployment, however, obliged the federal government to review its position. Between 1932 and 1936, the funds approved for public works projects diminished, only to increase again in 1939. Altogether, direct relief absorbed 60 percent of aid expenditures on the part of the three levels of government.[13]

The fifteen families in our sample who received public assistance received help in the form of vouchers, cheques, or in return for work benefits, according to when it was that they needed support. In every case, the steps required to obtain aid were undertaken by the man, who, as the head of the family and breadwinner, was the only one qualified to request it.[14] The women interviewed were not, however, offended by being excluded in this way. On the contrary, to appear before a Saint Vincent de Paul Society volunteer or a municipal clerk to claim benefits in fact represented a kind of degradation for most of those who had to bring themselves to do it. This is why the women were not particularly anxious to assume this responsibility. As one of the informants explained, "It wasn't me who would have gone—I would have starved to death before going to ask for direct relief. . . . He knew perfectly well that he was the head of the family—it was up to him to go see them. It wasn't up to me" (E19). In this very special circumstance, breadwinner status was nothing to envy.

Remitting aid to the head of the family only confirmed the economic dependence of wives. For those whose husbands drank, entrusting them with this money, which was all the more precious because there was so little of it, could have dramatic consequences, as was the case for one of the women interviewed:

> The dole was given in the husband's name, not the wife's. So that meant that he went to collect it and if he spent it, then you had nothing. It happened a lot—he went to get relief money and when he came home, he didn't have a penny left.... They gave it to the man, they didn't give it to the woman. Maybe they didn't have enough information ... maybe if I had gone, then I would have been the one to get it. (E22)

In fact, article 23 of the Montreal Unemployment Commission regulations stipulated that "If the husband drinks or gambles away his aid cheque, then the registrar should immediately be informed. He will see to it a new registration is made in the spouse's name or that of another responsible person or Society that can replace the head of the family."[15] The complete list of commission regulations does not appear to have been widely circulated, however, with the exception, of course, of those articles dealing with conditions of admissibility and cases of fraud.[16] Only one of the women in the sample whose husband refused to provide for her was able to get aid benefits paid to her directly. She had been directed toward the relief offices by the Grey Nuns, to whom she had regularly gone for food. Her circumstance represents a good example of the transference of "charity cases" to governmental responsibility that was taking place at the beginning of the Depression. In the second half of the decade, the state would move to eliminate cases of this sort from its benefit rolls. Thus, after 1937, couples living in common-law marriages and those incapable of work had once more to approach the charitable organizations while "needy mothers" and the aged were provided with a pension, however minimal.[17]

The majority of the men had trouble accepting the loss of their status as breadwinner and their new condition as part of the "deserving poor."[18] One of the few husbands who was present for part of the interview with his wife and who had experienced this situation recalled:

> When I got to be one of the "deserving poor," I went to get my ticket from Saint Vincent de Paul in the church basement, I went with my head hanging and my eyes were as red as if I had been bawling before I left the house....

> When we went on relief . . . when they came to the house, I lay down on the
> sofa and I cried like a baby. I would say to myself, I have two strong arms,
> two strong legs—(E20)

This reminiscence sums up very well the feelings that filled these men
when they had to go and apply for the dole and then appear week after
week before the same volunteers or civil servants to receive their vouchers
or their cheque. The comments of most of the women communicated
much the same feeling:

> He had to haul himself down there and line up, that was humiliating. The
> first few times he really hated it. . . . He found it humiliating to go get his
> tickets to have something to eat, but if he didn't go, we wouldn't have had
> any food. I wasn't the one who had to go, eh? It was him. As for me, I
> wouldn't have liked to go at all, either. (E23)

More than any regulation, it was this feeling of failure and humiliation
that acted as a powerful check on any attempt to abuse the system. Even
after fifty years, a number of the women recalled this period in their lives
only reluctantly. Their memories became rather vague and only after a
certain degree of prodding were they more specific:

> I don't remember any more how long he was [out of work]. Sometimes you
> forget that kind of thing. Like that—there are things you don't want to
> remember more often than [you have to], which means you forget them
> quicker than when you go back to a good memory. . . . It lasted . . . it must
> have been . . . a year. (E23)

The shame which some couples experienced because of their destitution was nevertheless mitigated by the extent of unemployment and by
the need to ensure their children's welfare: "If you had children, you said,
we're doing it for the children. Well, we got something out of it too, of
course. If we'd known other people who had jobs, that would have made
it worse. But everyone was the same. It wasn't as humiliating in those
days" (E5). "I wasn't up in arms, not at all. That's what the times were
like, that's what life was like. What could you do? You had to take it. No,
the main thing was whether you could eat and pay your rent. . . . No, it
didn't make me upset" (E29).

Contrary to the fears of the government and those in power, the
majority of the couples resigned themselves to asking for help only as a
last resort, when their personal savings were exhausted or when any possibility of a job had evaporated. "When the Depression started, we had a
little money put by—we ate up all our money" (E20). Some of the couples passed through periods of unemployment without going on the dole:

one of them chose to invest their savings in a plot of land; one of the women was helped by her grandfather while a third approached her old boss, who employed her husband as a chauffeur for several years. Finally, a former farmer, who had come to Montreal to join his wife after several months of separation, took advantage of the government's "back to the land" scheme rather than live off public assistance:

> My husband couldn't find any work—when he didn't have anything left, he had to go get a paper for food because they didn't give money then—they didn't have welfare in those days. When he saw all that, he wrote to the Quebec government . . . and he got the land. . . . That's how we went back to the land. (E9)

In order to ascertain that applicants were genuinely poor, volunteers from Saint Vincent de Paul, and later civil servants specially hired by the municipality, made home visits to investigate the beneficiaries' declarations, even though they had been made under oath. This inspection was made in order to ensure that the family did not own any goods or furniture of value, like a piano, that they could have sold, and that the home was well kept, a way of measuring if its occupants had high moral standards and if they could manage the aid that they would be provided with. "They looked in all the rooms, to see if they were clean" (E5). Even if wives were not able to claim assistance in their own names, the inspectors thus implicitly recognized the importance of the role played by housewives in the proper management of family affairs.

This visual inspection was in addition to the questions applicants had to answer to demonstrate that they were altogether without resources and unable to obtain any help from their families. As one informant stressed, "We felt as if we were asking for charity and it was very hard" (E6). With but two exceptions, all of those who were visited by an inspector were visited only once, and several were never visited at all. Despite the claims of the public authorities, the ever-increasing numbers of the unemployed made an investigation into every case extremely difficult. One of the informants who had never been inspected stated that the civil servants did not find these visits necessary: "They knew everyone was the same," but she went on to say, "Only, the men, they had to watch out not to work. If they did some work . . . if they made some money, they took it off their cheque. If they did odd jobs, they had to work on the sly" (E12).

Despite the implications of these last remarks, "fraud" was not very common and the amounts involved were very small indeed.[19] In general, when a man found a job, even a temporary one, he was just happy to see his name stricken from the relief list. Out of the fifteen families in this sample who received public assistance, only one man worked as a watchman two nights a week while he was receiving benefits, which earned him a visit from an inspector who was not, however, able to establish his guilt. Most of the men preferred to augment their income by doing odd jobs, as mentioned before, and which hardly provided them with the three dollars permitted by the commission regulations. Just one of them lost a week's benefits because, according to his wife, he gave a haircut at home that made him only twenty-five cents.

Even if the women interviewed were by and large not subjected to harassment by the inspectors, documents and newspapers of the period give evidence of a kind of pathological fear of "profiteers" and a frequently expressed desire to carry out strict checks. The state was much less concerned with the welfare of the families it was aiding, for whom a meagre cheque seemed quite sufficient. As one informant pointed out, it was only during the Second World War that the government undertook an extensive campaign in the newspapers and on the radio to advise housewives on how to make the best of the fewer available resources, like cloth, food, and soap. All of these tips would, however, have been extremely useful during the Depression.

A few of the families in the sample received aid in the form of goods while most came under the system of vouchers or cheques. Of the three modes of assistance, distribution of goods in kind was the least liked, not only because of the poor quality of the products distributed, especially meat, and the limited quantity, but also because this method reeked of charity and exposed their situation to the whole neighbourhood. The voucher system, adopted thereafter, was not without its drawbacks. For one thing, the family was labelled indigent among the dealers who supplied them (the grocer, the wood or coal dealer, the milkman, and the baker), and, for another, it limited the variety and quantity of most of the products that could be bought.[20] "Even so, when you'd put your order in and ask for a pound of tea and a pound of coffee, they'd send you a quarter of a pound. So much a person, that was it. We put the rest on the account" (E20). As this recollection indicates, some families got the quantities or the products they wanted by going into debt at the grocer's for the value of the supplies not covered by their vouchers. But many of the couples were loath to go into debt, especially when out of work, as we shall see later on in the chapter. None of the informants, however, ran into any difficulty in exchanging their vouchers, regardless of the many problems merchants encountered being reimbursed for them. The cheque system, while being less conspicuous, also allowed mothers of families on relief to buy the kinds of food they were used to eating. Whatever system was in use, the amounts dispersed remained minimal and the women, as we have already seen, had to move mountains to manage to feed their families. When they received a cheque covering all expenses, they could, however, decide to allot a greater proportion of it to food, even if it meant going short on clothing and fuel.

In return for obtaining relief, a third of the husbands took part in public works. These were men who lost their jobs at the beginning of the Depression or at the end of the decade, when unemployment was being reduced and governments were tightening up access to relief. Their husbands' participation in these projects seems to have aroused mixed feelings in the informants. On the one hand, as one of them remarked, the fact of having worked in exchange for money received constituted a kind of pretext that allowed him to save face. "He was never, ever happy about it, but what could you do? He did it a lot. It was always a little less of a disgrace than the dole. At least he was working for what he got" (E29). But some of the respondents also felt that these public works projects represented a kind of exploitation: "He had to go work for nothing, for that six bucks. A truck came to pick them up and he went to work all day, I don't know where, for nothing, for the six bucks a week they gave us" (E22). Even for those who were participating, hiring was irregular. "He had [work] from time to time. He was working on the canal from the aqueduct, digging the canal. I saw my husband go out for a dollar a day if the city had something to do—on the roads, Hydro,[21] the canal. . . . And then they would cut his relief cheque" (E5). As this recollection suggests, participating in public works projects did not substantially increase benefits. In the early days of the Depression, men working at municipal sites were earning forty cents an hour and were supposed to be hired on for thirty-two hours a week, which means that, theoretically, they were making a weekly wage of $12.80.[22] In practice, however, an ever-increasing number of unemployed men had to share a shrinking number of jobs, so that very few of them were able to work full-time or for long stretches.[23] Distributing these jobs also seems to have been subject to considerable patronage and at least two women reported that their husbands had obtained work at the municipal yards thanks to friendly relations with an alderman.[24] The majority of the men preferred to rely on their own initiative to find a job:

> He grabbed onto little jobs here and there but never anything regular before signing on with the city. He worked at R—. . . . That was iron, steel. As soon as there was a little slump then the last hired were the first fired. You understand, there wasn't a lot of work around at the time. It was the Great Depression. (E19)

Some of these families survived in this way for several years—on a combination of direct relief, public works, and temporary or part-time jobs: "We lived on hope" (E20), one informant stated.

The families that did not experience a lengthy spell of unemployment were able to benefit from the drop in the cost of living that characterized the 1930s; despite cuts in wages and hours, their lot did not substantially deteriorate. For many of these couples, however, these years also corresponded with a critical stage in their family life cycle, marked by the arrival of children and thus of new dependents, which to some degree nullified the favourable effects of deflation. It was for this reason that one of the women interviewed admitted to having experienced periods during the thirties when she was deeply discouraged and even asserted that prices had gone up:

> Children came along, and wages went down but the cost of living went up. In the end (around 1936), my husband was earning forty-five dollars every two weeks. I had four children and my husband always had to have his car. His car—that was really important. . . . I had a lot of things to be worried about. What with the cuts in wages, it became very discouraging. (E2)

The economic situation of those who were living on relief during these years, as was the case for seven of the households in the sample, can be termed desperate. In every case, but especially for those on the dole for many years, the family played an essential role in helping them get through this difficult period.

Unemployment and Husband-Wife Relations

Before going on to the other forms of help that couples received in this period, we should briefly consider the repercussions that unemployment had on the relationship between marriage partners. In general, we may observe that the oral narratives tend to confirm the conclusions of studies undertaken in the United States during the 1930s, revealing that previous relationships between husbands and wives represented the determining factor in explaining how they got along during the Depression.[25]

Indeed, for those couples whose roles were clearly defined and accepted and where the relationship was founded on mutual respect (which does not exclude relationships of domination), the Depression did not have any particularly destructive effects. Comments collected on this subject bear witness to this fact: "We both cheered each other up. In the first place, I'm not the sort of person to criticize or put the blame on someone else. Never, ever, ever did I criticize him, whatever happened. It wasn't his fault—it was the same for everybody" (E20). "It was like I told you. I loved my husband so much. And he was so good. Provided I had my husband at my side, I never lost heart. We made it through as if it were nothing" (E29). Several even asserted that these dismal years, looming over the early days of their marriage, forged stronger bonds between themselves and their husbands. "We talked to each other more. We didn't have much choice. . . . He was out of work, he was always around the house, and that meant we got closer to one another like that. In the evening, after the kids were in bed, we would play cards. . . . We would talk and cheer each other up" (E25). According to another of the women, the fact of their being barely adult and, in her case, being the product of a poor background, also helped them get through this difficult period of their lives: "We were both young and I came from a poor family—we were always contented with very little" (E6).

The impossibility of their husbands' carrying out their role as breadwinner did not cause these women to start resenting or despising them. But those who were in this situation over several years did sometimes question the amount of effort their husbands put into finding work:

> Six and a half years, that was a pretty long time. Sometimes, I would get discouraged. I'd tell him, "Get out and look for a job . . . look in *La Presse*. . . ." He didn't feel like it. At last, I would nag him, "You have to get a job." In those days, he would go out, he would look around. . . . Everyone was saying that there wasn't any work . . . but I thought that if no one took a chance, if they didn't go to the factories, if they didn't show up, then. . . . (E25)

> There were times when I would get mad and say, "It seems to me that you aren't looking hard enough. You should be able to find something. . . ." But there weren't any jobs. It wasn't that he wasn't looking, it wasn't that he was lazy. It was because he wasn't finding anything. (E19)

The economic dependence of women presumed by the breadwinner/ housewife model explains these women's anxieties when faced with their husband's prolonged unemployment. As we have already seen, the majority of them did not dream of looking for work during the Depression; in any event, their husbands would have been against it. They had only their husbands to turn to redress a situation that was daily becoming more and more insupportable, thus this insistence that the men find themselves a new job.

If the wives played an important role in preserving their husbands' self-respect, by avoiding criticizing them, for example, then the men very often comforted their wives when discouragement overwhelmed them. "Sometimes, I would cry. . . . He would say, 'Keep your chin up, we may be having hard times now, but we'll be better off by and by, you'll see'" (E25). Indeed, several of the women confessed that their husbands had been in better spirits than they were, or at least appeared to be: "He wasn't a man who got depressed very easily—he kept his morale up" (E19). It is certainly possible that some of these men had kept their feelings of insecurity or desperation to themselves in order to preserve their image as a protector able to cope with any situation. The man whose words were quoted earlier did, furthermore, acknowledge that he frequently cried in secret. It should also be noted that the men could take advantage of a range of organizations, like the clubs for unemployed men that existed in\some of the city districts, to find emotional support. According to one of the informants, this was why her husband remained in good spirits: "He had a lot of friends. And he also had a club on Notre Dame Street between Bourget and [Ste. Rose] de Lima. . . . They used to play cards in the afternoon" (E5). These networks of masculine solidarity probably allowed these men to distract themselves from the problems they were experiencing, something which their wives, constantly faced with the realities of the Depression and the need to cope with it, were not able to do.

In contrast, the women whose husbands were irresponsible or drunken, or whose marital relationship was based on fear, saw their resentment or indifference increase during this period. One of these women, who had taken her husband to court three times for abuse and non-support, admitted with difficulty that the Depression could be used as an excuse for not finding work:

> He had some good jobs . . . but after two months it was all over. [I asked him]: "Why aren't you working anymore?" [He said]: "There's no more work." He was telling me a pack of lies. There was work all right—he'd quit his job. So, there we were, back on relief. Some of our hard times were his fault. (E27)

The recollections of another woman, whose husband drank, suggests that she was completely resigned to this situation and no longer tried even to communicate with him. Thus, she did not know exactly why he had lost his job, or what he did with his days when he was not working any-more, or which of the public works projects he was on: "He'd come home and he'd say, 'No more work for me.' I'd never ask him why. . . . Some-times he went to his brother's place. . . . There's no way I could tell you how he spent his time. . . . I don't know where he was working—I never asked him where he went" (E22). With her entire concern the survival of her children, she concentrated all of her energies on making sure that they had at least the minimum of what they needed.

> I managed even though I didn't have very much. I knew what to expect—I knew my husband! That meant you had to be prepared. . . . I had children and they were my kids. Let me tell you, they didn't deserve to have so little. They weren't the ones who asked to be born. I gave my whole life to them. (E22)

Finally, those women whose husbands kept their jobs do not appear to have been excessively worried that they might lose them: "He had such a good job, I didn't worry very much" (E8). "The whole place would have had to shut down—he had the union and the union was very strong" (E15). This optimism about the security of their husbands' jobs had its source in the rationalizatons that the men proposed in order to reassure their wives. This confident attitude can also be explained by the very human tendency to believe oneself proof against disaster. In this way, another woman, whose husband in fact did lose both his job and his busi-ness, stated, "I was never afraid [of having to go on relief]—that hap-pened to other people. No, I was never afraid, I never thought about being afraid" (E7).

The Family

Recent work in the history of the family has stressed the enormous capac-ity of the family to adapt to the conditions imposed by industrialization and has particularly observed that certain elements of its internal dynamic inherited from the rural past, rather than disappearing, have been rein-forced. For this reason, the working-class family at the turn of the century is seen as a work unit in which each of its members old enough to do so make a contribution to the collective budget. From this perspective, child labour does not appear so much an aberration of industrialized society as a transference into an urban context of a long-tested survival strategy.

Among these strategies, family networks appear as "the cornerstone of help and social assistance in times of crisis before the state took over these functions."[26] The support that could be contributed by the family and especially by the immediate family (parents, brothers and sisters) did not occur merely during depressions—it was more a matter of habit, made necessary by inadequate incomes, and one that could only become more significant when looking at an economic period as particularly difficult as the 1930s.[27]

For this sort of mutual support to be readily available, it was at least convenient, though not essential, if the family lived nearby. This is why urban families had the tendency to settle in the same neighbourhoods. In Andrée Fortin's words, "the neighbourhood is enclosed in the meshes of the family network."[28] These connections were strengthened by the exodus from the countryside and as new families were established and maintained in the face of frequent changes of address. When you first came to the city, you looked for housing in the same neighbourhood, on the same street, as your relatives. These would, moreover, often provide shelter for a period of time, easing the transition from country to city and fostering the establishment of the rural family in the neighbourhood.[29] When you got married or moved, you chose generally to remain in the same parish or neighbourhood. At the worst, you could go and live in a nearby district, even if it meant dying of boredom, as one informant recounted: "I was bored stiff in Pointe Saint Charles. I was used to Saint Henri—I knew everybody. . . . That's why I didn't want to stay there. I didn't know anyone. [Well], there was my brother—his wife came from the Pointe" (E29). As this comment reveals, the family collected in the same area according to the female connections; but if the bride's parents were still living in the country or were no longer alive, then the couple usually went to live near the husband's parents. In any event, the pair frequently came from the same neighbourhood, which allowed them to live close to both their families and to maintain close ties to each of them:

> I lived next door to my mother—there was a passage into the courtyard and I lived in a little place right next to it there. . . . When I was stuck and if I needed to know something, I could go to my mother's and she would explain it to me, or else my mother-in-law, she lived across the street. (E12)

This visiting back and forth, sometimes daily in the early days of the marriage, mostly involved the mother and her daughters. "Well, my mother didn't live very far away. . . . I would go over there a lot but I came back home in the evenings" (E29). These visits, which provided both advice and company, also allowed the young bride to brush up her household skills as she often discovered certain shortcomings in that area.

Few of the couples tried to distance themselves from their immediate families when they were first married by going to live in a neighbourhood distant from their original one. Those who did so rather rapidly came to regret their decision, as was the case for one informant, originally from Verdun, who moved to Villeray after her wedding:

> We were young and we didn't want to live near the family—when you're young, you're cocky. After I had my first baby, it wasn't so funny—then after the second one, it got serious! Take the streetcar to Christophe Colomb, then change at Place d'Armes, then take the number 25 . . . it went on and on! . . . And then I didn't have a washing machine at the time. Mama did my wash. My husband worked on Saturdays. That meant my sisters used to come on Saturday . . . to get me and the children and they would carry the suitcase full of dirty laundry. But when I went back home again, I went with my husband—and we had a child each plus the suitcase full of clean clothes, plus of course the bag full of diapers. That was why we decided to come back to Côte Saint Paul. It was better. (E6)

Another woman, who was living with her mother-in-law when she was first married, decided to move a distance away because of conflicts with her that were likely to explode. The Depression and her husband's unemployment were a harsh reminder to her that this distance could also involve a number of inconveniences:

> I remember one Sunday, he wanted to go see his mother and we didn't even have the twenty-five cents for the street car. So we walked—from Rachel all the way to St. Henri. Let me tell you, that was quite a walk with the baby in the carriage. It was quite a hike. And remember, the streetcars weren't expensive—four tickets for a quarter at the time—but you had to be careful with your money. (E19)

Even if their choice did not work out as well as it might have, given the circumstances, it does illustrate a desire for autonomy on the part of certain couples. Their attitude is, however, far from representative of that of the majority.

Several couples were the first of their family to migrate to Montreal and thus they found themselves rather more isolated, although they did have cousins or aunts to whom they could turn. Moreover, distance did not prevent them from keeping up the relationship with their families and it was not unusual for the couple in the early years of their marriage to take the train every weekend to go visit their family. As the family grew and it became more difficult and more costly to make the trip, these visits became less frequent, but the wives and their children continued to spend part of the summer with their mothers or sisters in the country. The men, who did not as yet get paid vacations, stayed by themselves in the city and went to join their wives on Friday nights.

The family still living in the country was not always in a position to help those who were living in the city, even when it came to gifts of farm produce. In the first place, getting it to the city posed certain problems: it might be impossible to send perishable or fragile items to the family in the city, not to mention that the cost of doing so could obviate any savings such gifts might represent. Some vegetables, like potatoes and onions, hold up relatively well for long periods of time, but the tight quarters in which working-class families lived often prevented them from finding sufficient and adequate space to store them. One informant, who on the advice of her doctor went back to live for a few years in the village where she was born, could get help there from her father and uncles, who provided her with milk, vegetables, meat, and maple products. But when she went back to the city, the aid came to an end: "They couldn't send the stuff to the city. As long as we lived close by, they sent it to us" (E17), she explained. Another, who had spent several years on relief, observed:

> Oh, they helped me a lot because they brought me lots of vegetables from the country. I had a sister . . . who was married to a farmer and that meant she could bring me lots of vegetables. She would do that in the summer, but in the winter! . . . Winter was the worst because we had to pay for the heat, too. (E19)

These contributions of food were generally limited to the good weather. Putting up the city family for several weeks in the summertime, as well as gifts of clothing, were also among the ways that the rural family most frequently helped out.

The proximity of urban families made it easier to exchange favours, which could also be more varied: babysitting during childbirth or in case of illness and swapping or giving clothing were probably the most common, but we note very frequent references to the sharing of certain household tools, like sewing or washing machines, or the use of the telephone. Although the women did most of their housework by themselves, sharing certain appliances meant that chores were sometimes exchanged or done communally. A mother-in-law might do her daughter-in-law's wash while the younger woman might do the ironing for both families; some mothers did their daughters' laundry if they did not have a machine; a number of women went to sew at their mother's or mother-in-law's house while one used her godmother's machine. Although exceptional, the experience of one of the informants, whose husband's family owned a bakery, is worth noting:

> On Sunday evenings, we would go and have supper at his mother's. I would take my laundry and go wash it on Mondays along with his mother. Every Monday, I would go and help her.... We did the laundry. As soon as it was dry, we both took it down and ironed it.... Then on Tuesday... I'd go help her do her housework.... I would spend the whole day helping her. She had twelve kids, and none of them married young, that's what made so much work for her.... On Wednesdays, we went to the bakery and washed the showcases and all the glass in them and the shop windows and put back the shelves—all of that.... Then we'd go back home for lunch. After that, in the afternoon, sometimes she had mending to do. I did all kinds of things—sometimes I went out and ran errands. I did all that. I had my own little baby and still I went to help her out. (E21)

This informant was compensated for the help she provided her mother-in-law, both with the housework and in keeping up the bakery, by gifts of food: "We got all our sugar from them, and our flour, eggs, butter, shortening. Not to speak of the desserts—my father-in-law was always sending me cakes." (E21)

Generally speaking, food was given less frequently than clothing, and was not considered the same sort of thing. Swapping or receiving clothing, especially children's clothes, made a certain economic sense, even if it often involved at the same time a degree of charity; in fact, children grow faster than they can wear out their clothes and to throw them out while they were still wearable seemed like wastefulness. This is why two of the informants who experienced no particular economic difficulty (one of them, in fact, was quite well off) nevertheless were given clothing for their children. More often, however, it was the better off members of the family, or the mothers with fewer children, who gave to the poorer ones or those with more children, though of course the two circumstances often went hand in hand. Donations of food only came about in the case of extreme poverty and those who received them felt dependent on their families: "It was my mother who had me under her wing. Mama would send over food to eat—we didn't have anything to eat—he was out of work" (E27). Another remarked, "I didn't like it very much. If I had been on my own, that's OK, but there was my husband and my little boy" (E9).

Within the family circle, direct relief vouchers were also exchanged:

> [Both my parents and his parents] really liked tea and coffee with sugar—they used a lot more than I did. So I would give them my coupons.... Like butter ... I would buy my butter and pass it on to my mother, and she would buy me fruit for the children.... My mother-in-law, she would come over for vouchers for coffee and then she would buy some meat for me. (E25)

Loans and gifts of money among family members did not occur very often and primarily were intended to deal with exceptional circumstances. In every case, it was the informant's father who was asked for or who offered his aid. Two of the women borrowed money to settle urgent debts or to get through a tight spot caused by the husband's illness, while two others received sums of money "as a present," in one case to avoid the bailiffs. Finally, one woman lived for several years on the weekly allowance from her grandfather, who had raised her.

Like donations of food, loans or gifts of money were more difficult to accept because they were a last recourse that exposed not merely extreme poverty but also the husband's failure to provide for his family's needs. The couple felt it humiliating to be on the receiving end of this kind of favour that went beyond the range of ordinary exchanges. The ideal of financial autonomy, a measure of respectability, could even impel them to hide their financial problems from other members of the family. Thus, a woman stated that her father could have helped them avoid the loss of their house, had he known about the foreclosure: "[My father told me]: 'If he'd called me, I would have given him the money and you wouldn't have lost your house.' But my husband was too embarrassed to ask for the money" (E17). Another couple hid the fact that they were on relief from their friends and relations, which led to a rather embarrassing situation: when the informant's mother was visiting, the milkman employed by Saint Vincent de Paul to deliver milk to those on its rolls arrived, shouting, "It's Saint Vincent de Paul, madame!" Rather than tell her mother the truth, she told her that he had come to the wrong address: "I was too proud, you know" (E20), she concluded.

Some of the couples could not get material help from their parents. "My parents had no more money than we did, far from it. When my father died and then my mother, they didn't even have a penny of insurance. My husband and my brothers and sisters paid for the funerals" (E29). "You couldn't feel sorry for yourself. You didn't complain in those days. Me complain? Who was I going to go crying to? I had no mother and no father. My parents were gone. I had nobody left" (E22). In fact, in one case, the young couple saved the husband's father from bankruptcy by buying back, for "one dollar and other considerations," the last house that this man, a contractor, had succeeded in retaining. For the next two years, they took over the mortgage as well as working on the electricity and plumbing, after which they sold it back to the original owner on the same terms.

Shelter, either temporary or long-term, represented another form of quite considerable assistance. As we saw in chapter 3, eighteen of the couples in the sample lived with one or the other of their families, generally that of the groom, for periods ranging from a few months to two years. The husband's losing his job or falling ill, as well as a temporary marital separation, forced four of the women to go back to live with their parents for a number of months. In return, though more often after the end of the Depression, almost half of the women took into their homes members of their family or their husband's family (parents and parents-in-law, brothers, sisters, brothers- and sisters-in-law, sometimes with their children, nephews, and nieces), either free of charge or in return for board which was often token.

In addition to the help extended in all these areas, there were other kinds of assistance, which could take various forms: a handyman brother-in-law who could help install a new electric motor on an old manual washing machine, another who found a temporary job for his sister's husband, a third who provided free firewood, an aunt who paid her nephews' high school fees, a father-in-law who was happy to take advantage of his job at a biscuit factory to bring some home to his grandchildren, a father who let his daughter live rent-free in one of his flats. These kinds of assistance seem to have increased tenfold because of the Depression, which also encouraged an increase in barter. Thus, one of the informants who was especially broke was able to swap a lace tablecloth for the sewing machine she desperately needed. In another case, tenants traded a dining-room set and a sewing machine for the rent they could not pay. Another woman worked in exchange for rent for the landlord of her parents who were living on relief and in whose house she had gone back to live.

Quite as much as the state, the family made a large contribution to the support of couples in trouble by finding them clothing, food, or even a roof over their heads. In this connection, the stories and commentaries are very eloquent:

> We would go over to my mother's, sometimes for weeks at a time. . . . If we didn't go, she'd send someone over to us. . . . She'd say, "Come over, I want some company." Then I'd do a lot of little things while we were there . . . like sewing, knitting. I made a lot of things when I was at my mother's. . . . We were lucky to always have my mother-in-law. . . . If we didn't have enough to eat, we would go and eat at her house, and that was that. . . . My mother-in-law would come for my little girl. . . . Sometimes she'd keep her for three or four days. (E19)

In fact, relief payments were so small that it was impossible to live on them for extended periods, at least not without going seriously into debt. After they had exhausted all of their resources and whatever tactics they could use to reduce their expenses, these couples turned to their families, most often their mothers. It was these who took up again the responsibility of sheltering, feeding, and maintaining their children. The domestic labour of these women, which had begun to diminish as their children left home, increased once more as a result of the Depression and its unemployment.

The Neighbours

As we have seen, the neighbourhood was most often indistinguishable from the relatives, and "neighbourly visits" in reality meant dropping in on the parents. Indeed, it appears that "one is not close to the neighbours,"[30] who might be viewed with a certain distrust. Many of the informants in fact stated that they didn't bother about their neighbours or that they had only limited contact with them: "We knew all of them and spoke to all of them, but we didn't visit back and forth" (E19). " I didn't have time when I was young to go over to the neighbours" (E23). "I was always the type of person who got along with everyone, but I wasn't someone to go by the neighbours . . . and, you know, gossip" (E30). "I didn't bother with the neighbours. I stayed home in peace and did my work. . . . Anyway, the way I look at it, our money problems, what's going on in our life, are our business. Other people don't have to know about them" (E22).

These remarks indicate that while it was generally desirable to "get along" with the neighbours, relations with them were limited to greetings on the street or a "bit of chat" on the balcony in the summertime. This attitude reflects the women's concern to keep their private lives private, in order to camouflage their problems and their poverty; it carried with it a consequent deep isolation. Speaking of her mother-in-law, who took in washing and went out to work by the day (as a cleaning woman), one woman remarked, "Nobody knew. Everybody kept everything hidden in those days" (E16). Another woman said of her mother, "My mother's poverty never showed" (E2). Being broke was hidden as much as possible, as it was seen as shameful and synonymous with failure, and the attempt was made to project an image of an economically independent family, which was the symbol of success in social terms. Women were not only reluctant to open their doors to their neighbours, but some of them even refrained from enlisting their help when they needed it, on the grounds that the request could be seen as evidence of an inability to shoulder domestic responsibilities.

These various considerations might lead to the conclusion that a genuine barrier was erected between unrelated families in the same district or even the same street. In fact, comments about relations with the neighbours are often contradictory and coloured with considerable ambiguity. The reality is much more complicated and a more detailed analysis of the oral narratives shows that in fact, the neighbours did nevertheless occupy a place in the network of mutual aid. "Not interference, but not indifference" it would seem is the key to good neighbourly relations:

> If we were in a fix, they would help us out, but we didn't get involved in each other's business. (E16)

> It's like a small town here—they were good people—no one had any money, but we helped each other out.... But we did keep to ourselves.... But in the street then, if someone was in trouble, we would have helped them out. It's not like that today. But that was not because we used to visit one another. I would go to Madame M. upstairs but not to the others, no. (E28)

If it was going to be acceptable, the help the neighbours provided must not imply any direct intrusion in the recipient's private life and had to take place on neutral ground, like the street or the balcony. The examples of favours that were exchanged reflect this code, to which most of the women interviewed appear to have adhered. Using a neighbour's phone was a noteworthy exception, but the women were quick to point out that they did not abuse the privilege and that "as soon as I was off the phone, I went right back upstairs to my house" (E20). As well, two of the informants learned to sew at their neighbours', which required joint sewing sessions and therefore several visits. But by and large, these exchanged favours did not involve going to one another's homes. A neighbour might, for example, take care of the children when their mother was giving birth, or was sick, or needed to go to the doctor's or the store. The ways in which they might help each other out were not, however, confined to just these. One informant, for example, frequently did the shopping for a neighbour who had difficulty getting about; another would go to the market with one of her neighbours so they could share the cost of the taxi on the way back. Another took care of her landlord's dog and chickens when he was away; in exchange, he provided her with fruit and took her and her children on excursions in his car on Sundays. One neighbour who worked in a laundry brought an informant's washing to his place of work. One neighbour did a respondent's washing during her first couple of deliveries; another could also depend on a neighbour to do part of her ironing. This recollection is particularly interesting, since it describes very clearly how the whole undertaking would happen without the privacy of either party being violated:

> There was a lady who lived next door—when I would hang out the shirts, sometimes a dozen of them, she would say, "Send the shirts over here and I'll iron them for you. . . . I only have girls, I don't have any men around." Sometimes, I'd put them in a pillowcase and send them over to her by the clothesline and when she was finished, she put them on hangers and send them back the same way. (E30)

Thus, neighbours helped each other in a variety of ways. If there is a reluctance to recognize this right away, it is not only due to pride, but also because the women who regularly provided aid and support or with whom a continuing relationship was established to some degree changed their status—they were no longer considered neighbours but friends or members of the family. Several of the informants who received help from older neighbours identified them with their own mothers: "She was like a mother to me" (E6), "As if I were her own daughter" (E7) and, "I thought of her as the mother I no longer had" (E22). The following personal narrative is interesting because it shows how, after denying the existence of any form of mutual aid, the informant goes on to describe a series of exchanges with a neighbour whom she was careful to identify as a friend:

> We didn't help each other out much to speak of. Well, we did look after each other's kids. My neighbour had three and I had four. When she had somewhere she had to go, I would look after her kids. We were together all the time. You see, my husband worked nights in the taxi and her husband worked days—they would come over to my place—they didn't have a radio and they'd come to listen to the programs with me. We'd play cards together—we used to play three-handed. Her husband, he'd rock my baby the whole night long. She'd put hers to bed before coming over—we were next door to each other on the same floor. She didn't have a washing machine and I did. When she wanted to do her wash, her husband would come and get my machine—we were on the same landing and she would do her laundry. . . . She'd come to see me and if I had some dirty clothes, she'd take them and do them because I would lend my machine. That was her, not any of the others. . . . But she was my very good, close friend. (E29)

The informants who had a close relationship with their neighbours are, however, an exception and generally lived far from their relatives or had lost their parents, especially their mothers. Those who were living at the centre of a close family network rarely developed bonds of friendship with their neighbours, although this does not mean that they never helped each other out. On the subject of babysitting, for example, one of the respondents declared, "That didn't happen in those days. No, because everyone had such large families, they were so big that you wouldn't dare get a babysitter. If they did need to be looked after, it would more likely be by one of the children in the house" (E27). Another remarked, "There weren't any sitters except for my mother-in-law who would take care of my kids because she was used to us. Aside from that, I never had a sitter. Oh, no!" (E23).

Whether or not they became friends, the help neighbours gave each other took the form of an exchange of material aid and always excluded loans of money. In general, the help was intended to assist in the carrying out of household tasks: taking care of the children, lending the telephone or other household appliances, sharing the shopping, and so on. There certainly were exceptions: one very poor informant, for example, depended on her landlord to supply her with coal; another, who had suffered a fire, could turn to a neighbour for temporary shelter;[31] yet another helped out the neighbours by illegally reconnecting their electric meter. But more often than not, it was to the immediate family that they turned when they needed money, food, clothing, fuel, or lodging.

Debt

The 1920s marked the beginning of delayed payments (the installment plan), a tactic newly conceived to encourage consumption at a time when increases in productivity had not been translated into raises in wages.[32] In Canada as in the United States, specialized financial institutions appeared that advanced capital to retailers so that they could sell on credit. The department stores followed close behind, offering their own credit systems, while other corporations, like the Central Finance Corporation (CFC), created in 1928, made loans directly to consumers.[33] These new sales techniques were added to the possibilities for credit offered by the small neighbourhood merchants. Working-class families, however, still viewed using credit and going into debt, especially just to satisfy a desire for consumer goods, with fear. The following statement sums up very well the feelings of the majority of the informants on this subject:

> We were never in debt. I never bought anything on credit because I told myself that if I didn't have the money today, I wasn't going to have it tomorrow. You mustn't go into debt. If we had, I don't know how we could have paid it. In our day, we always thought that maybe tomorrow we

wouldn't have a paycheque. There wasn't anything to fall back on, you
know. You couldn't count on anybody. You could only count on yourselves.
That's why we often had to go without things we would have liked to have.
But listen—we couldn't buy it, we didn't have it and that was that. (E17)

Therefore, the absence of social policies that would compensate for the
loss of income meant that these women and their husbands were acutely
aware of their financial limitations. Employment insecurity, especially in
the 1930s, intensified their fear of being unable to repay their debts. As
was mentioned previously, one couple chose to sell their restaurant rather
than ask their suppliers for credit, even though such credit is common
business practice. Another couple preferred to sell an insurance policy
when the husband was on strike for five weeks in the 1930s rather than
take a loan on the policy as the company agent suggested. At least half the
couples went without certain things rather than buy them on credit:

> We never went into debt. No, we never ran a bill in any grocery store. Well,
> my husband bought something on time one year during the Depression—
> he bought a suit. He paid fourteen dollars for it. We couldn't pay the whole
> thing. But that was the only time. Don't talk to me about being in debt. It
> makes me feel like someone is creeping up on me. He didn't like debts, and
> I didn't either—we never went into debt. We may not have had so much,
> but what we had was ours. (E23)

The women had other reasons as well to justify their refusal to resort
to credit. One of them, for example, stated that she was both too embarrassed and too proud to put their groceries "on the tab," a remark that
reveals that credit was closely associated with poverty. Another remarked
that her husband was against it (as did a number of others) and that the
use of credit encouraged merchants to cheat their customers as well as
fostering impulse buying or the substitution of more extravagant alternatives:

> My husband never would do that. I felt the same way, because it was well
> known that most [of the shopkeepers] would rather you ran a bill. You had
> to check on them though, because I'm telling you, they would cheat you. If
> you wanted something, and they didn't have it, then you would take some-
> thing more expensive, while if you were paying cash, then you would go
> somewhere else and find what it was you wanted. And then my husband's
> opinion was that if you were paying cash, then you were living on the
> money you had while otherwise sometimes you would get carried away and
> buy more than you could afford. (E29)

But once again, what was done was often far from what was enunciated
as a principle. Thus several informants, after having declared that they had

never gone into debt, admitted that they would buy their groceries "on the tab," that they would spread out the payments for their deliveries, that they would buy furniture and clothing on the installment plan, that they had sometimes been late with their rent or that they had borrowed against an insurance policy. It must be said that advertising and certain merchants encouraged the use of credit by playing with words in order to get around the consumer's fears. This is why one respondent, who always bought her furniture by paying half down and the half in three months could state, "That didn't become credit for ninety days. They didn't call that a debt—they called it a current account. And I always managed to pay the whole thing in ninety days" (E25). In her mind, as in that of many of the others, having debts meant paying interest, which was not charged if one succeeded in paying the whole sum off by the due date. Generally, however, it did cost more to buy on extended payments, which allowed the retailer to cover the cost of providing this service.[34]

Those who did use credit did so most of the time to buy furniture and groceries and did so, especially in the 1940s, when their financial situation had improved and they were able to rely on a more regular cash income. During the Depression, a few women bought clothing on credit from pedlars, some others owed money to their landlords or their doctors, and just one went into debt to buy an automobile. The sums they owed were tiny compared to present-day standards—they rarely exceeded one or two weeks' wages. In fact, it can be said that credit was not as yet a part of the consumption habits of the majority of these households which would rather confine what they thought of buying to what their means allowed.

---

*F*or the first time in the course of the 1930s, the state was obligated to contribute directly to the family economy of an impressive number of families, particularly of the working class. This contribution, however critical, was obviously insufficient and could not as yet be placed in the very precise perspective of the redistribution of the collective wealth that was the case for various social programs after the Second World War. In principle, the state extended aid only to those unemployed who were wholly without other recourse and who could not expect help from their families; in practice, these families contributed in a range of ways to meet the needs that the meagre relief allowances paid to the unemployed could not cover. The Depression thus made it more common and more frequent to turn to those traditional resources of mutual aid that rested on the household labour of the women of the previous generation. Through their labour, these women made a contribution just as essential as that of the state to maintaining a minimum standard of living for those on assistance. To put it another way, all of the women within the family circle, and not just the wives of the men who were out of work, absorbed the impact of the Depression.

Conclusion

*T*he interviews collected in the course of this study provide support for the hypotheses of other researchers, and particularly have permitted us to revise our view of the women of this generation by revealing, for example, the lack of training in household tasks given to girls, the importance of paid work for "housewives," and the extent to which contraceptives were employed at a time when the Catholic Church was firmly in control of Quebec society.

The oral narratives also highlight the complexities of certain phenomena and the virtual impossibility of grasping their outlines with the aid of only written sources, regardless of their reputation for superior objectivity. Among other things, they have demonstrated beyond all doubt the necessity, previously expressed in various works, to turn to criteria other than the occupation of the principal breadwinner to establish the family living standard; the domestic and paid labour of women and children, but also the size of the family, moonlighting on the husband's part, and the help contributed by relatives appeared as equally determining factors in developing an accurate picture of living conditions for these families.

In this regard especially, it can be stated that, at least during the 1930s, the standard of living for a number of the families in the sample was more alike than different, regardless of what sort of job the principal breadwinner held. The Great Depression probably contributed to this phenomenon as it brought with it a reduction in the clientele of the small shopkeepers, when they did not lose their trade altogether, as well as unemployment not only for unskilled labourers but also for certain skilled workers, particularly in construction, and for white-collar workers as well.

Note to the Conclusion is on p. 212.

As has already been stressed, the Depression coincided also with a critical stage in the life cycle of these families, one marked by the arrival of children; the presence of numerous dependents in the better off families sometimes contributed to reducing their standard of living to one approaching that of poorer but smaller families or those in which the mother was making a financial contribution.

Another factor enters into the balance to explain why the gap between the families was quite narrow during this period: the thrifty practices of those who enjoyed higher incomes. In fact, even women who had enough money at their disposal did not buy more than what was absolutely necessary and would produce the most for their money, which permitted them not only to put a little aside, but also meant that their families' living standards were limited for a longer or shorter period of time. After the war, however, these savings allowed some of the couples pay for their children's education or to buy a house, which differentiated them clearly from the others: "We were always very careful with money," one of the women stated, whose husband bought a barber shop in 1926 and a house in 1953. "I only got one dress a year, and I made it myself. I made all the children's clothes. I didn't find this hard, because everyone was doing the same thing. . . . People today don't believe in saving their pennies anymore" (E4). On the other hand, especially among the families of unskilled workers, neither women's paid labour nor a smaller number of children was sufficient to generate a surplus that could be invested in education or property.

The economic mobility of certain families is explained in part by women's domestic and paid labour and by their careful management of the family finances, something which few studies have taken into account;[1] changes in the principal breadwinner's employment (either after a promotion or additional training) are another significant variable. This phenomenon, relatively frequent according to the oral narratives, highlights the arbitrary nature of social status assignments when they are applied to an individual or a family without taking into account their evolution over time.

Otherwise, the analysis of the recollections of the women interviewed demonstrates that, at least in their eyes, the Great Depression did not have a particularly catastrophic effect on their work in the home, or, for that matter, on their standard of living. Several factors explain this apparently paradoxical phenomenon. On the one hand, it is necessary to recall that even before these households were affected by job losses or salary cuts, they were already dependent on the contribution made by women's domestic and paid labour and on other strategies without necessarily being assured of achieving a minimum level of comfort and well-being. Of course, the relative poverty in which the majority of these families lived, even before the Depression intervened, meant that they were obliged to cut back on essential expenses rather than just the inessentials. But at the same time, this impoverishment had accustomed them to live frugally and certainly contributed to softening the impact of the Depression. For these women, the conditions brought about by unemployment were not in such stark contrast to their previous quality of life. Moreover, even if, at the moment the Depression began, a number of these couples had been married only a short time and none had as yet experienced unemployment, most of the women interviewed had grown up in poor families where unemployment was a constant reality. Faced with poverty from childhood, they had learned to come to terms with it and were familiar with the strategies required to deal with it. The oral narratives of women who had lived through the Depression when they were older might have provided other indicators of its consequences on their domestic work and brought to light other strategies for coping with it (like sending their children to work, for example), but on the grounds of their age alone, it is impossible, even through the techniques of oral history, to access their experience.

How the informants judged the impact of the Depression on their work and on how they lived goes back to their previous experience of life. The fact that the Depression coincided with the beginning of the married life of the majority of these women also plays an important role. At this stage, it was still possible for couples to put off having children in order to lessen their financial obligations and few of them had as yet accumulated any possessions that the Depression might jeopardize. Still on the threshold of their adult lives, they could entertain hopes for better days, something which surely helped them bear up under the difficulties they were encountering. That, at least, is what emerges from the set of narratives collected here. If this period was particularly striking in our collective history, it certainly left its mark on each individual destiny, though, it may be said, in less specific and predictable ways. All of the women interviewed recalled this period very clearly as well as the extent of unemployment, but closer questioning revealed rather more measured comments regarding the personal consequences of the Depression. Summing up the general sentiment, one of the women, asked if the Depression was a particularly traumatic period in her life, answered:

> No. As I said, I don't know if it was because we were young . . . but I can't say that it left its mark on us. We always had hope that things would change. I think that if the Depression were to happen today, we would panic more than in those days because we weren't so spoiled. That's how it was in those days. We got along with very little, because we had to, to tell the truth. Those who lost a lot were the ones who had money and who lost it all. There were some who took their own lives—it was serious. But when you don't have any money then you don't worry about it, eh? (E29)

Appendices

Appendix A: Interview Guide

Part One: General Information

A. *Identification*

1. Last name, first name
2. Year and place of birth
3. Number of siblings, place in birth order, other persons living in home
4. Year first arrived in Montreal; district lived in, reason for moving to Montreal and subsequent moves; return to the countryside
5. Father's occupation; mother's occupation before marriage

B. *Education*

1. Age on entering school
2. Years completed
3. Type of school attended (country, neighbourhood, convent, private or public school)
4. Training received (especially in domestic science)
5. Siblings' education
6. Age on school leaving; reasons for leaving
7. View of the experience; would she have liked to continue?

C. *Work Experience before Marriage*

Paid work

1. Age at first employment
2. Was the decision voluntary or made by parent; agreement to leave school
3. How first job obtained: contacts, classified ads, etc.
4. Other members of the family working at the same place

5. Kind of work, kind of company
6. Situation of workplace; close to or distant from home
7. Work performed
8. Hours, days of work, general work conditions
9. Why this work was chosen; other possibilities
10. Training: who provided it; for how long?
11. Wages: amount, how paid (by the hour, by the piece) how spent
12. Did status in family change?
13. Unionized premises? participation in union? in strikes? causes of strikes; settlements? causes of non-participation?
14. Relationships with other workmates; any lasting friendships? leisure activities and excursions with workmates?
15. Length of employment; reason for leaving
16. Feelings about work experience

Note: points 4-16 to be repeated for each different job

Domestic work

1. Tasks performed; training; frequency
2. Voluntary help or not
3. Who else helped out (siblings, father, etc.)? what did they do? how often?
4. Feelings about domestic work

Chapter 5: *Note: These questions should be repeated in regard to three possibilities: domestic work while still at school, while still at work, between the end of school and marriage.*

Part Two: Dating and Marriage

A. Dating

1. Dating before meeting husband
2. Meeting husband: where? under what circumstances? why chosen?
3. Age at which partners met
4. Origin of partner: area, neighbourhood, family, number of siblings, father's and mother's occupation; years of schooling
5. Occupation of husband when first met: kind of job, company, duties, wages
6. Length of engagement; reasons for long engagement: unemployment, family reasons, etc.
7. Desire to enter a convent? If not, why not?
8. Premarital sexual experience; out-of-wedlock pregnancies; abortion; child placed in orphanage; "shotgun wedding"
9. Economic effects of marriage on birth families
10. Parental approval?

B. *Marriage*

1. Age at marriage for both partners; if the couple was married after 1929, awareness of economic conditions
2. What kind of wedding? clothes worn? honeymoon?
3. Matrimonial regime
4. Husband's occupation at marriage; wages
5. Occupation of informant; cessation of paid work; why? willing or not to quit. In cases where she continued to work: why? husband's attitude?
6. Financial situation of the couple: savings, debts, trousseau; furniture and domestic appliances; whether bought or received; description
7. Aid offered by parents or others when couple set up housekeeping; what form did this take—presents, financial gifts, other?

Part Three: Family Economy during the Thirties

A. *Housing*

1. First residence with parents of one of the pair; why? for how long? what space did couple occupy? Feelings about the experience
2. First house and subsequent housing: location (close to or distant from family; why?) who was responsible for finding the housing? how much rent?
3. Physical description of the premises: number of rooms and how used, condition of the premises (cleanliness, dilapidation, presence of vermin); amenities: hot and cold running water, electricity, gas, kind of heating, toilets, bathroom, number of sinks
4. Number of years spent in each lodging; reason for leaving
5. Expectation of owning a home: if not, why not; if yes, after how many years of marriage did the project materialize? lost due to Depression?

B. *Motherhood, Contraception, Care and Raising of Children*

1. Discussion between partners regarding number of children desired?
2. Number of children; sex, years of birth; miscarriages; deaths of infants or children; number and ages of children at home between 1929 and 1939
3. Place of childbirth; who performed the delivery?; cost
4. Aid received following childbirth: who provided it? for how long? was it free or paid? who took care of the children for subsequent childbirths?
5. Nursing experience with first child; if no experience, who helped and advised (mother, doctor, nurse, government pamphlets, etc.)? was the advice welcome?
6. Birth control: level of awareness of contraceptive methods; learnt from whom? were any of the methods used? if yes, which? if no, why not? were the attempts successful? awareness of and opinion of the Church's position on this matter
7. Influence of the economic climate on the number and spacing of children

8. Help by the father in the care and raising of children: baths, bottles, diaper-changing, babysitting, discipline, games, help with homework
9. Husband's unemployment: did he concern himself with the children more?
10. Work outside the home: who looked after the children (free or paid babysitter); feelings about leaving child with a sitter
11. Feelings about the experience of motherhood

Note: other points in this third part cover one of the three following possibilities and were not raised in every interview:

1. Wives whose husbands were never out of work
2. Wives whose husbands experienced brief periods of unemployment or short weeks but did not have to go on relief
3. Wives whose husbands experienced prolonged periods of unemployment that obliged the couple to go on relief

C. *Income and Source*

Couples who did not experience unemployment

1. Husband's employment during the Depression: hours and work schedule; impact on housework and married life; wages; management of salary; who decided how to spend money: on food? furniture? clothing? rent? other expenses?; who controlled the purse strings?
2. Insufficient wages to live on: among the following, which were used when money was short?
   a *Children's working*: age at first job; how many worked between 1929 and 1939?; how much of the wage was given to the parents? how was the money used? agreement to work? feelings about their children's contribution
   b *Mother's work in the home*: during what period? why? room used; payment; how was money used? effect on housework, child care, on the use of space; husband's opinion; length of employment
   c *Mother's work outside the home*: during what period? why? kind of work? hours of work? wages and how used; reactions of husband and family; child care, effect on domestic tasks; help from husband
   d *Renting rooms and taking in boarders*: parents or strangers; why?; in what period? for how long? effect on housework; amount charged; how was the money used? advantages and disadvantages of having roomers
   e *Debt*: who was owed? how much? how often were debts incurred? for what? how were payments made? credit possibilities
   f *Outside help*: from whom?; in what form? how often? feeling about this kind of aid
   g *Other stopgaps*: which?

3. Situations of financial difficulty when wives did not work: why

Couples experiencing unemployment

1. Loss of husband's job: what year? for how long? reactions of the couple faced with the situation; steps taken to find work; results; support provided; consequences on the couple's relationship
2. Means of survival: savings; parental aid; wife's paid employment (refer to questions in previous section); going into debt
3. Wife's paid work during husband's unemployment: sufficient wages to live on?; reactions of husband and wife to this role reversal; involvement of husband in domestic chores and child care
4. Other stopgaps: outside help, from whom? moving house; where? differences in rent; description of new housing; sale of furniture; how much obtained?; reductions in expenditures; which? (food, clothing, health care); cuts in services (gas, electricity); impact on family life, on housework

Couples living on direct relief

1. Steps taken to obtain aid; what happened?; inspection visits; aid received (money, vouchers, provisions); conditions imposed; relations with those in charge of applying the rules; being checked up on
2. Direct relief; amount received (by the week); what was done to live on the sums provided
3. Payment in kind: provisions distributed; quantities; did the provisions accord with family's habitual eating patterns?
4. Vouchers: limitations imposed by this method of distribution
5. Going back to the land; reasons for choosing this solution; year of departure; previous experience with living on the land; effect on domestic work
6. Feelings about help received

D. Housework: Tools Tasks, Organization, and Distribution

For all situations:

1. Tools of work: household articles and appliances on marriage or acquired during the 1930s: washing machine, stove (gas, coal, wood, electric), refrigerator or icebox, dishes, pots and pans in sufficient quantities, telephone, radio, iron and ironing board, toaster, rugs, floor covering, sewing machine, furnace (oil, gas, coal, electric)
2. Amenities: see description under housing
3. Organization of work: description of a typical day, a typical week; same routine as mother?
4. Description of chores: washing, housework, ironing, cooking, length of time; assessment
5. Purchases: who made them?; what was bought (food, clothing); delivery service; who made purchases of food, furniture, clothing?

6. Meals: products bought; made at home?; grown in garden? menus; source of recipes used; examples of recipes; lack of food: how dealt with (cutting portions, skipping meals)

7. Clothing: which were bought; where?; which made at home? from new or used fabric? received from whom?; knitting, crochet, other needlework

8. Sharing of tasks: husband, children, domestic help; chores done by these persons; how often?; tasks done outside the home (laundry, for example): how often? for how long? cost?; tasks undertaken in common with other women: which ones?; how often?; tasks which took the most time, the least time; feelings about tasks.

Couples having experienced a period of unemployment; add the following questions:

1. Supplementary work required by lack of money; what sort?; tasks most affected; concrete effects on housework, laundry, meals, purchases

2. Husband's help while out of work: estimation of his presence in the home; absence of husband; how did he spend his days?

B. Community Life

1. Leisure activities: movies, outings, all-night parties, visits from family; effect of Depression on leisure activities

2. Mutual aid—parents, neighbours: what kind?; favours exchanged; concrete examples; impact of the Depression on mutual help

3. Awareness of the extent of the Depression; where information obtained (radio, newspapers, personal effects) feelings about the Depression; acquaintance with people on relief; help provided; what sort; for how long?

4. Participation in or awareness of unemployment demonstrations in Montreal.

5. Awareness of the back-to-the-land campaign; contemplated as a solution? acquaintance with anyone who went

6. Opinion at the time of the measures taken by governments to end the crisis.

7. Church discourse on the subject of the Depression

8. Other recollections of the era and influence of the period on later life.

Appendix B: Thumbnail Biographies of the Women Interviewed
(in chronological order of interview)

Note: *These biographies have been attached in order to situate the quotations drawn from the interviews within the larger context of the life course of the informants and thus restore their full sense. In order to preserve confidentiality, names of places, companies, or any other details that might aid identification of the informants have been omitted.*

Informant E1

Born in rural Quebec in 1904; elder of two girls; father a farmer and logger; mother died when informant was two years old; raised by her grandparents, separately from her sister. At thirteen, she left school and came to live in Montreal with them. For sixteen years she worked in different factories until her marriage in 1933 to a factory worker. Her marriage was delayed for three years because her fiancé was out of work. She continued to work for the first year of her marriage as her husband was working short weeks. Unable to have a child, she adopted a daughter in 1939.

Informant E2

Born in rural Ontario in 1905; came to the Montreal region in 1908; second girl in a family of eight children; father a foreman, mother let rooms. At twelve, she left school and worked as a domestic until she was eighteen, then in a factory until her marriage in 1926 to an automobile mechanic, a widower with no children. Mother of eight children (nine pregnancies), born between 1927 and 1941. Her husband worked short weeks for several years. In the 1940s, she worked part time and also took in lodgers.

Informant E3

Born in rural Quebec in 1899; second child and first girl of a family of eleven; father a farmer. At twelve, she left school to help her mother at home until she married a farmer-logger in 1919. The couple arrived in Montreal in 1925. Widowed in 1930, with three children to support, she opened a little restaurant-convenience store; she did dressmaking and took care of relatives to support herself until her remarriage in 1933 to a construction worker, a widower and father of five. He lost his job and the couple decided to go back to the country to live on a piece of land bought with the husband's savings, where they were to live for thirty years. Four other children were born in this marriage, the last in 1939.

Informant E4

Born in rural Quebec in 1903; last of a family of seven living children (thirteen births); father a farmer; raised in part by her sister who was fifteen years her senior. At fourteen, she left school to assist her ailing mother until she married a barber in 1923 who took her to live in Montreal. In 1926, he bought his own barber shop. Mother of eight children (nine pregnancies) born between 1924 and 1940.

Informant E5

Born in Montreal in 1907; eldest of a family of six surviving children (fourteen pregnancies, nine births); father a carpenter, later a contractor; mother a former teacher. At the age of fourteen, she quit school and worked as a saleswoman until her marriage to a factory worker in 1926. During the Depression, her husband lost his job and for six years the family was obliged to live on direct relief, public works employment, or other temporary jobs. At this time, she took in boarders and did sewing at home. Mother of two (five pregnancies) born in 1927 and 1929.

Informant E6

Born in an urban area outside Montreal in 1914; came to Verdun in 1917; eldest of a family of eight (nine pregnancies); father and mother both weavers. At thirteen, she left school and worked as a saleswoman and then as an office clerk until she "had" to get married in 1932. For the first three years of her marriage, her husband worked only part-time and the family had to live for some weeks on direct relief. Mother of three children (eight pregnancies) born between 1932 and 1952.

Informant E7

Born in the United States in 1910; came to Maisonneuve in 1914; younger of two children (five pregnancies) but only girl; her father, a machinist in the United States, opened a restaurant-convenience store when he moved to Maisonneuve. When she was eleven, she left school for health reasons and helped out at her father's store until she was sixteen. She worked as a dressmaker until her marriage to a shopkeeper in 1929. She managed the business while her husband worked another job. In 1933, they had to sell up to avoid bankruptcy. Mother of one son (seven pregnancies), born in 1930.

Informant E8

Born in Montreal in 1902; next to last of a family of seven; father a printer. At twelve, she left school and worked as a wrapper in a department store and then worked in a factory until she married a factory worker in 1923. He worked short weeks during the Depression. The couple had no children.

Informant E9

Born in Maisonneuve in 1904; next to last of a family of five, but the only girl; father a mason. At fifteen, she left school and went to work as a nurse's aide until she went to live with her family who were moving to the country because of her mother's illness. She married a farmer in 1920 and went back to live in Montreal in 1925, where her husband joined her a few months later. Between 1926 and 1934, she worked as a nurse's aide to support her husband, herself, and her only son, born the year she returned to Montreal. In 1934, the family went back to live on a farm, due to lack of work; she returned to the Montreal area in 1952. The couple lived for some time on relief before going to live in a region of colonization.

Informant E10

Born in rural Quebec in 1909; came to Maisonneuve in 1914; last of a family of six (second daughter). At seventeen, she finished her commercial course and stayed at home to help her ailing mother for the next two years before going to work in an office and then as a milliner until her marriage to a laboratory technician in 1932. Mother of five, born between 1934 and 1940.

Informant E11

Born in rural Quebec in 1901; fifth child of a family of nine; father a barber. Came to Montreal in 1916; whole family employed in a cotton mill; she worked there until her marriage to a machinist in the same factory in 1929. Mother of three, born between 1930 and 1933.

Informant E12

Born in Verdun in 1912; fourth in a family of nine (third girl); father a butcher. She left school at fifteen to help her mother at home until she was seventeen. She then held several different jobs as an apprentice seamstress until her marriage to a bricklayer in 1929. Mother of seven born between 1929 and 1940. Her husband lost his job in 1933 and remained unemployed throughout the Depression. The family lived on public works employment and relief until 1940, when she decided to go to work in a munitions factory.

Informant E13

Born in Montreal in 1912; third in a family of four (second girl); her father, a carpenter, died when she was eight; her mother worked as a dressmaker and put her children to board. At fourteen, she left school, worked for a few weeks in a shirt factory and then as a domestic until she "had" to get married in 1932 to a white-collar worker. Mother of five (seven pregnancies) born between 1932 and 1949. She took in a boarder and sewed at home during the 1930s.

Informant E14

Born in rural Quebec in 1904; second in a family of three (second girl); orphaned at the age of twelve, she and her two sisters were raised by her grandparents who owned a door and window factory. She left school at fifteen to help her grandmother until she married a grocer's son in 1928. She came to Montreal in 1930 with her husband, who worked for a while in construction, then became unemployed. Mother of three born between 1930 and 1934, she did embroidery for various companies at home and took in a boarder. Her grandfather's help allowed the family to avoid going on relief.

Informant E15

Born in Montreal in 1909; fourth in a family of six (second girl); father a furrier. She left school at fifteen to work as a stenotypist until she married a fellow employee in 1931. Mother of three boys (eight pregnancies), born between 1933 and 1941. Her husband worked short weeks during the Depression.

Informant E16

Born in the United States in 1909; came to Montreal at the age of six months following the death of her father; youngest of a family of three; her mother worked in textile and shoe factories before her remarriage. The family then went to live in a region of colonization until returning to Montreal when she was thirteen. She left school at fourteen and worked in a hat factory until her marriage to a butcher's clerk in 1932. Mother of three (four pregnancies), born between 1933 and 1938. After her marriage she did various jobs at home (sewing, laundry) and worked as a housekeeper.

Informant E17

Born in rural Quebec in 1899; next to last of a family of six (first girl); mother died when informant was sixteen; father a farmer and farm machinery salesman. She left school at fourteen and apprenticed as a seamstress for a year and filled her mother's place until she married a farmer's son in 1919. She came to Montreal in 1923, where her husband became a deliveryman. Mother of ten children born between 1921 and 1940, she took in sewing at home for thirty years, beginning in 1935.

Informant E18

Born in rural Quebec in 1913; second child and first girl in a family of ten; father a painter-decorator, mother a housekeeper and factory worker. When she was eleven, she left school to take care of her younger brothers and sisters. She came to Montreal when she was fifteen and worked as a domestic until she married a factory worker in 1930. Mother of seven children born between 1931 and 1957, she took in washing and sewing and worked as a housekeeper to support her family.

Informant E19

Born in rural Quebec in 1912; third child (second girl) in a family of eleven; father a carpenter. She finished her high school diploma at the age of seventeen and taught for a year before marrying a clerk-salesman in 1931 and went to live in Montreal. Mother of four born between 1932 and 1951. Her husband lost his job in 1933 and they lived on relief until 1936.

Informant E20

Born in Montreal in 1904; fifth child (third daughter) of a family of eleven; father a machinist. Her family left Montreal when she was very young and she spent the greater part of her childhood in Ontario. Her family then moved to a rural area south of Montreal. When she was twelve, she left school to help her mother at home, then, at fourteen, she went to work in a local woollen mill until she married a lathe operator in 1927. Mother of two daughters, born in 1928 and 1930; her husband lost his job in 1930 and the family was obliged to go on relief for about six months.

Informant E21

Born in rural Quebec in 1905; second daughter in a family of fifteen children; father a farmer and blacksmith. She left school at fourteen to work in a stocking factory until she married a clerk in 1929 and they came to live in Montreal. Mother of eight children born between 1930 and 1946; during the war she worked with her husband making figures for Christmas crèches.

Informant E22

Born in rural Quebec in 1906; last in a family of ten; father a farmer. When she was seventeen, she finished her normal school course and taught for two years before filling in for her deceased mother for her unmarried brothers and her father. She married a plasterer and carpenter in 1930 and came to live in Montreal. Mother of eleven (sixteen pregnancies) born between 1931 and 1947, she did needlework and sewing at home during the early years of her marriage. Her husband lost his job in 1937 and the family was obliged to go on relief until they returned to the country in the early 1940s.

Informant E23

Born in rural Quebec in 1906; sixth child of a family of nine (third girl); father an "engineer" in the sawmills. She left school at eleven and stayed at home until she came to Montreal when she was thirteen, where she went to live with her sister. The following year, she went to work in a ribbon factory until she married a factory worker in 1925. Mother of five children born between 1932 and 1945 (seven pregnancies). Her husband lost his job for a year and the family had to go on relief.

Informant E24

Born in Montreal in 1905; fourth child and first girl in a family of seven; father a baker. She left school when she was fourteen to learn the trade of chocolate-making, which she engaged in until she married a barber in 1932. Mother of five born between 1932 and 1945 (seven pregnancies). The family was on relief for six months during the Depression.

Informant E25

Born in Montreal in 1916; third child and second girl in a family of six (twelve pregnancies); father a clerk. When she was twelve, she left school to take care of her younger brothers as her father's illness obliged her mother to go to work. Between the ages of sixteen and eighteen, she worked in the same factory as her mother until she married a factory worker in 1934. Mother of seven children born between 1935 and 1954; her husband lost his job in 1936 and the family lived on relief and public works employment until 1941.

Informant E26

Born in Montreal in 1908; an adopted and only child; father a day labourer. She left school at thirteen and became a millinery apprentice and then a saleswoman until her marriage to a clerk in 1927. After her marriage she continued to work part time now and then. Mother of two (three pregnancies) born in 1928 and 1930. Her husband lost his job and the couple tried without success to open a little restaurant before going on relief for a couple of years.

Informant E27

Born in Ontario in 1907, she came to Montreal when she was four; third child and first girl in a family of nine; father a day labourer. At fifteen, she left school and became a domestic and then a saleswoman until she married an unemployed man in 1927. Mother of five (eleven pregnancies) born between 1928 and 1944. Because of the husband's chronic unemployment, the family always had difficulty supporting itself.

Informant E28

Born in Montreal in 1908; eldest of a family of eight; father a carpenter; on the death of her grandmother, who had taken the place of the informant's mother who had died the year before, the family was dispersed and she went to work, first as a domestic and then as a clerk, before marrying a cigar-maker in 1932. Mother of two sons (four pregnancies) born in 1934 and 1942. After her marriage, she worked for four years while her husband was unemployed.

Informant E29

Born in Verdun in 1908; last child in a family of six; father a painter. She left school at the age of twelve to help her mother at home before going to work in a cigarette factory until she married a widower, father of one child, in 1929. Mother of five (six pregnancies), born between 1930 and 1941. Her husband was obliged by the Depression to sell his taxis and the family lived on public works employment and other odd jobs for about four years.

Informant E30

Born in Montreal in 1897; fifth child and third daughter in a family of eleven; father a day labourer. She left school at twelve to help her mother at home until the age of nineteen. She then went to work in various factories until she married a cigar-maker, a widowed father of six, in 1927. Mother of one daughter (three pregnancies), born in 1929. During the Depression, her husband experienced short weeks.

Appendix C: Scale of Winter and Summer Rations
Approved by the City of Montreal (c. 1935)

Number	Food (weekly)	Fuel (weekly)	Clothing (weekly)	Total (weekly)	Rent (monthly)	Total (monthly)	Total (yearly)
Winter Rations							
1	1.65	0.00	0.15	1.80	6.00	13.80	165.06
2	2.50	0.90	0.30	3.70	7.00	23.03	276.40
3	3.15	1.15	0.45	4.75	7.50	28.08	337.00
4	4.15	1.15	0.60	5.90	8.00	33.57	402.80
5	5.05	1.35	0.75	7.15	8.50	39.48	473.80
6	5.80	1.40	0.90	8.10	9.00	44.10	529.20
7	6.60	1.50	1.05	9.15	9.50	49.15	589.80
8	7.35	1.55	1.20	10.10	10.00	53.77	645.20
9	8.00	1.80	1.35	11.15	11.00	59.32	711.80
10	8.65	1.85	1.50	12.00	12.00	64.00	768.00
11	9.25	2.05	1.65	12.95	12.00	68.12	817.40
12	9.85	2.05	1.80	13.70	12.00	71.37	856.40
13	10.45	2.25	1.95	14.65	12.00	75.48	905.80
Summer Rations							
1	1.65	0.00	0.15	1.80	6.00	13.80	165.60
2	2.50	0.60	0.30	3.40	7.00	21.73	260.80
3	3.15	0.70	0.45	4.30	7.50	26.13	313.60
4	4.15	0.70	0.60	5.45	8.00	31.62	379.50
5	5.05	0.75	0.75	6.55	8.50	36.88	442.60
6	5.80	0.75	0.90	7.45	9.00	41.28	495.40
7	6.60	0.75	1.05	8.40	9.50	45.90	540.80
8	7.35	0.80	1.20	9.35	10.00	50.52	606.30
9	8.00	0.80	1.35	10.15	11.00	54.98	659.80
10	8.65	0.80	1.50	10.95	12.00	59.45	713.40
11	9.25	0.85	1.65	11.75	12.00	62.92	755.10
12	9.85	0.85	1.80	12.50	12.00	66.17	794.10
13	10.45	0.85	1.95	13.25	12.00	69.42	833.10

Note: In 1933, the amount allocated for a family of five was $670 a year for rent, food, clothing, fuel, and lighting.

Source: Montreal Unemployment Commission, *Renseignements à l'usage des chômeurs nécessiteux et des propriétaires*, n.d. 10-11.

Appendix D: Furnishings Bought by an Informant upon Her Marriage in 1932

Furnishing	Price
Kitchen	
maple furniture including	
1 table	
4 chairs	
1 buffet	$78.50
Dining Room	
Gibbord-style polished walnut dining-room	
set with mahogany inlays including:	
1 table	
1 armchair and 5 sidechairs	
1 china cupboard	
1 buffet	$129.00
Living Room	
Chesterfield-brand suite	
in beige bouclé:	
1 three-seat sofa	
1 low-back armchair	
1 high-back armchair	$145.00
Bedroom	
American walnut suite:	
1 bed	
1 night table	
1 bureau with mirror	
1 dressing table with mirror	$135.00
Carpets	
Synthetic fibres	
living room	$26.00
dining room	$31.50
bedroom	$27.50
Occasional table	$1.00
Total	$573.50

Appendix E: Floor Plans of Working-Class Flats

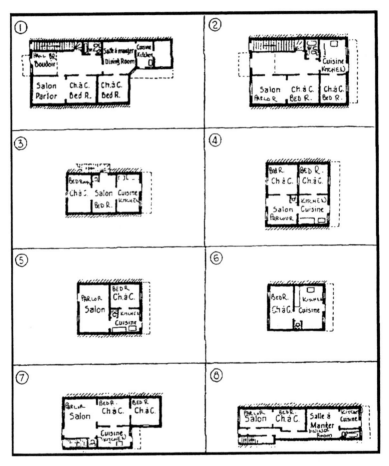

Source: Réal Bélanger, George S. Mooney et Pierre Boucher, *Les Vieux Logements de Montréal*, Montréal, Commission métropolitaine de Montréal, 1938

Appendix F: Percentage of Montreal Households Owning Various Equipment 1931-1958

Equipment	1931	1941	1948	1951	1958[b]
Heating					
By stove	—	51.5	—	54.8	55.5
Wood and coal	—	92.3	—	48.0	34.4
Cooking Fuel					
Wood and coal	—	17.7	50.9[b]	8.2	24.1
Gas and electric	—	80.6	39.8[b]	87.4	68.6
Bathtub	—	83.9	—	86.7	73.7
Hot and cold water	—	—	—	62.8	71.6
Refrigeration					
Mechanical	—	25.1	38.0	61.1	—
Icebox	—	65.0	—	36.2	89.7
None	—	5.1	—	2.3	2.2
Washer					
Electric	—	—	89.0[b]	—	87.1
Manual	—	—	8.7[b]	—	0.3
Gas	—	—	2.1[b]	—	0.4
Sewing Machine	—	—	—	74.0[a]	75.5
Electric	—	—	—	24.2[a]	—
Treadle	—	—	—	75.7[a]	—
Radio	—	85.5	—	96.1	96.6
Television	—	—	—	—	79.4
Telephone	10.5[b]	44.9	—	77.1	80.0
Vacuum cleaner	—	28.2	41.0	43.6	49.1
Automobile	—	15.7	—	24.2	46.7

a In 1950.
b Percentages for all Quebec.

Source: Canada, *Recensement du Canada 1931*, vol. 1: 1417; *Recensement du Canada 1941*, vol. 5: 50-85; *Recensement du Canada 1951*, vol. 3: 20-3 to 40-2; Canada, BFS, *Appareils de chauffage, appareils de TSF et téléphones dans les maisons canadiennes, août 1947* (Ottawa, 1948) 3; Canada, BFS, Accessoires ménagers, *novembre 1948. Appareils de cuisson, lessiveuses, réfrigérateurs, aspirateurs et radios dans les maisons canadiennes* 3-12; Canada BFS, *Appareils ménagers appareils de chauffage, machines à coudre, juin 1950*, 10-11 and 18; Canada, BFS, *Household Facilities and Equipment, May 1958* (Ottawa, 1959) Quebec, *ASQ 1939*, 396.

Appendix G: Household Appliances and
Other Articles Used by Housewives

The illustrations on the following pages are from *A Shopper's View of Canada Past. Pages from Eaton's Catalogue, 1886-1930 (Toronto: University of Toronto Press, 1969).*

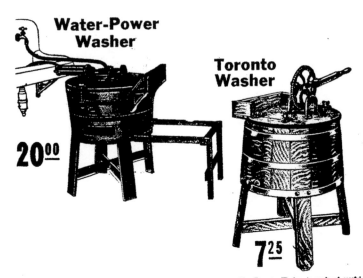

Eaton's Catalogue, Spring/Summer 1923, p. 221

188

Eaton's Catalogue, Spring/Summer 1929, p. 241

Eaton's Catalogue, Fall/Winter 1926-1927, p. 267

Eaton's Catalogue, Fall/Winter 1926-1927, p. 285

Notes

Introduction

1 "More than a million umemployed in December: the slump as great as the '30s." *Le Devoir* 9 Jan. 1982: 1; "Poverty indicators higher than in the 1930s," *La Press* 23 Jan. 1982: B1; "1,241,000 Canadians looking for work: highest unemployment since the Great Depression," *La Presse* 5 June 1982: B1.

2 Some of the more recent works on this period include Andrée Lévesque, *Virage à gauche interdit. Les communistes, les socialistes, et leurs ennemis au Québec 1929-1939* (Montreal: Boréal Express, 1984); Allen Seager and John H. Thompson, *Canada 1922-1939: Decades of Discord* (Toronto: McClelland & Stewart, 1985); James Struthers, *No Fault of Their Own: Unemployment and the Canadian Welfare State, 1914-1941* (Toronto: University of Toronto Press, 1983). For a more extensive bibliography of this period, see: Centre populaire de documentation, ed., Le Choc du passé. Les années trente et les sans-travail.

3 La Turlutte des années dures, dir. Richard Boutet and Pascal Gélinas, Vent d'Est, 1983.

4 Barry Broadfoot: *Ten Lost Years: 1929-1939* (Toronto: Doubleday, 1973)

5 See, for example; Tamara Hareven, *Family Time and Industrial Time: The Relationship between the Family and Work in a New England Industrial Community* (Cambridge: Cambridge University Press, 1982); Louise A. Tilly and Joan W. Scott, *Les Femmes, le Travail et la Famille* (Paris: Rivages, 1987); Bettina Bradbury, "L'économie familiale et la travail dans une ville en voie d'industrialisation: Montréal dans les années 1870," *Maîtresses de maison, maîtresses d'école: Femmes, famille, et éducation dans l'histoire de Québec*, ed. Nadia Fahmy-Eid and Micheline Dumont (Montreal: Boréal Express, 1983) 287-318 and "Pigs, Cows, and Boarders: Non-Wage Forms of Survival among Montreal Families," *Labour/Le Travail* 14 (1984): 9-48.

Chapter 1: Domestic Labour and Economic Crisis

1 M.C. Urquhart and K.A.H. Buckley, *Historical Statistics of Canada* (Toronto: Macmillan, Cambridge University Press, 1971) 303; Michiel Horn, "The Great Depression: Past and Present," *Journal of Canadian Studies/Revue d'études canadiennes* 11.1 (1976): 45; Canada, *Report of the Royal Commission into Relations between the Dominion and the Provinces* I (Ottawa: King's Printer, 1939): 149-50; Struthers, 215; Michiel Horn. *The Dirty Thirties: Canadians in the Great Depression* (Toronto: Copp Clark, 1972) 10.

2 C.H. Goldenberg, *Finances municipales au Canada* Study prepared for the Royal Commission of Inquiry into Relations between the Dominion and the Provinces (Ottawa: King's Printer, 1939) 68-71; Montreal: *Rapport de la Commission d'enquête du chômage* (Montreal, 1937); Horn, "Great Depression," 43.

3 L.C. Marsh. *Canadians in and out of Work: a Survey of Economic Classes and Their Relation to the Labor Market.* McGill Social Research Series 9 (Toronto: Oxford University Press, 1940) 345-46. These figures reflect the situation at the worst moment of the Depression, the winter of 1932-33. According to the distribution established by Marsh, only 2.6 percent of the unemployed receiving aid were of the professional class and 10.1 percent were clerks, 54.9 percent were unskilled labourers, 16.9 percent semi-skilled labourers, and 15.5 percent were skilled labourers.

4 Montreal Board of Trade and City Improvement League. *A Report on Housing and Slum Clearance for Montreal* (1935) 6. David Lewis and F.R. Scott. *Un Canada Nouveau* (Montreal: Valiquette, 1944) 88, cited in Lévesque, *Virage* 22. Between 1929 and 1933, the average industrial wage in Montreal dropped from $1022 to $777 a year (Marsh 198-99).

5 See Marsh, 193. Appendix C reproduces the table of summer and winter rations approved by the Montreal Unemployment Relief Commission.

6 Réal Bélanger, George S. Mooney and Pierre Boucher, *Les Vieux Logements de Montréal* (Montreal: Commission métropolitaine de Montréal, département d'urbanisme et de recherche, 1938); A. E. Grauer, *Hygiène publique,* a study prepared for the Royal Commission of Inquiry into Relations between the Dominion and the Provinces, 5 (Ottawa: King's Printer, 1939): 73.

7 Terry Copp, "The Health of the People: Montreal in the Depression Years," *Norman Bethune: son époque et son message,* ed. A.E. Sheppard and Andrée Lévesque (Ottawa: Association canadienne d'hygiène publique, 1982) 129; Lévesque, *Virage* 11.

8 L.C. Marsh, A. Grant Fleming and C.F. Blackler, *Health and Unemployment: Some Studies of Their Relationships*, McGill Social Research Series 7 (Toronto: Oxford University Press, 1938) 155-58, 163-64, 213-15.

9 Terry Copp, "The Montreal Working Class in Prosperity and Depression," *Canadian Issues* 1 (1975) n.p.

10 Bradbury, "Pigs, Cows, and Boarders," 9-48.

11 A number of writers observe that sexuality is an element in spousal psychological and emotional support. Veronica Strong-Boag clarifies the point, in my view a very important one: "Naturally, not all sexual exchange falls into the category of labour. Two critical distinctions between work and non-work for housewives would surely be reciprocity of pleasure and absence of coercion of any kind," "Keeping House in God's Country: Canadian Women at Work in the Home," *On the Job: Confronting the Labor Process in Canada*, ed. Craig Heron and Robert Story (Montreal: McGill-Queen's University Press, 1986) n. 49, 150.

12 This discussion has been developed in a number of publications since the early 1970s. For a synthesis of these works, see, among others, Nathalie Sokoloff, *Between Money and Love: The Dialectics of Women's Home and Market Work* (New York: Praeger, 1980); Sylvia Walby, *Patriarchy at Work* (Minneapolis: University of Minnesota Press, 1986) and Louise Vandelac, et al. *Du travail et de l'amour, Les dessous de la production domestique* (Montreal: Éditions Saint-Martin, 1985).

13 Monique Haicault, "Sexes, salaire, famille," in *La famille en question, Annales,* Université Toulouse-Le Mirail XVI, 4, 1980; Katherine Blunden, *Le Travail et la Vertu. Femmes au*

Foyer: une mystification de la Révolution industrielle (Paris: Payot, 1982) cited in Vandelac et al., "Problématique," 23-68.

14 Heidi Hartmann, "Capitalism, Patriarchy and Jobs Segregation by Sex," *Capitalist Patriarchy and the Case for Socialist Feminism,* ed. Zillah Eisenstein (New York: Monthly Review Press, 1979) 206-48.

15 Vandelac, et al., "Problématique," 28.

16 Catherine Hall, "The History of the Housewife," *The Politics of Housework,* ed. Ellen Malos (London: Allison and Busby, 1980) 45-71; Susan Strasser, *Never Done: A History of American Housework* (New York: Pantheon, 1982); Diane Bélisle et Yolande Pinard, "De l'ouvrage des femmes québécoises," Vandelac, et al., 99-133.

17 It was not, moreover, until the 1950s that the majority of Montreal households had the benefit of an electric stove and refrigerator. Appendix F presents a table of the percentages of Montreal homes possessing various appliances between 1931 and 1958.

18 Bélanger et al. 6-14.

19 Diane Bélisle, "Une histoire de ménagères," Vandelac et al. 85-90; Glenna Matthews, *Just a Housewife: The Rise and Fall of Domesticity in America* (New York: Oxford University Press, 1987) 145-71.

20 Ruth Schwartz Cowan, "Two Washes in the Morning and a Bridge Party at Night: The American Housewife Between the Wars," *Decades of Discontent: The Women's Movement, 1920-1940,* ed. Lois Scharf and Joan M. Jensen (Boston: Northeastern University Press, 1987) 179.

21 Marie Lavigne, "Réflexions féministes autour la fertilité des Quebecoises," Fahmy-Eid and Dumont 323.

22 Denyse Baillargeon, "Les gardes de la Métropolitain, les Gouttes de lait, et l'Assistance maternelle: l'encadrement de la maternité au Québec entre les deux guerres," *Bulletin du RCHTQ* 47-48, 16.2 (1990): 19-45.

23 Andrée Lévesque, *La Norme et les Déviantes: Des femmes au Québec pendant l'entre-deux-guerres* (Montréal: Éditions du remue-menage, 1989).

24 Terry Copp, *Classe ouvrière et pauvreté: Les conditions de vie des travailleurs montréalais, 1897-1929* (Montreal: Boréal Express, 1978) 108.

25 See Katherine Blunden, in Vandelac et al., 23-68.

26 Elizabeth Roberts, "Women's Strategies, 1890-1940," *Labour and Love: Women's Experience of Home and Family 1840-1940,* ed. Jane Lewis (Oxford: Blackwell, 1986) 223.

27 Marie Lavigne and Jennifer Stoddard, "Ouvrières et travailleuses montréalaises, 1900-1940," *Travailleuses et féministes: Les femmes dans la société québécoise,* ed. Marie Lavigne and Yolande Pinard (Montreal: Boréal Express, 1983) 102.

28 Tamara Hareven, "Les grands thèmes de l'histoire de la famille aux États-Unis," *Revue d'histoire de l'Amérique française,* 39.2 (1985): 185-209.

29 Examples of this sort are not lacking. Andrée Léveseque's *La Norme et les Déviantes* presents an excellent synthesis of the normative discourse formulated by the Quebec elites regarding motherhood and female sexuality. See also Sylvie Van de Casteele-Schweitzer and Danièle Voldman, "Les sources orales pour l'histoire des femmes," *Une histoire des femmes est-elle possible?* ed. Michelle Perrot (Paris: Rivages, 1984) 60-70.

30 Interviews undertaken in France have thus demonstrated that people remember rather little about events such as the Popular Front, the rise of Nazism, or the Resistance but have retained memories of their impact on daily life. Philippe Joutard, *Ces voix que nous viennent du passé* (Paris: Hachette, 1983) 174-75; 179, 181.

31 On this question, see Paul Thompson, "Problems of Method in Oral History," *Oral History* 1.4 (n.d.) 5-12.

32 Hareven, *Family Time* 374; Isabelle Bertaux-Wiame, "Mémoire et récits de vie," *Pénélope, Mémoires de femmes* 12 (1985): 51; Alessandro Portelli, "The Peculiarities of Oral History," *History Workshop Journal* 12 (1981): 102.

33 In this connection, see Portelli 102; Hareven, *Family Time* 376-77.

34 Regarding specifically female memory and the way it is structured, see Bertaux-Wiame 47-54 and Anne-Marie Devreaux, "La mémoire n'a pas de sexe," *Pénélope* 55-68; Michelle Perrot, *Histoire orale et histoire des femmes*, (Bulletin de l'Institut d'histoire du temps présent 3, 1982) 47-50.

35 In the course of their research into the economic behaviour of working Quebec families during the 1950s, Fortin and Tremblay also noted that only women could provide them with the details necessary to their research. [Gérard Fortin and Marc-Adélard Tremblay, *Les Comportements économiques de la famille salariée du Québec* (Quebec: Laval University Press, 1964).]

36 A wing of the Communist party which attempted to mobilize women around questions of housing and feeding the unemployed. For an historical review of this League, see Luc Chartrand, "Au temps où les femmes prenaient les tramways d'assaut," *Châtelaine* 19.10 (1978): 56-57, 76, 79.

37 On the relationship between interviewer and interviewee, see Casteele-Schweitzer and Voldman 60-70; Joutard 196 ff.

38 Joutard 201.

39 See Appendix A.

40 On this issue, see Hareven, *Family Time* 371.

41 Daniel Bertaux, "L'approche biographique, sa validité méthodologique, ses potentialités," *Cahiers internationaux de sociologie. Histoires de vie et vie sociale* 69 (1980): 205.

42 J. Poirier, S. Clapier-Valadon and P. Raybaut, *Les Récits de vie. Théorie et pratique* (Paris: PUF, 1983) 144; Also: J.-C. Bouvier, H.-P Bremondy, P. Joutard, G. Mathieu, J.-N. Pelen, *Tradition orale et identité culturelle, problèmes et méthodes* (Marseille: Éditions CNRS, 1980) 67, cited in Joutard 227.

43 The class affiliation of the respondents posed a particular problem because women of that generation were generally not involved in the market economy following marriage. We had to confine ourselves to the husband's class, which made it difficult to make class a specific criterion from the beginning. This is why place of residence prevailed as a criterion since it has a general effect on the way of life and constitutes an excellent indicator of the standard of living. Isabelle Bertaux uses the expression "women of ordinary circumstances" precisely because it is imprecise. According to Bertaux, the term "refers . . . to the difficulty of classifying women who ply different trades in the course of their lives and often do so in a discontinuous fashion." [Isabelle Bertaux, "Mobilisations féminines et trajectoires familiales: une démarche ethnosociologique," *Les Récits de vie. Théorie, méthode et trajectoires types*, ed. Danièle Desmarais and Paul Grell (Montreal: Éditions Saint-Martin, 1986) n.5 98.]

44 To be precise, the majority of the respondents lived during this decade in St. Henri, Hochelaga, Maisonneuve, Rosemont, and in Verdun, which was included not only because of its proximity to Montreal and its primarily working-class character, but also because a number of the respondents who lived there at the beginning of the Depression also lived in St. Henri, or Pointe Saint Charles before, during, or after the Depression.

Moreover, Verdun forms part of a larger subsection (called the Southwest) inside of which the border between the two municipalities is largely absent in determining the natural "territory" of these women and their families.

45 Bertaux-Wiame "Mémoire," 50.

Chapter 2: From Birth to Marriage

1 Denise Lemieux and Lucie Mercier, *Les Femmes au tournant du siècle, 1880-1940: Ages de la vie, maternité et quotidien.* (Quebec: Institut québécois de recherche sur la culture, 1989) 58.

2 The mother of one of the informants was a forewoman in a shirt factory; another returned to the job as a weaver she had before she was married; three others had several jobs in the garment trade or in shoe factories and one of these also worked as a domestic.

3 It appears to be especially difficult to establish the numbers of live and stillbirths. When informants were among the younger members of the family and were not present at every birth, a baby who lived only a few hours, or even a few weeks, might easily be considered "stillborn" although demographically it would count as a live birth.

4 Jacques Henripin and Yves Peron note that French Quebec women born around 1887—that would be about the same generation as the mothers of our informants—who were still alive at the 1961 census had had an average of 6.4 children. This average includes all the women who were alive in 1961, regardless of whether or not they had had children. [Jacques Henripin and Yves Peron, "La transition démographique de la Province de Québec," *La Population du Québec: études rétrospectives,* ed. Hubert Charbonneau (Montreal: Boréal Express, 1973) 40.]

5 As Marie Lavigne has observed, if it is true that almost half of Quebeckers born around the turn of the century were raised in families of more than ten children, these were borne by only 20 percent of married women born about 1887 (Lavigne 324).

6 On this question, see Bettina Bradbury, "L'économie familiale," 300.

7 The informants were not always aware of the financial arrangements made with their parents. In general, it appears that younger adults (uncles, aunts) paid board, while grandparents, if they had no means of their own, were dependent on the family, which took them in since in this period there was no old-age pension.

8 In her study of Saint Brigide's parish, Lucia Ferretti also observes this rupture in the birth family. Her study of 1,105 couples married in this parish between 1905 and 1914 reveals that in 45 percent of the cases, one or even both parents had died before their children were married. [Lucia Ferretti, "Mariage et cadre de vie familiale dans une paroisse ouvrière montréalaise: Sainte-Brigide, 1900-1914," *Revue d'histoire de l'Amérique française* 39.2 (1985): 244-45.]

9 In Montreal in 1926, 94 percent of francophone students left school after the sixth grade. [P.A. Linteau et al., *Histoire du Québec contemporain,* vol. 1 (Montreal: Boréal Compact, 1989) 618]; Veronica Strong-Boag notes that English Canadian working-class girls also quit school at the same age to go to work. [Veronica Strong-Boag, *The New Day Recalled: Lives of Girls and Women in English Canada, 1919-1939* (Toronto: Copp Clark Pitman, 1988) 48].

10 Bettina Bradbury, who has studied child labour in Montreal in the nineteenth century, notes that in the working-class districts of Sainte-Anne and Saint-Jacques, "Almost every boy older than twenty was working, whereas only half the girls of the same age were employed. About 75 percent of the boys aged between sixteen and twenty had a job, and

only about 40 percent of the girls. If there were boys in the family, the older girls commonly stayed home to help with the housework and the care of the younger children. Boys of any age were far more likely to work than girls." (Bettina Bradbury, "L'économie familiale et le travail" 295.)

11 In the nineteenth century, Bettina Bradbury observes, "finding a job for the children seemed to be a family responsibility. . . . It was apparently common for mothers to look for work for their sons and daughters and to act as an agent." (Bradbury, "L'économie familiale," 295). See also Denise Lemieux and Lucie Mercier, "Familles et destins féminins. Le prisme de la mémoire, 1880-1940," *Recherches sociographiques, La Famille de la Nouvelle-France à aujourd'hui* 28.2-3 (1987): 259-62.

12 Hiring by the family seems to have been especially frequent in the textile sector. In this regard, see Hareven, *Family Time;* Jacques Rouillard, *Ah, les États! Les travailleurs canadiens-français de l'industrie textile de la Nouvelle-Angleterre d'après le témoignage des derniers migrants* (Montreal: Boréal, 1985).

13 Piecework seems to have been especially common in Canada in the 1920s and 1930s (Strong-Boag, *New Day* 57-58).

14 According to David M. Katzman, the very word "servant" is in conflict with the democratic spirit of nineteenth-century America. [*Seven Days a Week: Women and Domestic Service in Industrializing America* (Chicago: University of Illinois Press, 1981) 238.]

15 Few of the informants broached the question of sexual harassment. One mentioned that the male workers "bothered them" sometimes. But with other people around, it was easier to defend yourself. "We put them in their place" (E1). The sexual segregation on the shop floor and as the workers entered and left the factory seems also to have contributed to a lessening of this problem. "There was one staircase at the back and another at the front for the men and the women" (E1). No one mentioned being subjected to sexual harassment on the part of a foreman.

16 Tamara Hareven also observes the same phenomenon. According to American statistics in 1923, boys gave 83 percent of their wages to their families while the girls gave 95 percent (*Family Time* 189).

17 It was on the basis of similar observations that the ladies of the Fédération nationale Saint-Jean-Baptiste decided to open a school to teach housekeeping. See Nicole Thivierge, *Écoles ménagères et instituts familiaux: une modèle féminin traditionnel* (Quebec: Institut québécois de recherche sur la culture, 1982) 122.

18 Training homemakers was the subject of a brief thesis during the 1940s. According to the author, women generally were badly trained, especially in nutrition and dressmaking, to fulfill their role (Madeleine Mercier, "Étude de la formation domestique de quinze mères de famille de Québec," MA thesis Université Laval, 1946). In this connection, also see Denise Lemieux, "La socialisation des filles dans la famille," Fahmy-Eid and Dumont: 237-61.

Chapter 3: Beyond Romance: Courtship and Marriage

1 In Montreal, the rate of marriage declined from 9.9 percent to 6.9 percent between 1929 and 1933 (Quebec: *Annuaire statistique* 1930 et 1934, 75, 80).

2 Two of the informants had saleswomen's jobs in a business near where their fiancés were working, another was working as a domestic in the home of her future sister-in-law, whereas only two couples were working in the same factory; the sexual division of the job market probably explains why few women met their husbands at work.

3 In her study of English working-class women between 1890 and 1940, based on oral histories, Elizabeth Roberts also reports evidence which stresses the importance of the walk as an opportunity for young people to socialize. This sort of activity was approved by adults, according to Roberts, because it takes place in public, thus permitting effective control to be exercised over the young. In working-class districts, it could also get round the cramped lodgings, where it was less easy to organize the social evenings which allowed young people to meet in rural areas. See Elizabeth Robbins, *A Woman's Place: An Oral History of Working-Class Women, 1890-1940* (Oxford: Blackwell, 1984) 72.

4 The suitors of three of the informants had cars when they were dating. Two of them, who were widowers, had inherited a small insurance payment which they had invested in buying an automobile; except for one of the widowers, who made his living driving a taxi, the other two sold their cars when they got married or when their first child was born.

5 In his study of the village of Saint Denis, Horace Miner describes this reality in these terms: "The girl is not obliged to marry any one of her suitors, but as she has no direct way of getting to know candidates, she must be happy with their initiative." [Horace Miner, *Saint-Denis: un village québécois* (Montreal: Hurtubise HMH (1985) 276.]

6 Lemieux and Mercier 136.

7 Ignorance of sexual matters, however, meant that, while worried about what their fiancés might do, the young women were not too sure what they were afraid of. The next chapter, on motherhood, will go into greater detail on this question.

8 Only one of these two women told me about her experience during the interview. In the other case, it came to my notice through a diary that the informant entrusted to me after the interview was over. This reluctance to broach the subject more than fifty years later conveys the disgrace which attached to the reputation of the "unwed mother." If there were two premarital pregnancies, we may suppose that a larger number of couples engaged in sexual relations before marriage without suffering the consequences. It is, however, difficult to ascertain how widespread such behaviour was, since it represents a transgression of moral standards, a phenomenon which is frequently kept hidden. We observe that the number of illegitimate births (that is, outside of marriage) for Quebec as a whole between the years 1929 and 1939 varied between 2,055 and 2,668 (Lévesque, *La Norme* 121).

9 That is, 28.9 years old for men and 25.4 for women in Quebec in 1930. [Canada, BFS, *Annuaire du Canada 1933* (Ottawa: King's Printer, 1933) 165.] Note that these averages are based on the age at first marriage while the sample includes three couples in which the men, aged respectively twenty-eight, thirty-two, and forty-three, were widowers.

10 "The average age of those married for the first time between 1905 and 1914 in Saint Brigide's parish was almost twenty-five for men and twenty-two for women." She notes as well that more than a third (35.2 percent) of the young women were minors when they married compared to only 13.3 percent of the young men (Ferretti 247).

11 Lemieux and Mercier, *Les Femmes,* 130.

12 These would be in place in the diocese of Montreal by the end of the 1930s (Lévesque, *La Norme* 52-53).

13 Elizabeth Roberts notes that English couples at the beginning of the century shared the same vision of marriage: "marriage was seen as a life-long working partnership, both husband and wife having different, clearly defined roles, both of which were critical for the well-being of each other and of any children. The man was seen as the basic wage-earner and the woman as the household manager with prime responsibility for rearing the children" (*A Woman's Place* 83).

14 According to a study carried out in the 1950s by Philippe Garigue, wives generally accepted the husband's authority if he fulfilled his duty as provider: "The role of the man as familial authority ... is ... the result of the recognition, especially on the part of women, that it is the "normal" role of the man to the degree that he fully carries out his responsibilities." [*La Vie familiale des Canadiens français* (Montreal: University of Montreal Press, 1970) 38.]

15 Blunden 33.

16 In fact, no law forbade all work to married women. In certain sectors, however, like teaching and the public service, a woman who married was deemed to have "resigned." See: Carolle Simard. *L'Administration contre les femmes* (Montreal: Boréal Express, 1983); Maryse Thivierge, "La syndicalisation des institutrices catholiques, 1900-1959, Fahmy-Eid and Dumont, 176. During the 1930s, a member of the legislature named Francoeur tried without success to have a law passed that would have seriously limited the hiring of women on the pretext that they created unemployment [Collectif Clio, *L'Histoire des femmes au Québec depuis quatre siècles* (Montreal: Quinze, 1982) 255]. The Confédération des travailleurs catholiques du Canada likewise adopted a resolution to this effect (Lavigne and Stoddart, "Ouvrières et travailleuses" 111).

17 Jacques Rouillard notes the same ignorance concerning the Church's disapproval of French-Canadian emigration to the United States (Rouillard 30-31).

18 We should recall that it was though the agency of the parish retreats and the confessional that the Church disseminated its message regarding contraception and that this position was reinforced by the medical profession. According to Church rule, violating this prohibition was a grave, that is, mortal sin, one that had to be confessed, of the same degree of seriousness as murder or theft. Regarding the confessional as a means of controlling female sexuality, see Eli Zaretsky, "Female Sexuality and the Catholic Confessional," *Signs* 6.1 (1980): 176-84.

19 According to Lavigne and Stoddart, in 1931, 12 percent of the working women in Montreal were widows or married, while 87.7 percent were unmarried ("Ouvrières et travailleuses," 392, n.4). These examples of women's hiding their matrimonial status in order to work are a good illustration of the strategies of resistance to the confinement to the domestic sphere that was imposed on women.

20 Strong-Boag, *New Day* 95.

21 In Saint Brigide's parish at the beginning of the century, this group gave the bride a crown to wear at her wedding; in return, the bride offered her bouquet to adorn the Lady Altar. For other advantages enjoyed by Children of Mary at their weddings, see Ferretti 249.

22 In the Quebec City region, couples made several round trips on the Lévis ferry (Lemieux and Mercier, *Les Femmes* 164).

23 Agnès Fine, "À propos du trousseau: une culture féminine?" *Histoire des femmes*, Perrot, ed.: 155-89. A study of marriage contracts in southwest France between the sixteenth and twentieth centuries and the use of oral sources for the more recent period enable her to demonstrate that the trousseau was a very old and widespread tradition, one that at first was a legal obligation before being transformed into a moral one.

24 Fine 165, 168.

25 The study of marriage contracts in France shows that at a certain period, the wedding dress, generally black, formed part of the trousseau (Fine 165).

26 Two exceptions must be noted: the husband of one of the informants, a laboratory technician in an oil company, had accumulated around one thousand dollars in stocks offered

by the company as a bonus; another, employed by a railway company, had more than three hundred dollars in his account.

27 As we have already seen, three of them were given it by their parents, while a fourth, who boarded with family friends, had her own furniture.

28 Appendix D contains a complete description, with prices, of good quality furniture bought for cash by one of the couples in the sample.

29 Households comprised of two families represented 4.1 percent and 6.4 percent of all households in Verdun and Montreal respectively in 1931 and 4.9 percent and 6.3 percent in 1941 (Canada, *Recensement du Canada* vol. 5, 998-91; and *Recensement du Canada 1941*, vol. 5, 102-103, 106-107). Certainly the census figures provide a snapshot of a population in a given period of time. In fact, the sample supports the idea that a higher percentage of young couples lived with one or the other of their parents, most often with the husband's family, in the early months of their marriage.

30 Feretti 250.

Chapter 4: Motherhood

1 In the second chapter of *La Norme et les Déviantes*, Andrée Lévesque provides an excellent overview of the medical and clerical discourse on the subject of motherhood (Lévesque 25-59).

2 An expression used by 'Fadette," (Henriette Dessaulles) in a paper entitled, "L'éducation familiale," presented during the "Semaines Sociales du Canada" (*Semaine sociale du Canada*, 4th session, *La Famille*) (Montreal: Bibliothèque de l'Action française, 1923: 290).

3 Dr. Gaston Lapierre, "La limitation des naissances et les lois de stérilisation," *Annales médico-chirurgicales de l'hôpital Sainte-Justine*, 2.2 (1935) quoted in Lévesque, *La Norme* 31.

4 In his study of Saint-Denis, Horace Miner notes also that parents usually kept young children away from this sort of "show" (Miner 271-72).

5 Elizabeth Roberts remarks correctly that this ignorance, which she also observed, is practically a miracle when we take into account the crowded living conditions of the English working class at the beginning of the century (Roberts 16). The same remark applies to working-class Quebec families whose children often shared the same room, if not the same bed. Even if they were separated according to sex, it is amazing that this crowding did not facilitate a knowledge of the anatomy of the opposite sex. Even if the fear of sin was enough to stifle a perfectly natural curiosity, unquestionably the mother had to expend boundless ingenuity in seeing to it that everyone dressed and undressed, washed and slept, while respecting very strict rules regarding modesty at all times. The works denouncing cramped worker's lodgings make frequent reference to the moral dangers they represented, in order to alert families: "There the family loses its privacy and becomes depraved, the innate sense of dignity of the children withers and fades, modesty is destroyed, and decency and virtue are so outrageously offended that they yield to vice," writes Thomas Watson, health inspector-in-chief of Saskatchewan (Cited in J.A.Beaudoin, "La famille et l'habitation," *Semaine sociale* 4th session: 103).

6 According to Denise Lemieux and Lucie Mercier, the term "to buy," used in this sense, refers to the visit of the "Indians," who would leave the mother a baby which she had to accept, even buy (*Les Femmes au tournant du siècle* 195).

7 Elizabeth Roberts has observed the same phenomenon: "for some women, the most admired men seem to have been those who 'indulged' themselves the least" (*A Woman's Place* 84).

8 According to Jacques Henripin, French-Canadian couples in Montreal did not begin to control their fertility before 1925. The use of contraceptive methods became more common after a certain number of children had been born and when the wife was over thirty ["From Acceptance of Nature to Control: The Demography of the French-Canadians Since the Seventeenth Century," *French-Canadian Society*, vol. 1, ed. Marcel Rioux and Yves Martin (Toronto: McClelland and Stewart, 1964) 204-16]. Veronica Strong-Boag also stresses that the fertility rate of Canadians between the ages of thirty and thirty-four fell by 20 percent between 1921 and 1931 and fell a further 18.7 percent during the following decade. Between the ages of thirty-five and thirty-nine, the reduction was nineteen percent and 25.1 percent and 23.9 percent and 30.6 percent for those between forty and forty-four (*New Day* 147).

9 The 1930s nevertheless was marked by a reduction in the birthrate from 29.9 percent in 1929 to 25.1 percent in 1939 while the overall fertility index dropped from 4.09 to 3.28 during the same period [Suzanne Messier, *Les Femmes, ça compte. Profil socio-économique des Québécoises* (Quebec: Éditeur officiel, 1984) 172-73]. This reduction is attributable in part to a lower rate of marriage.

10 In a study carried out in the 1960s, Colette Carisse noted that there was "no direct link between the number of children in the families from which they came and the number of children they wanted, expected to have, or thought was ideal" but that "the fact of coming from a large family had a negative influence on the spouse's attachment to this cultural model [of a large family]" [Colette Carisse, *Planification des naissances en milieu canadien-français* (Montreal: University of Montreal Press, 1964) 118].

11 These were the methods in most general use throughout Canada. According to Agnus McLaren and Arlene Tigar McLaren, the lower birthrate registered in the 1920s and 1930s is due not to the dissemination of new forms of birth control, like that based on the calculation of the menstrual cycle, which had been worked out in the 1920s, but on a wider use of traditional methods [*The Bedroom and the State: The Changing Practices and Politics of Contraception and Abortion in Canada, 1880-1980* (Toronto: McClelland and Stewart, 1986) 22].

12 The Roman Catholic Church accepted this form of family limitation during the 1930s as it involved abstinence (Lévesque, *La Norme* 31).

13 Thirteen of the twenty-eight fertile women had miscarriages, four of them more than five.

14 See, for example, "La mère et l'enfant," *La Patrie* 20 Mar. 1926.

15 In the course of a study carried out in 1970 among married women between the ages of fifteen and sixty-five, Colette Carisse discovered that 47.9 percent of 720 women born between 1905 and 1935 answering the question approved of birth control and 40.8 percent admitted to having used contraceptive methods, while 9.5 percent either did not answer or refused to answer the question [*La Famille: mythe et réalité*, vol. 1. Report submitted to the Conseil des Affaires sociale et de la Famille (Quebec: Éditeur officiel, 1979): 79-80].

16 In her study carried out at the beginning of the 1960s, Colette Carisse noted that a family was not considered large until it contained at least five or even six or seven children (*Planification* 57).

17 According to Évelyne Lapierre-Adamcyk the period of family composition (that is, the

time elapsing between the birth of the first child and that of the last) dropped from twenty years to nine between the seventeenth and twentieth centuries. (Nine of the twenty-eight informants who had children took close to twenty years to complete their families.) In contrast, the period called "parental," that is, the years separating the birth of the first child from the departure of the last only diminished by four years, dropping from forty to thirty-six years in the course of the same period ["Le cycle de la vie familiale au Québec: vues comparatives XVIIᵉ—XX ᵉ siècles," *Cahiers québécois de démographie* 13.1 (1984): 59-76].

18 In this connection, see Lavigne, "Réflexions féministes"; Henripin and Peron, "La transition," 40. As a matter of information, let us stress that, according to the latter, married women whose mother-tongue was French and who were between the ages of fifty-five and fifty-nine in 1961 had 5.06 children on average (live births) for both rural and urban areas and 4.33 children, if only the metropolitan areas are counted.

19 In 1922, the infant mortality rate rose to 213 per thousand in the working-class districts of Montreal, went to 133.7 and then to 59.3 per thousand between 1928 and 1940 (Copp, "Health of People," 129).

20 In Quebec City, for example, in 1922 the company had issued 80,000 life insurance policies for a population of 100,000. The visiting nurse service, first begun in the United States as an experiment, met with such a success that the company decided to extend it to the whole of North America. Again in 1922, Metropolitan nurses had visited 11,472 new mothers in Greater Montreal. Additionally, this company published numerous pamphlets on the precautions to take to avoid deadly diseases like tuberculosis or more simple contagions and how to treat them. In the area of child care, the company published the first edition in 1922 of a book successively entitled *The Child*, then *The Baby*, and *Your Baby*. By 1945, there would be 31,872,000 copies in circulation in a number of languages. In a book published in 1947 on the history of the company, the author makes no bones about bluntly declaring the company's motives, "Healthy people live longer and pay more premiums than sick people do." See James Marquis, *The Metropolitan Life: A Study in Business Growth* (New York: Viking, 1947) 188, as well as The Metropolitan Life Insurance Company, *Report on Industrial Insurance*, Dec. 1921 and *More than a Century of Health and Safety Education*, Health and Safety Education Division. I was able to consult these publications in the company's uncatalogued archives thanks to the kindness of the present archivist, Mr Michel Barsalou. Additionally, see Mme L.-E. Warren, "Comment venir en aide aux mères de familles," *La Bonne Parole* 10.7-8 (1922): 6-7.

21 J.-E. Dubé, "Les débuts de la lutte contre la mortalité infantile à Montréal, Fondation de la première *Goutte de Lait*," *Union Médicale du Canada* 65 (1936): 879-91, 986-93, 1088-1102.

22 The functioning of this organization and the services it offered are described in "L'Assistance Maternelle," *La Bonne Parole* 10.5 (1922): 4.

23 *La Presse* 8 April 1925.

24 *La Patrie* 20 Feb. 1934.

25 Hélène Laforce, *Histoire de la sage-femme dans la région de Québec* (Quebec: Institut québécois de recherche sur la culture 4, 1985) 111.

26 J. Jill Suitor, "Husbands' Participation in Childbirth: A Nineteenth Century Phenomenon," *Journal of Family History* 6.3 (1981): 278-93.

27 The percentage of hospital births went from 4.8 percent in 1926 to 15.6 in 1940 to 32.2 in 1945, more than doubling during the Second World War. In 1955, by which almost all of the

women in this study had completed their families, it was 66.6 percent [France Laurendeau, "La médicalisation de l'accouchement," *Recherches sociographiques* 24.2 (1983): 205].

28 Many articles on the women's pages of *La Patrie* encouraged women to breast-feed and made a direct connection between the practice and the rate of infant mortality. See for example, "La majorité des maladies infantiles sont évitables," (The majority of childhood illnesses are preventable) (*La Patrie* 23 May 1921, 25). According to Dr Joseph Gauvreau, "infant mortality is the direct result of the breast-feeding strike" and "the mother who places her child . . . in this all too evident danger of death [is guilty]" if her dereliction of duty is voluntary and conscious." He did recognize, however, that breast-feeding "is a bondage beloved by mothers whose hearts are in the right place" ("La mortalité infantile," *Semaine sociale du Canada*, fourth session, 162, 171).

29 According to Carole Dion, the well-baby clinics only contained a limited amount of equipment; a baby scale, a ruled board to measure the babies with, a clinical thermometer, and some tongue depressors ("Les femmes et la santé de la famille au Québec 1890-1914," Master's thesis, University of Montreal, 1984, 149).

30 For a description of the care provided by the midwife, see the oral histories reported by Miner, 231-34.

31 According to demographers, in fact, 10 percent of couples are sterile. See Charles Enid, *The Changing Size of the Family in Canada*, Canada DBS *Canada Census 1941* (Ottawa: King's Printer, 1948) 37ff.

Chapter 5: Working for Pay and Managing the Household Finances

1 The average family, used as a point of reference to establish the minimum budget necessary to support a working-class family, generally comprises five persons: two adults and three children, a composition that does not correspond to the reality of every family. For a discussion of wages before the Great Depression see Copp, *Classe ouvrière* 149-63 and the publication of the Federal Ministry of Labour: *La Gazette du Travail et Salaires et Heures de travail au Canada*.

2 Marsh 345-46.

3 Quebec, *Annuaire statistique du Québec*, 1930, 1934: 400, 426; *La Gazette du Travail*, Canada, ministère du Travail, Feb. 1933, 249.

4 Lévesque, *Virage* 22.

5 According to a study carried out in 1935, eighty-five percent of the population of Montreal was dependent on an income of less than $1250 a year (around twenty-four dollars a week) and fifty percent on an income of less than $850 (about sixteen dollars a week) (Montreal Board of Trade, *Housing and Slum Clearance for Montreal*, cited in Lévesque, *Virage* 22).

6 Montreal Unemployment Relief Commission, *Renseignements à l'usage des chômeurs nécessiteux et des propriétaires*, n.d.10-11. In other directives issued in 1937, the amounts went to $8.51 a week in summer and $9.11 in winter, always for a family of five.

7 Investigations into workers' wages carried out by government agencies and charities obviously did not take into account the money that derived from these activities as well as the savings produced by the domestic labour of housewives. See Martha May, "The 'Good Manager': Married Working-Class Women and Family Budget Studies, 1885-1915," *Labour History* 25 (1984): 351-72.

8 Bettina Bradbury, "Women's History and Working-Class History," *Labour/Le Travail* 19 (1987): 38.

9 We have virtually no data on the incidence of men working two jobs before the Second World War. In the 1950s, Fortin and Tremblay state that 18.4 percent of the heads of households in their sample had a second job (72).

10 It should be noted that it was not prohibited to earn a little money while receiving aid from Saint Vincent de Paul, since the society provided only food or food vouchers but did not pay for rent or other expenses. According to the rules laid down by the Unemployment Relief commission of Montreal, the head of the family and his wife could earn up to three dollars a week each without losing their benefits. Still, the commission deducted 50 percent of the income derived from renting rooms from the relief payment, even if this income did not exceed three dollars a week (*Renseignements à l'usage* 6).

11 Unlike boarders, roomers only got a place to stay; they had to take their meals elsewhere and do their own washing, though not all the boarders automatically had their laundry done for them.

12 A.J. Pelletier, F.D. Thompson and A. Rochon, *La Famille canadienne, Recensement du Canada 1931* 12 (Ottawa: King's Printer, 1942) 69. Bettina Bradbury likewise notes that in nineteenth-century Montreal, the poorest familes were more likely to live with other families than to take in boarders, whereas the property-owning and professional families, perhaps influenced by the ideology of the home, were less and less involved in this activity. (Bradbury, "Pigs, Cows, and Boarders": 33-35). For a discussion of the decline in this practice among the middle class in the United States in the nineteenth century, see John Modell and Tamara Hareven, "Urbanization and the Malleable Household: An Examination of Boarding and Lodging in American Families," *Journal of Marriage and the Family* (1973): 467-79. This article notes that the Depression temporarily reversed the tendency, observed in all social classes, to cease taking in boarders, in the United States at least.

13 We must emphasize that the Depression involved an increase in the proportion of women working in the personal service sector where domestics are classified. In Montreal, for example, 20.2 percent of female labour was listed in this sector in 1921, compared to 29.3 percent in 1931 and 26.9 percent in 1941 (Lavigne and Stoddart, "Ouvrières et travailleuses" 101). These census figures do not always permit us to establish what proportion of them were married.

14 The observations only confirm the theories about the invisibility of married women's work that several scholars with an interest in paid female labour have advanced. See for example, Bettina Bradbury, "L'economie familiale;" Suzanne D. Cross, "La majorité oubliée: le rôle des femmes de Montréal au 19e siècle;" Lavigne and Pinard 99-114; Lavigne and Stoddart, "Ouvrières et travailleuses"; Strong-Boag, *New Day* 41-71.

15 In this regard, see Roberts 229.

16 In fact, this informant had taught for a year before getting married, but she did not seem to consider this a real job.

17 That is, as a daily cleaning woman.

18 Concerning the impossibility of reversing these roles during the Depression, see Mirra Komorovsky, *The Unemployed Man and His Family* (New York: Arno, 1971); Ruth Milkmann, "Women's Work and Economic Crisis: Some Lessons of the Great Depression," *Review of Radical Political Economics* 8 (1976): 85.

19 Meg Luxton, *More than a Labor of Love: Three Generations of Women's Work in the Home* (Toronto: Women's Press, 1980) 161-99; Strong-Boag, *New Day* 133-44; Roberts 125-68; Pat Ayers and Jan Lambertz, "Marriage Relations, Money, and Domestic Violence in Working-Class Liverpool, 1919-39," in Lewis 195-219.

20 Ayers and Lambert 197.

21 Jennifer Stoddart, "Quand des gens de robe se penchent sur les droits des femmes: le cas de la commission Dorion 1929-1931," in Lavigne and Pinard 321.

22 This statement must, however, be qualified as three informants intervened to find work for their husbands while another called her husband's boss to get him a raise.

23 Philippe Garigue also observed that women did not feel that they had more authority, even when they controlled the purse strings (*La Vie familiale* 38).

24 Andrée Fortin, for example, states, "It may well be said that this administrative power is not large, managing poverty not being a secure job; one notes that "queen of the home" is not merely a symbolic title—she is the regent and the steward" ["La famille ouvrière d'autrefois," *Recherches sociographiques, La Famille de la Nouvelle-France à aujourd'hui* 28. 2-3 (1987): 283].

25 Quebec, *Annuaire statistique du Québec*, 1930 and 1934, 400 and 426. According to a federal study in 1938, francophone families in Montreal devoted on average 34 percent of their budget to this expenditure [Canada, BFS, *Family income and Expenditure in Canada: A Study of Urban Wage-Earner Families, Including Data on Physical Attributes* (Ottawa: King's Printer, 1941) 26].

26 The study undertaken in 1938 also looked into consumption habits regarding foodstuffs noted that, compared to the sample as a whole, among French-Canadian families in Quebec, "Purchases per person . . . were noticeably above the average for meat, white bread, potatoes, canned fruit, and bananas. They were below the average for brown bread, cheese, milk, and oranges" (Canada BFS 54). We should note that it was rare that wages would permit buying in bulk; in any event, cramped quarters hardly encouraged the storage of provisions.

27 Roberts, "Women's Strategies": 223.

28 Strong-Boag, *New Day* 137.

Chapter 6: Housework

1 Danielle Chabaud-Rychter, Dominique Fougeyrollas-Schwebel and Françoise Sonthonax, *Espace et temps du travail domestique* (Paris: Librairie des Méridiens, 1985) 23.

2 According to data provided by a plant situated in one of the districts surveyed about housing in 1937 by the city, the majority of the workers lived a short distance from the factory, to which they could easily walk. Indeed, 1201 of the 1382 male and female workers lived less than two miles away (Bélanger et al. 18). The large number of retail business is a good indication of their accessibility. Thus in 1930 in Montreal there were 2180 groceries, 665 combination grocery and butcher shops, and 391 butcher shops for a population of 818,577 inhabitants, or one retail food business for every 253 residents In 1941, this proportion was one business for every 293 residents [Canada, *Recensement du Canada 1931* vol.11, 213 and *Recensement du Canada 1941*, vol. 10, 21; Gérald Bernier and Robert Boily, *Le Québec en chiffres de 1850 à nos jours* (Montréal: ACFAS, Coll. Politique et économie, 1986) 56].

3 This kind of housing existed well into the 1930s. Out of the 4216 workers' homes that were visited during the municipal inquiry of 1936-37, they accounted for 379, or 8.9 percent of the total. Furthermore, some of the women interviewed had lived in them (Bélanger 9).

4 Lyse Pelletier, "Au sujet des espaces féminisés," *Cahiers de géographie du Québec* 31.83: 177-88; Anne-Marie Séguin, "Madame Ford et l'espace: lecture féministe de la surburbanisation," *Lieux et milieux de vie. Recherches féministes* 2.1: 51-68.

5 At the beginning of the thirties, more than half of the informants were paying less than fifteen dollars a month in rent for a four-room flat. According to *La Gazette du Travail*, a six-room flat without modern facilities or with some of them absent would cost, in Montreal, from sixteen to twenty-five dollars a month in 1929 and from fifteen to eighteen dollars a month in 1933 (Canada, Minister of Labour, *La Gazette du Travail* Feb. 1929, 256 and Feb. 1933, 257).

6 Appendix E presents some of the floor plans taken from the municipal inquiry of 1937.

7 In 1941, 51.5 percent of Montreal flats were heated exclusively by a stove, which was the case for almost every flat visited in 1937 during the course of the municipal inquiry carried out in seven working-class districts of Montreal (Canada, *Recensement du Canada, 1941* 5, 54, and Bélanger 11).

8 The municipal inquiry of 1936-37 noted that in the 4216 lodgings visited, only 1716 had a completely separate toilet; in 1431 cases, it had been added to a corner of the kitchen, in 112 cases in the parlour, in 536, in a bedroom, and in 239, in the hallway (Bélanger 12). The floor plans in Appendix E, taken from the report, demonstrate these additions well.

9 Strong-Boag, "Keeping House," 132.

10 According to the 1937 municipal inquiry, 91.5 percent of the lodgings surveyed had softwood floors (Bélanger 10).

11 In another connection, this crowding reminds us that the poorest classes do not have the benefit of any sort of privacy: "room is lacking to provide a private space for each member of the group—private space is thus only the public space of the domestic group," (Antoine Prost, "La famille et l'individu," *Prost and Gérard* 72).

12 This saying reminds us that working-class families in this period did not carry fire insurance. Mentioned in "Housing," a column by Louise in *La Patrie*, 13 Feb. 1932: 14 and in a talk by Mme Louis-F. Coderre on "The Home" for the *Semaine sociale du Canada* Fifth Session, *La Propriété* (Montreal: Bibliothèque de l'Action française 1924: 146). According to Mme Coderre, "A principal way of saving money is to have a steady place of residence, or in other words, to avoid moving house."

13 The number of relocations in Montreal was in fact constantly on the rise during the first years of the Depression: 54,000 in 1930, 55,000 in 1931, 65,000 in 1932, and almost 82,000 in 1933 according to data furnished by Montreal Light, Heat and Power (*La Patrie*, 17 Apr 1931:7 and 17 Apr 1933: 3). Moreover, the economic situation meant that most of these families were looking for less expensive accommodations. Thus during the Depression, the best flats remained vacant while an overpopulation was noted in the old housing. In this connection, see Marc Choko, *Les Crises du logement à Montréal* (Montreal: Éditions Saint-Martin, 1980) 109.

14 One couple made major renovations thanks to a government renovation scheme. Unfortunately, the informant could not say exactly what this consisted of since her husband took care of the family finances. According to what she could recall, he would send the bills for the materials to the bank which would deduct the amount from his mortgage.

15 In the forties and fifties, three other couples became owners of houses in Montreal, one through inheritance, three went back to the countryside to live where they bought or built a house, and four would come to own a summer cottage.

16 Canada, *Recensement du Canada 1931 et 1941* 5: 989 and 11: 98, cited in Choko 114.

17 Thus the number of permits issued by the city of Montreal for domestic renovation and construction went from 5755 in 1929 to 2196 in 1933, later to rise to 2981 in 1939. Construction of new houses was the most affected as the permits declined from 4116 to 875

between 1929 and 1933 (from 1639 to 1321 for renovation). Moreover, a number of houses in the working-class areas was destroyed during this period to permit the building of public facilities or work on the infrastructure—the Atwater market, the Jacques Cartier Bridge, and so on (Montreal construction statistics cited by Choko, 107 and 146).

18 Margaret Hobbes and Ruth Roach Pierson, "A Kitchen that Wastes No Steps: Gender, Class and the Home Improvement Plan 1936-40," *Histoire sociale/Social History* 21.41 (1988): 34.

19 Susan Strasser, "An Enlarged Human Existence? Technology and Housework in Nineteenth-Century America," *Women and Household Labor*, ed. Sara Fenstermaker-Berk (London: Sage, 1980) 29-51, cited in Diane Bélisle and Yolande Pinard, "Un peu d'histoire," in Vandelac 90, 120; Jessie Bernard, *The Female World (New York: The Free Press, 1981)* n.1 409.

20 Appendix F includes a table showing the proportion of Montreal (or Quebec) households that enjoyed various conveniences or domestic equipment at different periods between 1931 and 1958.

21 The item that the Woodhouse store advertised as "the famous Fisher electric icebox" retailed for between $225 and $736, depending on the model, in 1930 (*La Patrie* 1 March 1930: 37).

22 The tubs of these machines had to be agitated by a wooden handle.

23 Only four owned a washing machine when they married. Seven had to wait between one and two years, four between two and three years, eight between three and five years, and seven for more than five years. These figures do not take into account the period of shared accommodations, when the bride might have been able to take advantage of her mother's or mother-in-law's machine.

24 Elizabeth Roberts recalls that the sewing machine was for a long period the only technological innovation possessed by working-class families ("Women's Strategies," 232).

25 Other items, like laundry baskets, stepladders, washtubs and wash benches were also offered, which would seem to imply that the merchants knew that women continued to do some laundry by hand even after they bought a machine. See, for example, the ad for Beatty's in *La Presse* 31 October 1930: 27.

26 In 1941, 17.7 percent of Montreal households used wood or coal for cooking and only 8.2 percent in 1951. There are no figures for this subject in the 1931 census. On the other hand, the municipal inquiry of 1937 concluded that almost all the housing visited was heated only by a stove and that in 68.6 percent of these cases, either wood or coal was used as fuel (Bélanger 11).

27 Montreal Light, Heat and Power exercised a virtual monopoly in the Montreal region which allowed it to maintain high rates and to disconnect customers who did not pay their bills with impunity. According to Robert Rumilly, more that 20,000 families were deprived of electricity in the depths of the Depression [Robert Rumilly, *Histoire de Montréal* (Fides, 1974) cited in Claude Larivière, *Crise économique et contrôle social: le cas de Montréal 1929-1937* (Montreal: Éditions Saint-Martin, 1977) 175].

28 P.A. Linteau et al. *Histoire du Québec contemporain* vol. 2: *Le Québec depuis 1930* (Montreal: Boréal Compact, 1989) 41.

29 A number of others have already observed this phenomenon in English Canada and in the United States. See Strong-Boag, *New Day* 50; Komorovsky 28-130.

30 According to Maïté Clavel, "Contrary to those societies which allowed them space, industrialized societies, excluded dirt, the buried, the hidden. Only what was clean was

valued, promoted, and celebrated . . . the current value attributed to cleanliness for its own sake would date from the seventeenth century" ["Propreté: mots, rites, images," *Cahiers internationaux de sociologie. Le détour anthropologique féminin-masculin* 80 (1986): 43].

31 Coderre, 139-51.

32 Lemieux and Mercier 282.

33 Several authors who have studied the evolution of domestic labour have often associated the increase in frequency of certain household tasks, like laundry, with the appearance of more sophisticated machinery. In this regard, see Bélisle and Pinard, 91 and 125; Bernard 395 and n.4, 410; Ruth Schwartz Cowan, "The 'Industrial Revolution' in the Home: Household Technology and Social Change in the 20th Century," *Technology and Culture* 17 (1976): n.10, 5.

34 The number of commercial laundries, moreover, would diminish. In 1931, there were 358 laundries in Montreal and eighteen in Verdun; in 1941, their number had shrunk respectively to 308 (of which 262 were classified as "Chinese laundries") and eleven, while in 1951, there were 185 Chinese laundries in Montreal (seven in Verdun) and ten "hand laundries" (Verdun: six), twenty-six machine laundries (Verdun: 1) and twenty laundries where women could do their own wash (Verdun: 2). These self-service laundries had begun to appear in the 1940s [Canada: *Recensement du Canada 1931* 11: 206; *Recensement du Canada 1941* 11: 462, 482 and *Recensement du Canada 1951* 8: 22-14, 22-15 and 22-41, 22-42. For Chinese laundries in Montreal, see Denise Helly, *Les Chinois à Montréal 1877-1951* (Quebec: Institut québécois de recherche sur la culture, 1987)].

35 As Ruth Schwartz Cowan has observed: "Studies of energy expenditure during housework have indicated that by far the greatest effort is expended in hauling and lifting the wet wash, tasks which were not eliminated by the introduction of washing machines" ("Industrial Revolution," n.10, 5). These operations were not without their risks. Newspapers of the period frequently carried stories about children who were scalded when they tipped a washtub over on themselves. In the months of November and December 1929 alone, *La Patrie* reported five accidents of this kind (*La Patrie* 20, 23 Nov. 1929: 3, 11, 24; Dec. 1929: 1 and 26 Dec. 1929: 23). Moreover, one of the families in the sample experienced a similar accident.

36 According to Keith Walden, the Toronto-based *Canadian Grocer*, a weekly trade journal, recommended clearly visible price tags on products " 'Nowadays, every well-informed grocer makes it a point to have everything marked.' This would avoid the embarrassment to customers who would have to ask the shopkeeper for the price, which might turn out to be too expensive" (Keith Walden, "Speaking Modern: Language, Culture and Hegemony in Grocery Window Displays, 1887-1920," paper presented to the Congress of the Historical Society of Canada, Quebec, June 1989: 10).

37 According to Ruth Schwartz Cowan, delivery services began to disappear in the United States during the 1930s, due to the rise of the automobile and to the ferocious competition among retailers trying to capture the market. This led to their cutting back their costs of operation in order to lower their prices. [*More Work for Mother: The Ironies of Household Technology from the Open Hearth to the Microwave* (New York: Basic Books, 1983) 79-85]. The compulsory school attendance of the children who did this sort of work was probably also responsible. According to the oral histories, it was not until the 1940s, in any event, that delivery services began to disappear in Montreal, which coincided with the application of the school attendance law of 1943. In this regard, see Dominique Jean,

"Familles québécoises et politiques sociales touchant les enfants de 1940 à 1960: obligation scolaire, allocations familiales et travail juvénile," diss. University of Montreal. 1989.

38 Compared to men, women always occupy more reduced space. After retirement, for example, men no longer go to work but start doing the shopping while their wives will become more sedentary, saving even on movements: "everything proceeds as if the social space assigned to women, a space delimited by housework, should be further reduced by age in order to retain its separation from masculine space" (Chabaud-Rychter 82).

39 The informants rarely mentioned remaking their own clothes, probably because they had very few of them and they wore them to shreds.

40 These figures are probably not correct—according to other informants who bought from the abattoir, this amount of meat would cost more like two or three dollars.

41 In this period, most shops stayed open until eleven o'clock on Saturday night.

Chapter 7: State, Family, Neighbours, and Credit

1 B.L. Vigod, "Ideology and Institutions in Quebec: The Public Charities Controversy, 1921-1926." *Histoire sociale/Social History* 11.21 (1978): 167-82; Huguette Lapointe-Roy, *Charité bien ordonnée. Le premier réseau de lutte contre la pauvreté à Montréal au 19e siècle* (Montreal: Boréal, 1987).

2 Copp, *Classe ouvrière* 117.

3 Struthers; Michel Pelletier and Yves Vaillancourt, *Les Politiques sociales et les Travailleurs.* Cahier 2: *Les années 30* (Montreal: Yves Vaillancourt, 1975).

4 Montreal, *Rapport de la Commission d'enquête du chômage*, 1937.

5 Thus, according to Robert Rumilly, the priest of the parish of the Nativity, Mgr. Lepailleur, required the unemployed to attend Benediction Friday evenings before receiving their vouchers [*La Plus Riche Aumône* (Montreal: Éditions de l'Arbre, 1946) 156-57].

6 Regarding the administration of direct relief in Montreal, see June MacPherson, " 'Brother, Can You Spare a Dime?' The Administration of Unemployment Relief in the City of Montreal 1931-1941," Master's thesis, Concordia University, 1976 13ff; *Rapport de la Commission d'enquête du chômage.*

7 Appendix C provides a list of rations allocated to families according to size.

8 Dorothy King, "Unemployment Aid (Direct Relief)," *Canada's Unemployment Problem*, ed. L. Richter (Toronto: Macmillan, 1939): 80-84; *Renseignements à l'usage des chômeurs.*

9 According to the Unemployment Commission report, the voucher system required city clerks to handle more than 200,000 documents a week. In 1935, the commission distributed 40,000 cheques a week to the unemployed and 17,000 cheques each month to landlords (*Commission d'enquête du chômage* 3; MacPherson, 19).

10 Suzanne Clavette, "Aide aux chômeurs et Crise des années trente à Verdun," paper presented to the Canadian Historical Society, June 1989: 10-17.

11 The amount allotted monthly for food for a family of five went to $23.22 compared with $21.88 in Montreal (Suzanne Clavette, "Des bons aux chèques: aide aux chômeurs et Crise des années 30 à Verdun," Master's thesis, University of Quebec at Montreal Press, 1986, 344).

12 Clavette, "Des bons" 20.

13 For all of Quebec, 15.6 million dollars were allocated to public works in 1931-32, which dropped to 6.5 million the following year and to 1.4 million in 1935-36. In 1938-39, the amount rose to 26.4 million (Pelletier and Vaillancourt, 199; 201).

14 According to the regulations laid down by the city of Montreal, "every head of the family capable of work but unable to find a job [was] considered as a needy person, eligible for direct relief" (*Renseignements à l'usage des chômeurs*, 1).

15 *Renseignements à l'usage des chômeurs*, 6.

16 As has already been said, households turned spontaneously to Saint Vincent de Paul for aid. Subsequently, the municipality made use of the newspapers to publicize its instructions and conditions of eligibility; the information was also spread by word of mouth.

17 MacPherson 63-64.

18 This expression encompassed those who were destitute because of circumstances beyond their control in order to distinguish them from those deemed chronically unemployed, lazy, or drunk.

19 In 1931, the minutes of a meeting of the Advisory Commission on Unemployment determined that of the 22,923 unemployed men and women duly registered in the several city offices during the week of 6 December 1930, 483 cases of fraud had been reported, or 2.1%. In 1937, when the city had 47,000 on its rolls in February and 36,700 in May, the Commission of Inquiry into Unemployment reported three hundred cases of fraud a week. Even according to the report, 50 percent of the "fraud cases" were in fact "charity cases," that is, persons who were receiving direct relief when they should have been requesting help from private charitable organizations because they were unfit to work. Cases of common-law couples, which did not represent financial fraud, constituted another 5 percent. The other cases divided as follows: the idle and the chronically unemployed: 10 percent; irregular cases: 15 percent; cases of fraud: 15 percent (the final 5 percent is not accounted for in the report). The average amount claimed fraudulently was established to be $10.84 for the year 1937 (Minutes of the meeting of the Advisory Commission on Unemployment, 18 Jan. 1931; *Commission d'enquête du chômage*, 12, 16, 33, 37).

20 In November 1932, the provincial government established the following list of acceptable products: beef (forequarter), salt pork, pigs' feet and heads, macaroni and noodles, milk, eggs, flour, buckwheat flour, cornmeal, oatmeal, Quebec-grown fruit, bread, potatoes, peas and beans by the pound, pepper, salt, lard, butter, baking powder, tea, coffee, molasses, sugar, Quebec vegetables, fish, vinegar, rice, and yeast (Clavette, Appendix C).

21 This cannot refer to Hydro-Québec, which was yet to be established.

22 "Les travaux de chômage," *Le Devoir* 27 Jan. 1932: 7, cited in Larivière, 236.

23 The number of jobs available at municipal yards went from a peak of 16,000 in March 1931 to 5,000 in July 1933, while on 26 July in that year, the city registered 64,000 unemployed ("Du travail à 16,000 hommes," *Le Devoir* 12 March 1933:3; "La Commission de chômage," *Le Devoir* 26 July 1933: 3). According to Claude Larivière's calculations, "except in 1931, never more than 15 to 20 percent of Montreal's unemployed had work on public projects and these percentages fall even lower if we take into account only the number of full-time jobs (236).

24 After 1933, the practice having the unemployed register with the aldermen's secretaries gave rise to such accusations of patronage (Larivière 228).

25 See Ruth Shonle Cavan and Katherine Howland Rock, *The Family and the Depression: A Study of One Hundred Chicago Families* (1938; New York: Arno Press and The New York Times, 1971). Mirra Komarovsky in particular notes that the loss of his role as breadwinner did not lead to a loss of status within the family for the husband except where the wife was already harbouring feelings of deep dissatisfaction toward him:

"Unemployment does not so much change the sentiments of the wife towards the husband as it makes explicit the unsatisfactory sentiments that already existed prior to the depression." Wives who accepted their husbands' authority solely on the grounds of his role as provider or whose relationship with their spouses was founded on fear were the ones most susceptible to losing all respect for their mates. In contrast, husbands who were able to maintain their authority despite their loss of status as a provider were able to do so due to the love and support of their wives (Komarovsky 54).

26 Hareven, "Les grands thèmes," 191.

27 Marc-Adélard Tremblay, "La Crise économique des années trente et la qualité de vie chez les Montréalais d'ascendance française," *Travaux et Communications* 3, *Progrès techniques et qualité de vie* (Montreal: Bellarmin, 1977).

28 Andrée Fortin, *Histoires de familles et de réseaux. La sociabilité au Québec d'hier à demain* (Montreal: Éditions Saint-Martin, 1987) 31.

29 The analysis of a series of interviews conducted by a team headed by Nicole Gagnon in the early sixties among working-class Montreal families reveals that: "You do not take up residence in a neighbourhood where you have no family or that is not close to where your family lives" (Andrée Fortin, "La famille ouvrière d'autrefois," *Recherches sociographiques* 282).

30 Denys Delâge, "La sociabilité familiale en basse-ville de Québec," *Recherches sociographiques* 28.2-3 (1987): 305.

31 This fire was, moreover, directly related to the Depression. Her neighbours, who were living on relief, were storing in their shed sacks of wood-shavings that they got free from a dealer. The sacks spontaneously combusted.

32 Stuart Ewen, *Captains of Consciousness: Advertising and the Social Roots of the Consumer Culture* (New York: McGraw Hill, 1976) 30.

33 Strong-Boag, *New Day* 114-15. According to the 1941 Census, 28.4 percent of retail sales in Canada were made on credit. This percentage climbed to 65.9 percent for sales of household appliances, furniture, and radios (Canada, *Recensement 1941* 10, 374-77).

34 Thus, a washing-machine valued at eighty-five dollars would cost $90.40 if bought on installments (*Eaton's Catalogue*, Spring-Summer, 1929, 395).

Conclusion

1 Here, see Bertaux-Wiame, "Mobilisations féminines," 85-102.

Bibliography

Books

Armstrong, Pat, and Hugh Armstrong. *The Double Ghetto: Canadian Women and their Segregated Work.* Toronto: McClelland and Stewart, 1984.

Belotti, Elena Gianini. *Du côté des petites filles.* Paris: Éditions des femmes, 1974.

Benson, John. *The Penny Capitalists: A Study of Nineteenth-Century Working-Class Entrepreneurs.* New Brunswick, NJ: Rutgers University Press, 1983.

Bernard, Jessie. *The Female World.* New York: The Free Press, 1981.

Bliss, Michael, and Linda Grayson, eds. *The Wretched of Canada: Letters to R.B. Bennett 1930-1935.* Toronto: University of Toronto Press, 1973.

Blunden, Katherine. *Le travail et la vertu. Femmes au foyer: une mystification de la Révolution industrielle.* Paris: Payot, 1982.

Boucher, J., and A. Morel, eds. *Le droit dans la vie familiale.* Montreal: University of Montreal Press, 1970.

Broadfoot, Barry. *La Grande Dépression. Témoignages des années perdues.* Trans. Jacques Fontaine. Montreal: Québec/Amérique, 1978.

Carisse, Colette. *La famille. Mythe et réalité,* Vol. 1. Report presented to the Council on Social Affairs and the Family. Quebec, 1979.

———. *Planification des naissances en milieu canadien-français.* Montreal: University of Montreal Press, 1964.

Cavan, Ruth Shonle, and Katherine Howland Ranck. *The Family and the Depression: A Study of One Hundred Chicago Families.* 1938; New York: Arno Press and *The New York Times,* 1971.

Chabaud-Rychter, Danielle, Dominique Fougeyrollas-Schwebel, and Françoise Sonthonnax. *Espace et temps du travail domestique.* Paris: Librairie des Méridiens, 1985.

Charbonneau, Hubert. *La Population du Québec. Études rétrospectives.* Montreal: Boréal Express, 1973.

Choko, Marc. *Les crises du logement à Montréal.* Montreal: Éditions coopératives Albert Saint-Martin, 1980.

Collectif Clio. *L'histoire des femmes au Québec depuis quatre siècles.* Montreal: Éditions Quinze, 1982.

Copp, Terry. *The Anatomy of Poverty: The Conditions of the Working Class in Montreal 1897-1929.* Toronto: McClelland and Stewart, 1974.

Cowan, Ruth Schwartz, *More Work for Mother: The Ironies of Household Technology from the Open Hearth to the Microwave.* New York: Basic Books, 1983.

Dalla Costa, Mariarosa, and Selma James. *Le pouvoir des femmes et la subversion sociale.* Geneva: Librairie adversaire, 1973.

De Bonville, Jean. *Jean-Baptiste Gagnepetit. Les travailleurs montréalais à la fin du XIXᵉ siècle.* Montreal: L'Aurore, 1975.

De la Broquerie, Fortier. *Au service de l'enfance. L'Association québécoise de la Goutte de lait.* Quebec: Éditions Garneau, 1965.

Desmarais, Danièle, and Paul Grell, eds. *Les Récits de vie. Théorie, méthode et trajectoires types.* Montreal: Éditions Saint-Martin, 1986.

De Vilaine, A.-M., L. Gavarini, and M. Le Coadic, eds. *Maternité en mouvement. Les femmes, la re/production et les hommes de sciences.* Grenoble and Montreal: Grenoble University Press; Éditions Albert Saint-Martin, 1986.

Dufrancatel, Christiane, et al. *L'Histoire sans qualités.* Paris: Éditions Galilée, 1979.

Dumais, Monique. *La mère dans la société québécoise. Étude éthique d'un modèle à partir de deux journaux féministes: La Bonne Parole, 1913-1958 et Les Têtes de Pioches, 1976-1979.* Ottawa: CRIAW, 1983.

Dumas, Evelyne. *Dans le sommeil de nos os.* Montréal: Léméac, 1971.

Dumont, Fernand, Jean Hamelin, and J.P. Montminy. *Idéologies au Canada français, 1930-1939.* Quebec: Laval University Press, 1978.

Dumont, Micheline, and Nadia Fahmy-Eid. *Les Couventines. L'éducation des filles au Québec dans les congrégations religieuses enseignantes 1840-1960.* Montreal: Boréal Express, 1986.

Ehrenreich, Barbara, and Deirdre English. *Des experts et des femmes. 150 ans de conseils prodigués aux femmes.* Trans. Louise E. Arsenault and Zita De Koninck. Montreal: Éditions du Remue-ménage, 1982.

Eisenstein, Zillah, ed. *Capitalist Patriarchy and the Case for Socialist Feminism.* New York: Monthly Review Press, 1979.

Ewen, Stuart. *Captains of Consciousness: Advertising and the Social Roots of the Consumer Culture.* New York: McGraw-Hill, 1976.

Fortin, Andrée. *Histoires de familles et de réseaux. La sociabilité au Québec d'hier à demain.* Montreal: Éditions Saint-Martin, 1987.

Fortin, Gérard, and Marc-Adélard Tremblay. *Les comportements économiques de la famille salariée du Québec.* Quebec: Laval University Press, 1964.

Garigue, Philippe. *La vie familiale des canadiens français.* Montreal: University of Montreal Press, 1970.

Gérin, Léon. *L'habitant de St-Justin.* Mémoires et Comptes rendus de la Société royale du Canada. Second series. Vol. 4, 1898.

Gittins, Diane. *Fair Sex: Family Size and Structure, 1900-1939.* London: Hutchinson, 1982.

Hareven, Tamara. *Family Time and Industrial Time: The Relationship Between the Family and Work in a New England Industrial Community.* Cambridge: Cambridge University Press, 1982.

Harvey, Fernand. *Révolution industrielle et travailleurs. Une enquête sur les rapports entre le capital et le travail au Québec à la fin du 19ᵉ siècle.* Montreal: Boréal Express, 1978.

Helly, Denise. *Les Chinois à Montréal, 1877-1951.* Quebec: IQRC, 1987.

Heron, Craig, and Robert Story, eds. *On the Job: Confronting the Labor Process in Canada.* Montreal: McGill-Queen's University Press, 1986.

Horn, Michiel, ed. *The Depression in Canada: Responses to Economic Crisis.* Toronto: Copp Clark, 1988.

———. *The Dirty Thirties: Canadians in the Great Depression.* Toronto: Copp Clark, 1972.

Ishwaran, K., ed. *Childhood and Adolescence In Canada.* Toronto: McGraw-Hill, 1979.

Joutard, Philippe. *Ces voix qui nous viennent du passé.* Paris: Hachette, 1983.

Katzman, David M. *Seven Days a Week: Women and Domestic Service in Industrializing America.* Chicago: University of Illinois Press, 1981.

Knibielher, Yvonne, and Catherine Fouquet. *Histoire des mères, du Moyen-âge à nos jours.* Paris: Éditions Montalba, 1980.

Komarovsky, Mirra. *The Unemployed Man and His Family.* 1940; New York: Arno Press, 1971.

Kuhn, Annette, and Ann-Marie Wolpe. *Feminism and Materialism.* London: Routledge, 1978.

Labrie, Vivian. *Précis de transcription de documents d'archives orales.* Quebec: Institut québécois de recherche sur la culture, 1982.

Lacelle, Claudette. *Les domestiques en milieu urbain canadien au XIXᵉ siècle.* Ottawa: Parks Canada, 1987.

Lachance, Gabriel, ed. *Mémoire d'une époque. Un fonds d'archives orales au Québec.* Quebec: Institut québécois de recherche sur la culture, 1987.

Laforce, Hélène. *Histoire de la sage-femme dans la région de Québec.* Quebec: Institut québécois de recherche sur la culture, 1985.

Lamonde, Yvan, and Raymond Montpetit. *Le parc Sohmer de Montréal, 1889-1919. Un lieu populaire de culture urbaine.* Quebec: Institut québécois de recherche sur la culture, 1986.

Lapointe-Roy, Huguette. *Charité bien ordonnée. Le premier réseau de lutte contre la pauvreté à Montréal au 19ᵉ siècle.* Montreal: Boréal, 1987.

Larivière, Claude. *Crise économique et contrôle social. Le cas de Montréal, 1929-1937.* Montreal: Éditions coopératives Albert Saint-Martin, 1977.

Lauzon, Gilles. *Habitat ouvrier et révolution industrielle. Le cas de village St-Augustin*. Montreal: Coll. du Regroupement des chercheurs et chercheures en histoire des travailleurs et travailleuses du Québec, Études et Documents 2, 1989.

Lavigne, Marie, and Yolande Pinard. *Travailleuses et féministes. Les femmes dans la société québécoise*. Montreal: Boréal Express, 1983.

Lazarsfeld, Paul F., Marie Johada, and Hans Zeisel. *Les chômeurs de Marienthal*. Trans. Françoise Laroche. Paris: Éditions de Minuit, 1981.

Lejeune, Philippe. *Je est un autre*. Paris: Seuil, 1980.

Lemieux, Denise, and Lucie Mercier. *Les femmes au tournant du siècle 1880-1940. Âges de la vie, maternité et quotidien*. Quebec: Institut québécois de recherche sur la culture, 1989.

Lévesque, Andrée. *La norme et les déviantes. Des femmes au Québec pendant l'entre-deux-guerres*. Montreal: Éditions du Remue-ménage, 1989.

———. *Virage à gauche interdit. Les communistes, les socialistes et leurs ennemis au Québec 1929-1939*. Montreal: Boréal Express, 1984.

Lewis, Jane, ed. *Labour and Love: Women's Experience of Home and Family, 1840-1940*. Oxford: Blackwell, 1986.

Linteau, Paul-André, et al. *Histoire du Québec contemporain*. Vol. 1: *De la Confédération à la crise (1867-1929)*, and Vol. 2: *Le Québec depuis 1930*. 1979; Montreal: Boréal Compact, 1986 et 1989.

Luxton, Meg. *More than a Labor of Love: Three Generations of Women's Work in the Home*. Toronto: Women's Press, 1980.

Marquis, James. *The Metropolitan Life: A Study in Business Growth*. New York: Viking Press, 1947.

Marsh, Leonard C., A. Grant Fleming, and C. F. Blackler. *Health and Unemployment: Some Studies of Their Relationships*. McGill Social Research Series 7. Toronto: Oxford University Press, 1938.

———. *Canadians in and out of Work. A Survey of Economic Classes and Their Relation to the Labour Market*. McGill Social Research Series 9. Toronto: Oxford University Press, 1940.

Matthews, Glenna. *Just a Housewife: The Rise and Fall of Domesticity in America*. New York: Oxford University Press, 1987.

McLaren Angus, and Arlene Tigar McLaren. *The Bedroom and the State: The Changing Practices and Politics of Contraception and Abortion in Canada, 1880-1980*. Toronto: McClelland and Stewart, 1986.

Michel, Andrée. *Les femmes dans la société marchande*. Paris: Presses Universitaires de France, 1978.

Miner, Horace. *St-Denis: un village québécois*. Trans. Édouard Barsamian and Jean-Charles Falardeau. Montreal: Hurtubise HMH, 1985.

Moreux, Colette. *La fin d'une religion. Monographie d'une paroisse canadienne-française*. Montreal: University of Montreal Press, 1969.

Neatby, Blair. *La grande dépression des années 30. La décennie des naufragés.* Trans. Lucien Parizeau. Montreal: Éditions La Presse, 1975.

Oakley, Ann. *The Sociology of Housework.* Oxford: Blackwell, 1985.

Ogden, Annegret S. *The Great American Housewife.* London: Greenwood Press, 1986.

Parr, Joy, ed. *Childhood and Family in Canadian History.* Toronto: McClelland and Stewart, 1982.

Pelletier, Michel, and Yves Vaillancourt. *Les politiques sociales et les travailleurs. Cahier II. Les années 30.* Montreal: Yves Vaillancourt, 1975.

Perrot, Michelle. *Histoire orale et histoire des femmes.* Paris: Bulletin de l'Institut d'histoire du temps présent, sup. 3, 1982.

Poirier, J., S. Clapier-Valadon, and P. Raybaut. *Les récits de vie théorie et pratique.* Paris: Presses Universitaires de France, 1983.

Prost, Antoine, and Gérard Vincent, eds. *Histoire de la vie privée.* Vol. 5: *De la Première Guerre mondiale à nos jours.* Paris: Seuil, 1987.

Provencher, Jean. *Les quatre saisons dans la vallée du Saint-Laurent.* Montreal: Boréal Express, 1988.

Reiter, R.R., ed. *Toward an Anthropology of Women.* New York: Monthly Review Press, 1975.

Richter, Lothar, ed. *Canada's Unemployment Problem.* Toronto: Macmillan, 1939.

Riley, Denise. *"Am I that Name?": Feminism and the Category of "Women" in History.* Minneapolis: University of Minnesota Press, 1988.

Roberts, Elizabeth. *A Woman's Place: An Oral History of Working-Class Women, 1850-1940.* Oxford: Blackwell, 1984.

Rosaldo, Michelle Zimbalist, and Louise Lamphere, eds. *Women, Culture and Society.* Stanford: Stanford University Press, 1974.

Rouillard, Jacques. *Ah les États! Les travailleurs canadiens-français de l'industrie textile de la Nouvelle-Angleterre d'après le témoignage des derniers migrants.* Montreal: Boréal Express, 1985.

Rumilly, Robert. *La plus riche aumône. Histoire de la société Saint-Vincent-de-Paul du Canada.* Éditions de l'Arbre, 1946.

Safarian, A. E. *The Canadian Economy in the Great Depression.* Toronto: McClelland and Stewart, 1970.

Scharf, Lois, and Joan M. Jensen, eds. *Decades of Discontent: The Women's Movement, 1920-1940.* Boston: Northeastern University Press, 1987.

Scott, Joan W. *Gender and the Politics of History.* New York: Columbia University Press, 1988.

Seager, Allen, and John H. Thompson. *Canada 1922-1939: Decades of Discord.* Toronto: McClelland and Stewart, 1985.

Sheppard, A. E., and Andrée Lévesque, eds. *Norman Bethune, son époque et son message.* Ottawa: Canadian Association for Public Hygiene, 1982.

Simard, Carolle. *L'administration contre les femmes.* Montreal: Boréal Express, 1983.

Sokoloff, Nathalie. *Between Money and Love: The Dialectics of Women's Home and Market Work*. New York: Praeger, 1980.

Stephenson, Marylee, ed. *Women in Canada*. Toronto: New Press, 1973.

Strasser, Susan. *Never Done: A History of American Housework*. New York: Pantheon, 1982.

Strong-Boag, Veronica. *The New Day Recalled: Lives of Girls and Women in English Canada, 1919-1939*. Toronto: Copp Clark, 1988.

Struthers, James. *No Fault of Their Own: Unemployment and the Canadian Welfare State (1914-1941)*. Toronto: University of Toronto Press, 1983.

Thivierge, Nicole. *Écoles ménagères et instituts familiaux. Un modèle féminin traditionnel*. Quebec: Institut québécois de recherche sur la culture, 1982.

Thompson, Paul. *The Voice of the Past*. Oxford: Oxford University Press, 1978.

————. *The Edwardians: The Remaking of British Society*. Bloomington: Indiana University Press, 1975.

Turkel, Studs. *Hard Times: An Oral History of the Great Depression*. New York: Pocket Books, 1978.

Vandelac, Louise, et al. *Du travail et de l'amour. Les dessous de la production domestique*. Montreal: Éditions Saint-Martin, 1985.

Walby, Sylvia. *Patriarchy at Work*. Minneapolis: University of Minnesota Press, 1986.

Ware, Susan. *Holding Their Own: American Women in the Twentieth Century*. Boston: Twayne, 1982.

Weiner, Lynn Y. *From Working Girl to Working Mother: The Female Labor Force in the United States, 1880-1980*. Chapel Hill and London: University of North Carolina Press, 1985.

Westin, Jeane. *Making Do: How Women Survived the 30s*. Chicago: Follet, 1976.

Articles

Ayers, Pat, and Jan Lambertz. "Marriage Relations, Money, and Domestic Violence in Working-Class Liverpool, 1919-39." In Jane Lewis, ed., *Labour and Love: Women's Experience of Home and Family, 1840-1940*, 195-219. Oxford: Blackwell, 1986.

Beaudoin, J. A. "La famille et l'habitation." *Semaine sociale du Canada*. 4th session. *La Famille*, 102-22. Montreal: Bibliothèque de l'Action française, 1923.

Bélisle, Diane. "Temps et tant." In Louise Vandelac et al., eds., *Du travail et de l'amour. Les dessous de la production domestique*, 135-83. Montreal: Éditions Saint-Martin, 1985.

Bélisle, Diane, and Yolande Pinard. "De l'ouvrage des femmes québécoises." In Louise Vandelac et al., eds., *Du travail et de l'amour, Les dessous de la production domestique*, 99-133. Montreal: Éditions Saint-Martin, 1985.

Benston, Margaret. "Pour une économie politique de la libération des femmes." *Partisans* 54-55 (1970): 23-31.

Bertaux, Daniel. "L'approche biographique, sa validité méthodologique, ses potentialités." *Cahiers internationaux de sociologie. Histoires de vie et vie sociale* 66
(1980): 197-223.

Bertaux-Wiame, Isabelle. "Mémoire et récits de vie." *Pénélope, Mémoires de
femmes* 12 (1985): 47-54.

———. "Mobilisations féminines et trajectoires familiales: une démarche ethnosociologique." In Danièle Desmarais and Paul Grell, eds., *Les récits de vie. Théorie,
méthode et trajectoires types*, 85-102. Montreal: Éditions Saint-Martin, 1986.

Bouchard, Gérard, and Christian Pouyez. "Les catégories socio-professionelles:
une nouvelle grille de classement." *Labour/Le Travail* 15 (1985): 145-63.

Bradbury, Bettina. "The Fragmented Family: Family Strategies in the Face of
Death, Illness, and Poverty, Montreal, 1860-1885." In Joy Parr, ed., *Child-
hood and Family in Canadian History*, 109-28. Toronto: McClelland and
Stewart, 1982.

———. "L'économie familiale et le travail dans une ville en voie d'industrialisation:
Montréal dans les années 1870." In Nadia Fahmy-Eid and Micheline Dumont,
eds., *Maîtresses de maison, maîtresses d'écoles. Femmes, famille et éducation
dans l'histoire du Québec*, 287-318. Montreal: Boréal Express, 1983.

———. "Pigs, Cows, and Boarders: Non-Wage Forms of Survival among Montreal Families." *Labour/Le travail* 14 (1984): 9-48.

———. "Women's History and Working Class History." *Labour/Le Travail* 19
(1987): 23-43.

———. "Surviving as a Widow in 19th-Century Montreal." *Urban History
Review/Revue d'histoire urbaine* 17.3 (1989): 148-60.

Bruchési, Charles-Emile. "Les bases juridiques de la famille." *Semaine sociale du
Canada*, 4th session, *La Famille*, 232-47. Montreal: Bibliothèque de l'Action
française, 1923.

Chartrand, Luc. "Au temps où les femmes prenaient les tramways d'assaut."
Châtelaine 19.10 (1978): 56-57, 76, 79.

Chodorow, Nancy. "Mothering, Male Dominance, and Capitalism." In Zillah
Eisenstein, ed., *Capitalist Patriarchy and the Case for Socialist Feminism*,
83-106. New York: Monthly Review Press, 1979.

Clavel, Maïté. "Propreté: mots, rites, images." *Cahiers internationaux de Sociologie. Le détour anthropologique féminin-masculin* 80 (1986): 41-52.

Clavette, Suzanne. "Aide aux chômeurs et Crise des années trente à Verdun."
Paper presented to the Congress of the Historical Society of Canada, June
1989.

Copp, Terry. "The Montreal Working Class in Prosperity and Depression." *Canadian Issues* 1 (1975): n.p.

———. "Montreal's Municipal Government and the Crisis of the 1930s." In
F. Allan, J. Artibise, and Gilbert A. Stetler, eds., *The Usable Urban Past:
Planning and Politics in the Modern Canadian City*, 112-29. Toronto:
Ottawa Institute of Canadian Studies, 1979.

————. "The Health of the People: Montreal in the Depression Years." In A. E. Shepard and A. Lévesque, *Norman Bethune, son époque et son message*, 129-37. Ottawa: Canadian Association of Public Hygiene, 1982.

Cowan, Ruth Schwartz. "The 'Industrial Revolution' in the Home: Household Technology and Social Change in the 20th Century." *Technology And Culture* 17 (1976): 1-25.

————. "Two Washes in the Morning and a Bridge Party at Night: The American Housewife Between the Wars." In Lois Scharf and Joan M. Jensen, eds., *Decades of Discontent. The Women's Movement, 1920-1940*, 177-95. Boston: Northeastern University Press, 1987.

Cross, Suzanne D. "La majorité oubliée: le rôle des femmes à Montréal au 19ᵉ siècle." In Marie Lavigne and Yolande Pinard, eds., *Travailleuses et féministes. Les femmes dans la société québécoise*, 99-114. Montreal: Boréal Express, 1983.

Darroch, A. Gordon, and Michael D. Ornstein. "Ethnicity and Occupational Structure in Canada in 1871: The Vertical Mosaic in Historical Perspective." *Canadian Historical Review* 61.3 (1980): 305-33.

————. "Family and Household in Nineteenth Century Canada: Regional Patterns and Regional Economies." *Journal of Family History* 9.2 (1984): 158-77.

Delâge, Denys. "La sociabilité familiale en basse-ville de Québec." *Recherches Sociographiques. La famille de la Nouvelle-France à aujourd'hui* 28. 2-3 (1987): 295-316.

Delphy, Christine. "L'ennemi principal." *Partisans* 54-55 (1970): 157-72.

————. "Travail ménager ou travail domestique?" In Andrée Michel, ed., *Les femmes dans la société marchande*, 39-44. Paris: Presses Universitaires de France, 1978.

————. "Agriculture et travail domestique; la réponse de la bergère à Engels." *Nouvelles questions féministes* 5 (1983): 3-16.

Devreux, Anne-Marie. "La mémoire n'a pas de sexe." *Pénélope, Mémoires de femmes* 12 (1985): 55-68.

Dubé, J.-E. "Les débuts de la lutte contre la mortalité infantile à Montréal. Fondation de la première Goutte de lait." *Union Médicale du Canada* 65 (1936): 879-91, 986-93 and 1088-1102.

Dumais, Monique. "Religion catholique et valeurs morales des femmes au Québec au XXᵉ siècle." *Religion/culture*. Special number, *Canadian Issues* 7 (1985): 164-80.

Dumont, Fernand. "Les années 30. La première révolution tranquille." In Fernand Dumont, Jean Hamelin, and J. P. Montminy, eds., *Idéologies au Canada français, 1930-1939*, 1-20. Quebec: University of Laval Press, 1978.

Dumont, Micheline. "Des garderies au 19ᵉ siècle: les salles d'asile des soeurs Grises à Montréal." In Nadia Fahmy-Eid and Micheline Dumont, eds., *Maîtresses de maison, maîtresses d'écoles. Femmes, famille et éducation dans l'histoire du Québec*, 261-85. Montreal: Boréal Express, 1983.

Eisenstein, Zillah. "Developing a Theory of Capitalist Patriarchy and Socialist Feminism." In Z. Eisenstein, ed., *Capitalist Patriarchy and the Case for Socialist Feminism*, 5-40. New York: Monthly Review Press, 1979.

Fadette (Henriette Dessaulles). "L'éducation familiale." *Semaine sociale du Canada*, 4th session. *La Famille*, 289-307. Montreal: Bibliothèque de l'Action française, 1923.

Farge, Arlette. "L'histoire ébruitée." In Christiane Dufrancatel et al., eds., *L'histoire sans qualités*, 13-40. Paris: Éditions Galilée, 1979.

Ferretti, Lucia. "Mariage et cadre de vie familiale dans une paroisse ouvrière montréalaise: Sainte-Brigide, 1900-1914." *Revue d'histoire de l'Amérique française* 39.2 (1985): 233-51.

Fine, Agnès. "Àpropos du trousseau: une culture féminine?" In Michelle Perrot, ed., *Une histoire des femmes est-elle possible?*, 155-89. Paris: Rivages, 1984.

Fortin, Andrée. "La famille ouvrière d'autrefois." *Recherches Sociographiques. La famille de la Nouvelle-France à aujourd'hui* 28.2-3 (1987): 273-94.

Gagnon, Nicole. "Un nouveau type de relations familiales." In Marc-André Lessard and Jean-Paul Montminy, eds., *L'urbanisation dans la société canadienne-française*, 59-66. Quebec: Laval University Press, 1967.

Gardiner, Jean. "Women's Domestic Labour." *New Left Review* 89 (1975): 47-58.

Garigue Philippe. "French Canadian Kinship and Urban Life." *American Anthropologist* 58.6 (1956): 1090-1101.

Gauthier, Anne. "État-mari, État-papa, les politiques sociales et le travail domestique." In Louise Vandelac et al., eds., *Du travail et de l'amour. Les dessous de la production domestique*, 257-312. Montreal: Éditions Albert Saint-Martin, 1985.

Gauvreau, Joseph. "La mortalité infantile." *Semaine sociale du Canada*, 4th session. *La Famille*, 162-76. Montreal: Bibliothèque de l'Action française, 1923.

Hall, Catherine. "The History of the Housewife." In Ellen Malos, ed., *The Politics of Housework*, 45-71. London: Allison and Busby, 1980.

Hamel, Thérèse. "Obligation scolaire et travail des enfants au Québec: 1900-1950." *Revue d'histoire de l'Amérique française* 38.1 (1984): 39-58.

Hareven, Tamara. "Les grands thèmes de l'histoire de la famille aux États-Unis." *Revue d'histoire de l'Amérique française* 39.2 (1985): 185-209.

Hartmann Heidi. "Capitalism, Patriarchy and Jobs Segregation by Sex." In Zillah, Eisenstein, ed., *Capitalist Patriarchy and the Case for Socialist Feminism*, 206-48. New York: Monthly Review Press, 1979.

Harvey, Fernand. "Technologie et organisation du travail à la fin du XIXe siècle: le cas du Québec." *Recherches Sociographiques* 18.3 (1977): 397-414.

Henripin, Jacques. "From Acceptance of Nature to Control: The Demography of the French-Canadians since the Seventeenth Century." In Marcel Rioux and Yves Martin, eds., *French-Canadian Society* 1, 204-16. Toronto: McClelland and Stewart, 1964.

Henripin, Jacques, and Yves Peron. "La transition démographique de la Province de Québec." In Hubert Charbonneau, ed., *La population du Québec: études rétrospectives*, 23-44. Montreal: Boréal Express, 1973.

Hobbs, Margaret, and Ruth Roach Pierson. "A Kitchen That Wastes No Steps . . . Gender, Class and the Home Improvement Plan 1936-40." *Histoire Sociale/ Social History* 21.41 (1988): 9-37.

Horn, Michiel. "The Great Depression Past and Present." *Journal of Canadian Studies/Revue d'études canadiennes* 11.1 (1976): 41-50.

Jewsiewicki, Bogumil Koss. "Le récit de la vie entre la mémoire collective et l'historiographie." In Jacques Mathieu, ed., *Étude de la construction de la mémoire collective des Québécois au XXᵉ siècle*, 71-99. Cahiers du CELAT 5 (1986).

Johnston, Wendy. "Keeping Children in School: The Response of the Montreal Catholic School Commission to the Depression of the 1930s." In Michiel Horn, ed., *The Depression in Canada. Responses to Economic Crisis*, 162-87. Toronto: Copp Clark, 1988.

Joutard, Philippe. "Historiens, à vos micros." *L'histoire* 12 (1979): 106-12.

Juteau, Danielle, and Nicole Laurin. "L'évolution des formes de l'appropriation des femmes: des religieuses aux mères porteuses'." *Revue canadienne de sociologie et d'anthropologie* 25.2 (1988): 183-207.

Kelly, Joan, "The Doubled Vision of Feminist Theory." *Feminist Studies* 5.1 (1979): 216-27.

Lapierre-Adamcyk, Evelyne, et al. "Le cycle de la vie familiale au Québec: vues comparatives, XVIIᵉ-XXᵉ siècles." *Cahiers québécois de démographie* 13.1 (1984): 59-76.

Laurendeau, France. "La médicalisation de l'accouchement." *Recherches sociographiques* 24.2 (1983): 203-34.

Lavigne, Marie. "Réflexions féministes autour de la fertilité des Québécoises." In Nadia Fahmy-Eid and Micheline Dumont, eds., *Maîtresses de maison, maîtresses d'école. Femmes, famille et éducation dans l'histoire du Québec*, 319-38. Montreal: Boréal Express, 1983.

Lavigne, Marie, and Jennifer Stoddart. "Ouvrières et travailleuses montréalaises 1900-1940." In Marie Lavigne and Yolande Pinard, eds., *Travailleuses et féministes. Les femmes dans la société québécoise*, 99-114. Montreal: Boréal Express, 1983.

Lavoie, Elzéar. "L'évolution de la radio au Canada français avant 1940." *Recherches Sociographiques* 12.1 (1971): 17-49.

Lemieux, Denise. "La socialisation des filles dans la famille." In Nadia Fahmy-Eid and Micheline Dumont, eds., *Maîtresses de maison, maîtresses d'école. Femmes, famille et éducation dans l'histoire du Québec*, 237-60. Montreal: Boréal Express, 1983.

———. "Des mythes de la mère à la parole des mères." *Questions de culture. Identités féminines: mémoire et création* 9, 71-84. Quebec: Institut québécois de recherche sur la culture, 1986.

Lemieux, Denise, and Lucie Mercier. "Familles et destins féminins. Le prisme de la mémoire, 1880-1940." *Recherches Sociographiques. La famille de la Nouvelle-France à aujourd'hui* 28.2-3 (1987): 259-62.

Leslie, Geneviève. "Domestic Service in Canada: 1880-1920." *Women at Work, 1850-1930,* 71-125. Toronto: Women's Press, 1974.

Lévesque, Andrée. "Mères ou malades: les Québécoises de l'entre-deux-guerres vues par les médecins." *Revue d'histoire de l'Amérique française,* 38.1 (1984): 23-37.

May, Martha. "The 'Good Manager': Married Working Class Women and Family Budget Studies, 1895-1915." *Labour History* 25 (84): 351-72.

Mercier, Lucie. "Quotidienneté et activités domestiques." *Questions de Culture. Identités féminines: mémoire et création* 9, 105-16. Quebec: Institut québécois de recherche sur la culture, 1986.

Milkmann, Ruth. "Women's Work and Economic Crisis: Some Lessons of the Great Depression." *Review of Radical Political Economics* 8 (1976): 73-97.

Modell, John, and Tamara Hareven. "Urbanization and the Malleable Household: An Examination of Boarding and Lodging in American Families." *Journal of Marriage and the Family* (1973): 467-79.

Moreux, Colette. "The French-Canadian Family." In Marylee Stephenson, ed., *Women in Canada,* 157-81. Toronto: New Press, 1973.

Morton, Suzanne. "The June Bride as the Working-Class Bride: Getting Married in the North End of Halifax in the 1920s." Paper presented to the Historical Society of Canada, June 1989.

Pelletier, Lyse. "Au sujet des espaces féminisés." *Cahiers de géographie du Québec* 31.83 (1987): 177-88.

Portelli, Alessandro. "The Peculiarities of Oral History." *History Workshop Journal* 12 (1981): 96-107.

Roberts, Elizabeth "Women's Strategies, 1890-1940." In Jane Lewis, ed., *Labour and Love. Women's Experience of Home and Family 1840-1940,* 223-47. Oxford: Blackwell, 1986.

Rosaldo, Michelle Zimbalist. "Women, Culture and Society: A Theoretical Overview." In Michelle Zimbalist Rosaldo and Louise Lamphere, eds., *Women, Culture and Society.* Stanford: Stanford University Press, 1974.

Rubin, Gayle. "The Traffic in Women: Notes on The Political Economy of Sex." In R. R. Reiter, ed., *Toward an Anthropology of Women,* 157-211. New York: Monthly Review Press, 1975.

Seccombe, Wally. "The Housewife and her Labour under Capitalism." *New Left Review* 83 (1974): 3-24.

Séguin, Anne-Marie. "Madame Ford et l'espace: lecture féministe de la suburbanisation." *Lieux et milieux de vie. Recherches Féministes* 2.1 (1989): 51-68.

Smith, Paul. "Domestic Labour and Marx's Theory of Value." In Annette Kuhn and Ann Marie Wolpe, eds., *Feminism and Materialism,* 198-220. London: Routledge, 1978.

Stoddart, Jennifer. "Quand des gens de robe se penchent sur les droits des femmes: le cas de la commission Dorion 1929-1931." In Marie Lavigne and Yolande Pinard, eds., *Travailleuses et féministes. Les femmes dans la société québécoise*, 307-36. Montreal: Boréal Express, 1983.

Strong-Boag, Veronica. "Intruders in the Nursery: Childcare Professionals Reshape the Years One to Five, 1920-1940." In Joy Parr, ed., *Childhood and Family in Canadian History*, 160-77. Toronto: McClelland and Stewart, 1982.

———. "Keeping House in God's Country: Canadian Women at Work in the Home." In Craig Heron and Robert Storey, eds., *On the Job: Confronting the Labor Process in Canada*, 124-51. Montreal: McGill-Queen's University Press, 1986.

Suitor, J. Jill. "Husbands'? Participation in Childbirth: A Nineteenth-Century Phenomenon." *Journal of Family History* 6. 3 (1981): 278-93.

Synge, Jane. "The Transition from School to Work: Growing-up Working Class in Early Twentieth Century Hamilton, Ontario." In K. Ishwaran, ed., *Childhood and Adolescence in Canada*, 249-69. Toronto: McGraw-Hill, 1979.

Thivierge, Maryse. "La syndicalisation des institutrices catholiques, 1900-1959." In Nadia Fahmy-Eid and Micheline Dumont, eds., *Maîtresses de maison, maîtresses d'écoles. Femmes, famille et éducation dans l'histoire du Québec*, 171-90. Montreal: Boréal Express, 1983.

Thompson, Paul. "Problems of Method in Oral History." *Oral History* 1.4. n.d. 1-47.

———. "Des récits de vie à l'analyse du changement social." *Cahiers internationaux de Sociologie. Histoires de vie et vie sociale* 66 (1980): 250-68.

Tremblay, Marc-Adélard. "Modèles d'autorité dans la famille canadienne-française." In Fernand Dumont et Jean-Paul Montminy, eds., *Le pouvoir dans la société canadienne-française. Recherches Sociographiques*, 215-29. Quebec: Laval University Press, 1966.

———. "La crise économique des années trente et la qualité de vie chez les montréalais d'ascendance française." Académie des sciences morales et politiques. *Travaux et Communications* 3, 149-65. Montreal: Bellarmin, 1977.

Van de Casteele-Schweitzer, Sylvie, and Danièle Voldman. "Les sources orales pour l'histoire des femmes." In Michelle Perrot, ed., *Une histoire des femmes est-elle possible?*, 59-70. Paris: Rivages, 1984.

Vandelac, Louise. "L'économie domestique à la sauce marchande ou les évaluations monétaires du travail domestique." In Louise Vandelac et al., eds., *Du travail et de l'amour. Les dessous de la production domestique*, 183-256. Montreal: Éditions Saint-Martin, 1985.

Vanek, Joann. "Time Spent in Housework." *Scientific American* 231 (1974): 116-20.

Vigod, Bernard. "Ideology and Institutions in Quebec: The Public Charities Controversy 1921-1926." *Histoire Sociale/Social History* 11.21 (1978): 167-82.

———. "The Quebec Government and Social Legislation During the 1930s. A Study in Political Self-Destruction." *Journal of Canadian Studies/Revue d'études canadiennes* 14.1 (1979): 59-69.

Walden, Keith. "Speaking Modern: Language, Culture and Hegemony in Grocery Window Displays, 1887-1920." Paper presented to the Historical Society of Canada, Quebec, June 1989.

Werner, Françoise. "Du ménage à l'art ménager: l'évolution du travail ménager et son écho dans la presse féminine française de 1919 à 1939." *Le Mouvement Social* 129 (1984): 61-87.

Zaretsky, Eli. "Female Sexuality and the Catholic Confessional." *Signs* 6.1 (1980): 176-84.

Bibliographies and Reference Works

Aubin, Paul. *Bibliographie de l'histoire du Québec et du Canada (1966-1975).* 2 vols. Quebec: Institut québécois de recherche sur la culture, 1981.

Aubin, Paul, and Louis-Marie Côté. *Bibliographie de l'histoire du Québec et du Canada/Bibliography of the History of Quebec and Canada (1976-1980).* 2 vols. Quebec: Institut québécois de recherche sur la culture, 1985.

Bernier, Gérald, and Robert Boily. *Le Québec en chiffres de 1850 à nos jours.* Montreal: Association canadienne-française pour l'avancement des sciences, 1986.

Centre populaire de documentation. *Le choc du passé. Les années trente et les sans travail. Bibliographie sélective annotée.* Quebec: Institut québécois de recherche sur la culture, Documents de recherche 11, 1986.

Lemieux, Denise, and Lucie Mercier. *La recherche sur les femmes au Québec. Bilan et bibliographie.* Quebec: Institut québécois de recherche sur la culture, 1982.

Urquhart, M. C., and K. A. H. Buckley. *Historical Statistics of Canada.* Toronto: Macmillan; Cambridge University Press, 1971.

Theses

Clavette, Suzanne. "Des bons aux chèques: aide aux chômeurs et crise des années 30 à Verdun." MA thesis. Université de Québec à Montréal, 1986.

Coulombe, Danièle. "Les femmes dans les années trente." MA thesis. University of Ottawa, 1981.

Couture, Claude. "La presse libérale au Québec entre 1929 et 1935. Analyse de contenu des éditoriaux de La Presse, du Soleil et du Canada, Montréal." Diss. University of Montreal, 1987.

Dion, Carole. "Les femmes et la santé de la famille au Québec 1890-1914." MA thesis. University of Montreal, 1984.

Jean, Dominique. "Familles québécoises et politiques sociales touchant les enfants de 1940 à 1960: obligation scolaire, allocations familiales et travail juvénile." Diss. University of Montreal, 1989.

Lavigne, Marie, and Jennifer Stoddart. "Analyse du travail féminin entre les deux guerres." MA thesis. Université de Québec à Montréal, 1973.

MacPherson, June. " 'Brother Can You Spare a Dime?' The Administration of Unemployment Relief in the City of Montreal 1931-1941." MA thesis. Concordia, 1976.

Martineau, Yvonne. "L'Assistance maternelle à Montréal." MA thesis. University of Montreal, 1948.

Meilleur, Pauline. "Un quartier de la cité de Montréal, Bourget, Montréal." MA thesis. University of Montreal, 1942.

Mercier, Madeleine. "Étude de la formation domestique de quinze mères de famille de Québec." MA thesis. University of Laval, 1946.

Thivierge, Maryse. "Les institutrices laïques à l'école primaire catholique au Québec 1900-1960." Diss. University of Laval, 1981.

Vandandaigue, Anna. "Un quartier ouvrier de Montréal: Papineau, Montréal." MA thesis. University of Montreal, 1941.

Vasil, Normande. "Femmes, prises de décision et pouvoir: analyse des relations entre époux dans la famille chicoutimienne pour la première moitié du XXe siècle." MA thesis. University of Québec at Chicoutimi, 1984.

Verret, Fernande. "L'Assistance maternelle de Québec." MA thesis. University of Laval, 1949.

Government Publications

Bélanger, Réal, George S. Mooney, and Pierre Boucher. *Les vieux logements de Montréal.* Montreal: Commission Métropolitaine de Montréal, Départe- ment d'urbanisme et de recherche, 1938.

Canada. Federal Bureau of Statistics. *Appareils de chauffage, appareils de TSF et téléphones dans les maisons canadiennes, August 1947.* Ottawa: King's Printer, 1948.

———. Federal Bureau of Statistics. *Appareils ménagers, appareils de chauffage, machines à coudre, June 1950.* Ottawa, King's Printer, 1950.

———. Federal Bureau of Statistics. *Canada Census 1931, 1941, 1951.* Ottawa: King's Printer, 1931, 1941, 1951.

———. Federal Bureau of Statistics. *Canada Yearbook, 1929-1939.* Ottawa: King's Printer, 1929-1939.

———. Federal Bureau of Statistics. *Accessoires ménagers. Appareils de cuisson, lessiveuses, réfrigérateurs, aspirateurs et radios dans les maisons canadiennes. November 1948.* Ottawa: King's Printer, 1948.

———. Federal Bureau of Statistics. *Family Income and Expenditure in Canada. A Study of Urban Wage Earners Families, Including Data on Physical Attributes.* Ottawa: King's Printer, 1941.

———. Federal Bureau of Statistics. *Household Facilities and Equipment, May 1958.* Ottawa: Queen's Printer, 1958.

Canada. Department of Labour. *Labour Gazette.* Ottawa: King's Printer, 1929-1939.

Charles, Enid. *The Changing Size of the Family in Canada. Canada Census 1941.* Ottawa: King's Printer, 1948.

Grauer, A. E. *Hygiène publique.* Study prepared for the Royal Commission on Relations between the Dominion and the Provinces 5. Ottawa: King's Printer, 1939.

———. *Logement.* Study prepared for the Royal Commission on Relations between the Dominion and the Provinces 7. Ottawa: King's Printer, 1939.

Greenway, H. F. *Le logement au Canada. Canada Census 1931,* Vol. 12. Ottawa: King's Printer, 1942. 423-590.

Messier, Suzanne. *Les femmes, ça compte. Profil socio-économique des québécoises.* Québec, 1984.

The Metropolitan Life Insurance Company. *More than a Century of Health and Safety Education. Highlights of Metropolitan Life's Health and Safety Activities 1871-1981.* n. p.: n. d.

———. *Report On Industrial Insurance.* December 1921.

Minville, Esdras. *La législation ouvrière et le régime social dans la Province de Québec.* Study prepared for the Royal Commission on Relations between the Dominion and the Provinces, Appendix 5. Ottawa: King's Printer, 1939.

Montreal Board of Trade and City Improvement League. *A Report on Housing and Slum Clearance for Montreal,* March 1935.

Montreal. CIDEM-Communications. *Voies de fer et voies d'eau. Quartiers du Sud-Ouest,* brochure 1. Coll. "Pignon sur rue." Montreal, n.d.

Montreal. CIDEM-Communications. *Au-pied-du-Courant. Quartiers Sainte-Marie, Saint-Eusèbe, Papineau et Bourget,* brochure 4. Coll. "Pignon sur rue." Montreal: n. d.

Montreal. CIDEM-Communications. *Le rêve industriel. Quartiers Hochelaga, Maisonneuve et Préfontaine,* brochure 5. Coll. "Pignon sur rue." Montreal: n. d.

Montreal. CIDEM-Communications. *Les villages du "Plateau." Quartiers du Plateau Mont-Royal,* brochure 6. Coll. "Pignon sur rue." Montreal: n. d.

Montreal. CIDEM-Communications. *La "cité du Nord." Quartiers Saint-Edouard et Villeray, Montcalm et Saint-Jean,* brochure 9. Coll. "Pignon sur rue." Montreal: n. d.

Montreal. CIDEM-Communications. *Fours à chaux et hauts fourneaux. Quartiers Rosemont et Saint-Michel-nord,* brochure 11. Coll. "Pignon sur rue." Montreal: n. d.

Montreal. CIDEM-Communications. *La côte Saint-Paul. Quartier Saint-Paul,* brochure 13. Coll. "Pignon sur rue." Montreal: n. d.

Montreal. *Les quartiers municipaux de Montréal depuis 1832,* document prepared by the municipal archives. Montreal: July 1973.

Montreal. Unemployment Commission. *Renseignements à l'usage des chômeurs nécessiteux et des propriétaires,* Montreal: n. d.

Montreal. *Rapport de la Commission d'enquête du chômage.* Montreal: 1937.

Pelletier, A. J., F. D. Thompson, and A. Rochon. *La famille canadienne.* Canada Census 1931. 12. Ottawa: King's Printer, 1931. 3-323.

Quebec. Dept. of Industry and Commerce. *Annuaire du Québec.* Quebec: King's Printer, 1929-1939.

Vandelac, Louise. *Production domestique,* document no. 1. Quebec. Council on the Status of Women. 1983.

Newspapers, Magazines, and Catalogues

A Shopper's View of Canada Past: Pages from Eaton's Catalogue, 1886-1930. Toronto: Toronto Press, 1969.

La Bonne Parole, 1920-1929.

La Patrie, 1929-1933.

La Presse, 1929-1933.

Index